Marxist Theory and Democratic Politics

Marxist Theory

and

Democratic Politics

Christopher Pierson

The University of California Press
Berkeley and Los Angeles

First published 1986 by The University of California Press
Berkeley and Los Angeles, California

Library of Congress Cataloging in Publication Data

Pierson, Christopher
  Marxist theory and democratic politics
  Bibliography: p.
  Includes index.
  1. Marx, Karl 1880–83. 2. Communism.
3. Democracy. 4. Partito comunista italiano.
5. Sverges socialdemokratiska arbetarepartia.
I. Title.
HX35.5.P487 1986   320.5′315   86–16059
ISBN 0–520–05957–3 (alk. paper)

Printed in Great Britain

For Meridee

Contents

Acknowledgements

I am especially grateful to Anthony Giddens for his generous help and wise guidance over a number of years. In large measure, his support has made the publication of this work possible. My particular thanks also to David Held who has helped in a variety of ways to make the writing of this book a more rewarding and less painful task than it might otherwise have been. A number of people have been kind enough to read and comment upon a part or the whole of the manuscript. These were: Richard Bellamy, members of the British Sociological Association Theory Group, G. A. Cohen, Paul Ginsborg, Gregor McLennan and Richard Scase, in addition to Anthony Giddens and David Held, both of whom have taken the trouble to read several drafts. I am very grateful to all these readers, even though I have not always felt able to follow their advice.

Thanks are also due to the Economic and Social Research Council and Jesus College, Cambridge, which supported my postgraduate research in Cambridge, to the University of Wales which funded my period as University of Wales Research Fellow in Sociology at University College, Cardiff, and to colleagues and students in Cambridge, Cardiff and Stirling.

Above all my thanks are due to my parents and to Meridee Peyton Jones for her constant kindness and support.

Introduction

Few propositions in contemporary social and political analysis could properly be claimed to be axiomatic. However, it is possible to identify a widespread, if not general, consensus that the past fifteen to twenty years have seen both an acute crisis in the political institutions of the advanced capitalist world and matching, at times, even surpassing this, a crisis of confidence in the capacity of the conventional tools of political analysis to diagnose, let alone to offer remedies for, this political malaise. This is quite clearly the sense of a number of recent contributions, from John Dunn's *Western Political Theory in the Face of the Future* to André Gorz's *Farewell to the Working Class*. It is a conviction most baldly stated by Andrew Gamble, who insists that 'for the present modern Western thought appears to have reached an impasse.'[1]

For some time, there was a broadly-held belief, 'on the left', that this was, in essence, an impasse confined to 'bourgeois' political science, whose predominantly consensual and pluralistic models of political life were quite unable to explain the widespread upsurge in political and industrial militancy in advanced Western capitalist societies from the late 1960s onwards. But in more recent years, confidence that, in contrast to this exhaustion of 'bourgeois' political science, Marxist political discourse was able to offer not only the means of interpreting but also the revolutionary medium for changing both the theory and practice of Western political institutions, has ebbed. It is now seen to be much more deeply implicated in the general crisis of Western political theory and, even among those who acknowledge its considerable strengths, both its theoretical and strategic cogency is now much more widely questioned. With the waning of confidence in Marxism, the edifice of socialist theory is now, as much as ever, a tower of Babel of competing ideologies and strategies.[2]

It is against this background that my consideration of the limitations of Marxist thinking, as a form of political analysis and of political advocacy, is set. In seeking principally to establish what are the major generic weaknesses of Marxism as a political theory and what, in the face of these inadequacies, remain its continuing strengths, I have two particular issues in mind: first, the extent to which the 'crisis of Marxism', rather than being a recent development issuing from changes in the structure of advanced capitalism, is premised upon deep-seated and long-standing generic weaknesses in the Marxist mode of explanation, and secondly, the extent to which these long-standing parameters of Marxist analysis stand in the way of the generation of an effective radical political strategy under contemporary circumstances. In the final third of the book, I discuss some of the recent initiatives that have been advanced to overcome these difficulties, assess their own prospects for success and offer some indications of those areas in which further advances might be sought.

In Part One, I consider the account of politics developed within 'classical' Marxism. Compared with his economic works, Marx's political writings have always seemed to offer his followers a much more uncertain heritage. Through a detailed consideration of his earliest writings on democracy and the state, a discussion of the impact of historical materialism and an assessment of the status of the political in his later writings, I set out to show that, if not quite so ambiguous as is sometimes supposed, Marx's political thought was bound to be acutely problematic for those who followed him. In subsequent chapters I consider the fiercely contested ways in which this political analysis was understood in what Kolakowski dubs the 'Golden Age' of Marxism and offer a general evaluation of the ambivalent political heritage that 'classical Marxism' was to bestow upon its inheritors.

In Part Two, I turn to a detailed consideration of the ways in which this classical tradition is able to inform contemporary political practice. Rather than considering its contribution to a primarily theoretical 'Western Marxism', through a detailed consideration of the continuing advocacy of the strategies of the Italian Communist Party and left social democrats in Sweden, I assess the difficulties entailed in adapting classical Marxism to generate a (party) political strategy for the circumstances of advanced capitalism. In particular, I look at the likely prospects for these quite differing strategies and the extent to which they are either assisted or retarded by their Marxist inheritance.

In Part Three, I summarise what I understand to be the major difficulties exposed in the opening two sections and consider some of the ways in which it has been suggested these weaknesses might be overcome. Here I consider a number of 'post-Marxist' initiatives that seek to redeem the acknowledged shortcomings of existing Marxist political thinking and subject these themselves to critical scrutiny. I offer an account of the kinds of new directions which appear to be both possible and desirable and assess the extent to which this re-consideration relates not only to a crisis of Marxist political thinking but also more widely to general difficulties in contemporary liberal democratic theory and conventional political science. I conclude with a tentative indication of those areas in which further advances might most usefully be sought. For some, such an undertaking will necessarily appear to be unduly speculative and programmatic. But the circumstances of contemporary theoretical disarray, as André Gorz has suggested, enjoin us 'to ask questions we cannot answer and to raise problems whose solutions remain to be found'.[3]

Part One
Origins

1
Marx
Democracy, State and the Transition to Socialism

Introduction

From the very earliest codification of Marxism, Marx's own writings on state, democracy and the transition to socialism have presented chronic difficulties for those who have sought to derive from them the bases for a systematic socialist political practice. In part, this is because they belong to a decisively different historical epoch, pre-dating what has been, within Western Europe at least, a very widespread twentieth century experience of well-established and party-dominated mass democracies. In part, it derives from the fact that, compared with the rigorous systematization of Marx's economics, the political writings are scattered, unsystematic and, at times, seemingly contradictory. But I intend to show, in this opening chapter, that it is, above all, weaknesses and misunderstandings in the very bases of Marx's analysis of the political that have made of it such an ambiguous and unsatisfactory source for a systematic socialist political practice. I begin with a detailed discussion of democracy and the state prior to 1845, then consider the impact upon Marx's political analysis of the advent of historical materialism and finally assess the nature of Marx's later political writings. Throughout, I focus attention upon those aspects – universalization of the suffrage and the 'parliamentary road to socialism', 'smashing the state' and 'the dictatorship of the proletariat' – which, though often quite secondary in Marx's own political writings, were to assume an urgent priority in the bitter disputes of subsequent generations of Marxists. I conclude by offering an overall assessment of the kind of account that Marx was to leave to socialist posterity and suggest why this has proven to be such a problematic heritage.

The Critique of Hegel

Lucio Colletti, in his 'Introduction' to Marx's *Early Writings*, argues that the *Critique of Hegel's Doctrine of the State*, written within the space of six months in 1843, contains 'a clear statement of the dependence of the state upon society, a critical analysis of parliamentarism accompanied by a counter-theory of popular delegation, and a perspective showing the need for ultimate suppression of the state itself'. He concludes that 'politically speaking, mature Marxism would have little to add to this.'[1] Though this position is almost certainly overstated, Marx's earliest writings do contain what is, in many ways, his most developed examination of democracy and, it is instructive, especially in the light of Hindess's complaint that 'marxist discussion of popular democracy has scarcely developed beyond Rousseau', that the writings of the more 'mature' Marx afford no comparable, *theoretical* account of democracy.[2]

To understand this early account of democracy, it is essential to recognize the way in which it emerged from Marx's much broader concern with the distinctive nature of political and civil relations in the 'modern world', which was the central concern of his critique of Hegel. The *Critique* is built upon a detailed textual criticism of paragraphs 261–313 of Hegel's *The Philosophy of Right*, the greater part of which deals with the distinctive nature of the modern state. Without entering into the dispute as to Marx's general characterization of Hegel's 'upside-down logic', it is clear that he was, in a general sense, critical of Hegel's attempt to derive empirical institutions from the development of 'the Idea', but, as importantly, that he did not see in Hegel's account of the state a wilful betrayal of his 'radical method' in an unprincipled rationalization of the contemporary Prussian state.[3]

Indeed, there was much in Hegel's morphology of the state which Marx endorsed, most notably the division between civil and political life, which both men characterized as distinguishing 'modern society' from feudalism. Both recognized that, under feudalism, economic and political life were intertwined, in what Marx styled 'the *democracy of unfreedom*' – where civil and political society were unified but the people were unfree – and both contrasted this unity with the separation of civil and political society which typified the modern world. Thus, Marx insisted that 'the identity of the civil and political classes in the Middle Ages' had given way to their 'separation', which alone was able to 'express the *true* relation of the civil and the political in modern society'.[4]

It is in their differing evaluations of this division between civil and political life that the substantive difference between Marx and Hegel emerged. The core of Marx's critique was that Hegel, having recognized the separation of civil and political life as a contradiction, had claimed to find this opposition resolved in the form of the modern state, whereas, for Marx, it was the *persistence* of this contradiction, characteristic of modern society, which called into being the modern state. The political state is not, as Hegel had depicted it, the means by which this contradiction could be overcome but is, rather, itself but one side of this opposition and its continued existence an expression of the *failure* to overcome it.

For Marx, 'the *constitution* of the *political state* and the dissolution of civil society into independent *individuals* – who are related by *law* . . . are achieved in *one and the same act*', these two aspects of 'modern society' being but the two sides of one contradiction.[5] The development of the political state is conditional upon and conterminous with the isolation of civil society, and the emergence of public life – the political state – is impossible without the concomitant development of private life – in civil society. Both issue simultaneously from the breakdown of the corporate life of feudalism. Political emancipation ensured the dissolution of the old order in which civil society had manifested a directly political character. Similarly, as civil society became increasingly relieved of its former political constraints, the political realm, liberated from the 'adulteration of civil life', grew into 'the universal concern of the people ideally independent of particular elements of civil life'. This process reached 'completion' in the French Revolution, following which '*class distinctions* in civil society became merely *social* differences in private life of no significance in political life.'[6]

But while the French Revolution established the universalization of the political realm it correspondingly generated universal particularization within civil society. It established 'juridical and political equality only upon the basis of a new and deeper inequality'.[7] Indeed, in this division of political and civil society, Marx identified the paradox of the individual's 'greatest freedom' which is at the same time 'the perfection of his slavery': 'The contradiction between the democratic representative state and civil society is the perfection of the classical contradiction between the public commonwealth and slavedom.'[8]

For in 'the modern world', the reality of the 'slavery of civil society' is in appearance the 'perfect independence of the individual'. What appears to the individual to be 'complete freedom' is really nothing but the free movement of 'his alienated life elements' – 'in reality, this is the perfection of his slavery and his inhumanity.'[9]

In this way, Marx argued, the individual in the 'modern world' comes to lead a double life. Just as Christianity had taught of an inequality on earth but equality in heaven, so did the people become '*equal* in the heaven of their political world, though unequal in their earthly existence in *society*.'[10] Unlike the Christian, however, the modern citizen experiences not simply a divided consciousness, but indeed a divided reality – being, in political society, 'a *communal being*' (with communal interests), but, in civil society, a private individual struggling in the *bellum omnia contra omnes* of competing private interests. But Marx did not confine himself to the positing of the individual as divided and these two spheres of political and civil life as in opposition. Continuing the religious analogy, he gave it a Feuerbachian twist:

> The (political) state stands in the same opposition to civil society and overcomes it in the same way as religion overcomes the restrictions of the profane world, i.e. *it has to acknowledge it again, reinstate it and allow itself to be dominated by it.*[11]

For Marx, it is not just that under modern conditions civil and political society become the opposing poles of a single contradiction but further that civil society is the *principal aspect* of this contradiction – just as man's earthly existence is the principal aspect of the contradiction with his heavenly being.

Individual 'Freedom' as Alienation

Marx's position may become clearer if we pursue his own further breakdown of the civil/political division into two sets of related oppositions. As cited above these are, first, 'the dissolution of civil society into independent *individuals* who are related by *law*', that is the reduction of civil society into a sphere of atomistic and legally enabled individuals, capable of exercising and protecting their rights under the rule of law, and secondly, 'the constitution of the political state', that is the more general estrangement of the state from (civil) society. We have already seen that Marx contended that the state cannot become the authentically universal sphere which Hegel envisaged because it is only called into being by, and is, as it were, the 'other side' of, the particularization of civil society. It is only the dissolution of civil society into mutually contending legal individuals which calls forth the modern state and it is only the persistence of the civil/political division which sustains it. Were this contradiction to be resolved, Marx argued, the very basis of the state would 'disappear'. Correspondingly, the general or universal interest which the state represents can be seen to be not a moment of authentic (that is 'truly human') unity – for such a unity could only be found in an undivided person – but is rather the estranged expression of the general interest of civil society, that is the interest which each individual shares over against all others in the *bellum omnia contra omnes* of a competitive market society.[12] The state does not overcome the contradictions and inequalities within civil society in establishing its realm of universal equality, it simply suspends them. Real differences in civil society are characterized as non-political and thus non-effective in the realm of the state. Thus, for example, the state 'annuls' private property when it abolishes the property qualification as a constraint upon suffrage. But, Marx insisted, 'the political annulment of private property does not mean the abolition of private property; on the contrary, it even presupposes it.' In a similar way, the state abolishes political distinctions based on birth, rank, education and occupation but it still allows these distinctions 'to act and assert their *particular* nature in their own way'. Thus, 'far from abolishing these *factual* distinctions, the state *presupposes them in order to exist.*'[13]

Rather than being the universal which overcomes the division between civil and political society, the state is then but the displaced representation of the general interest of civil society. This general interest cannot manifest itself directly in civil society, as this is the realm of dissociated and mutually competing individuals, but must rather find its *abstract* expression in the form of the state. However, since this general interest is formal and only obtained by abstracting from reality, 'the basis and content of such a "political society" inevitably remains civil society with all its economic divisions.'[14]

While civil society remains the unacknowledged and uncriticized premiss of the political state, this state will continue to be 'shot through' by the contradiction within this displaced base. Civil society is the real basis of human life and the political state its ethereal projection. Thus, not only are political and civil life, citizen and bourgeois, seen to be dissociated but, Marx argued, the individual as bourgeois is held to be the more fundamental, unmediated and *natural* person, whose nature political life and the citizen exist to guarantee. But in fact, the freedom of such rights-bearing persons – for whom the political state acts only as a means, as guarantor of this freedom – is, for Marx, only the freedom of alienated, egoistic individuals, unmediated only in so far as the limitations of such a freedom have not been confronted and overcome. While 'man' is indeed recognized as 'a sovereign and supreme being', this is only 'man in his uncultivated, unsocial aspect . . . man who is not yet a *true* species-being'. What is styled the freedom of the individual in civil society – for 'the civil society of the present is the principle of *individualism* carried to its logical conclusion' – is, in fact, the freedom of the individual's alienated life-activity. Thus, for Marx, the acknowledgement of the freedom of egoistic 'man' is rather 'the acknowledgement of the *unbridled* movement of the spiritual and material elements which form the content of his life'.[15]

'Purely Political Emancipation'

The consequences of this divided modern polity and of this 'partial' freedom for a democratic politics, Marx considered, at length, in his essay 'On the Jewish Question'. Here he confronted the opposition of the Young Hegelian Bruno Bauer to the extension of religious freedom to the German Jews. Such freedom was worthless, Bauer had argued, because it could yield only 'equality with slaves' – for 'the Germans were the slaves of the Christian state.' The German Jews should rather join in the struggle for the more general emancipation of the German people and the displacement of the (oppressive) Christian state by a 'totally free state'.[16]

Bauer's argument is flawed, Marx insisted, because he has failed to recognize the real (and limited) nature of political emancipation, (the extension of rights), and has erroneously identified it with fully *human* emancipation. For Marx, the supersession of religion – 'the devious acknowledgement of man through an intermediary' – is one aspect of a fully human emancipation. But it cannot be realized through a purely *political* emancipation. This Marx illustrated through the experience of the United States which proscribes state religion and yet which proved to be 'the land of religiosity *par excellence*'.[17] This seeming paradox arises, Marx suggested, from the fact that political emancipation *of* religion does not mean complete and consistent emancipation *from* religion, (which would be conterminous with fully *human* emancipation). Political emancipation of religion means only the freedom *to* worship as one chooses and not *freedom from* the superstition and alienation that religion is seen to express. In the 'free state' – under freedom *of* religion – the individual is liberated from religion only through the medium of the state and only in a political, and thus partial, way. This purely political annulment of religion, as of private property, consists only in declaring distinctions of religion/private property to be *non-political* – that is in confining these differences to civil society. Thus, 'the contradiction which exists between religious man and political man is the same as exists between the *bourgeois* and the *citoyen*, between the member of civil society and his *political lion's skin*.'[18]

The example of Jewish emancipation, Marx argued, helps in the more general task of understanding 'where the limit of political emancipation lies'. For this

> splitting of man into his *public* and his *private* self and the *displacement* of religion from the state to civil society is not one step in the process of political emancipation but its *completion* . . . The dissolution of man into

Jew and citizen, Protestant and citizen, is not a denial of citizenship or an avoidance of political emancipation: it *is political emancipation itself*, it is the *political* way of emancipating oneself from religion.[19]

'Truly Human Emancipation'

Quite as important as this insistence upon 'the incompleteness and contradiction' of purely political emancipation is the universality claimed, by Marx, for 'truly *human* emancipation', with which the former is so often contrasted. While political revolution is '*limited* and *contradictory*', social revolution achieves 'a *total* point of view'. For Marx, 'the *man* is greater than the *citizen* and human life than political life.' Correspondingly in 'On the Jewish Question', Marx insisted that while 'political emancipation is certainly a big step forward', it is not 'the last form of general emancipation'. For the perfection of political emancipation is the perfection of the division into 'bourgeois' and 'citizen'. It is 'the reduction of man on the one hand to the member of civil society, the *egoistic, independent*, individual, and on the other to the *citizen*, the moral person'. Thus, while the winning of the rights of the citizen represents a major advance over the structured inequalities of feudalism, freedoms of such a kind – secured to legally constituted persons under the jurisdiction of the state – express, in themselves, the partial nature of this emancipation. The great limitation of this purely political revolution, Marx insisted, is that 'it dissolves civil society into its component parts without *revolutionizing* these parts and subjecting them to criticism'.[20]

To aspire to 'general human emancipation', it is essential to go beyond this purely political emancipation and, for Marx, this means resolving the contradiction between civil and political society. Having rejected Hegel's 'semblance of a resolution' through the mediation of a 'universal' state, Marx insisted that this contradiction is only truly resolved when civil and political life are reunited, that is, when political society is reabsorbed by civil life. Only through this (renewed) coalescence of 'public' and 'private' life can the division of 'citizen' and 'bourgeois' give way to the individual '*real human being*'. He concluded that 'only when man has recognized and organized his *forces propres* as *social forces* so that social force is no longer separated from him in the form of *political* force, only then will human emancipation be completed.'[21]

For Marx, this human emancipation through the unity of civil and political life consummates the realization of democracy. Thus:

Democracy is the solution to the *riddle* of every constitution. In it we find the constitution founded on its true ground: *real human beings* and the real *people*; not merely *implicitly* and in essence, but in *existence* and in reality . . . Every other *political formation* is a definite, determinate *particular* form of the state [in which] the political man leads his particular existence alongside the unpolitical man, the private citizen. . . [But] in democracy the *formal* principle is identical with the substantive principle. For this reason it is the first true unity of the particular and the universal.[22]

The Early Marx: 'Radical Bourgeois Democrat'?

Marx's terminology here has led a number of commentators, notably Hunt and Avineri, to style the Marx of the *Critique* a radical bourgeois democrat. But such a reading is possible only if we divorce 'democracy' from Marx's understanding of it as the reunification of political and civil life and attribute to it instead a number of features typical of 'bourgeois democracy' – such as parliamentary government and representative elections. This terminological 'sleight of hand' is clearly exposed if we look at Marx's characterization of democracy in the broader context of the *Critique* in which, far from being an endorsement of 'bourgeois' democracy, it is the basis of Marx's attack upon parliamentarism and 'the representative principle'.

A second defence of this characterization of Marx as a 'bourgeois democrat' turns upon his seeming advocacy of universal suffrage as the medium of radical transformation. Evidence of this position is drawn from the closing pages of the *Critique* in which Marx argued that '*unrestricted* active and passive *suffrage*' raises civil society 'to the point of abstraction from itself, to the *political* existence which constitutes its true, universal, essential existence' which 'abstraction is also its transcendence'.[23] On the strength of this text, it is argued that Marx saw in the universalization of the suffrage the mechanism through which the division between civil and political society could be overcome. But a number of objections must be raised to such a claim. Firstly, there is an ambiguity in Marx's own usage – 'electoral reform', 'the Vote', 'unrestricted active and passive suffrage', are used in the *Critique* more or less interchangeably but each suggests a different shade of meaning. It seems clear that Marx did not hold that this 'universalization of the suffrage' was exhausted by the extension of the parliamentary franchise to the entire adult population. For Marx, indeed, universal suffrage was not, as in so many accounts, a means of expanding parliamentary representation, but was rather a means of overcoming the representative principle and of breaking the confines of a 'merely' parliamentary democracy. Secondly, Marx's own usage suggests that the aspiration to universal suffrage is a *symptom* of civil society's striving to realize its political existence, but that even its realization is *not* conterminous with the realization of democracy, (as this was understood by Marx), so long as the division between civil and political life persists. Thus:

> The efforts of *civil society* to transform itself into a political society, or to make the *political* society into the *real* one, manifest themselves in the attempt to achieve as general a participation as possible in the *legislature*.[24]

This is intimately related to a third objection, namely that while universal suffrage is now very generally seen to be a principle of representation, for Marx its pursuit is, rather, symptomatic of an attempt to overcome the representative principle. For, in characterizing democracy as the unity of civil and political life, Marx sought to avoid the classic conundrum of how 'all the people individually should take part in deliberating and deciding on political matters of general concern.' For Marx, this is a problem that can only arise where the political state is divided from civil society.[25] Where such a division exists, he argued, it is impossible for all as individuals to take part in the legislature. The fact that civil society is present in the political through deputies is itself an expression of this civil/political division. Thus, the 'separation of the political state from civil society takes the form of a separation of the deputies from their electors. Society simply deputes elements of itself to become its political existence.'[26]

This delegation entails a double contradiction: a formal contradiction – the deputies of civil society should be 'mandated' by their electors but, in fact, as soon as they take office they cease to be accountable to their electorate – and a material contradiction – they have authority as the representatives of the public interest, whereas in reality they represent private and particular interests. In this sense, representation is seen, by Marx, to be a measure of the *failure* to realize democracy. This he contrasts with a second possibility in which 'civil society is the *real* political society' and in which 'the *legislature* entirely ceases to be important as a *representative* body.' Here, the legislature is 'representative only in the sense that *every* function is representative' – that is, it is representative not in the sense of being elected or delegated, but rather in the sense that it is characteristic or typical of the people in general.[27]

Indeed, far from offering a vindication, Marx's early writings constitute a masterly critique of even the most radically conceived representative democracy. However, this critical strength is largely dissipated by Marx's pressing this radical critique towards a thoroughly

Hegelian resolution. For with the realization of democracy, as 'the first true unity of the particular and the universal', Marx anticipated that a whole series of classical political problems – the role of the state, the need of representation and/or delegation, the constraint of the ruling by the ruled – would be overcome. Increasingly, under 'True Demo-cracy', the age-old government of men, the circumstances of political rule, would be seen to yield to a Saint-Simonian 'administration of things', in which society could be organized according to purely technocratic, (neutral and non-controversial) imperatives. In this way, Marx painstakingly exposes the weaknesses and limitations of existing democratic practices, but offers a wholly unsatisfactory account of the way in which these can be overcome.

The Un-politics of Historical Materialism

This body of early writings, which probably constitutes Marx's most sustained and systematic work specifically on democracy and the nature of 'the political', draws to a close in 1844. Of course, ever since the belated publication of these early writings, their relation to Marx's work from the *German Ideology* onwards has been vigorously contested. For a time, it was fashionable to posit a profound discontinuity between the 'young' and the 'old' Marx.[28] More recently, Neil Harding has argued that the radically decentralist model of the early Marx, directed at the overcoming of alienation, was substantially displaced by 1848 and throughout Marx's maturity – with the brief exception of his commentary on the Paris Commune – by 'a second edition of Saint-Simon's organic labour state', which envisaged centralized state ownership, planning and control as the means of prosecuting a productivist strategy aimed not at the elimination of alienation but at the overcoming of exploitation.[29] While some such account of a centralizing (even if 'transitional') state is essential if we are to make sense of Marx's many references to centralizing ownership and control, from 'The Communist Manifesto' to 'The Critique of the Gotha Programme', repeated evidence of the 'earlier' model reappear-ing in the political writings of the mature Marx makes too clear-cut a 'rupture' seem improbable.

This having been said, it seems clear that the adoption of materialist assumptions from 1845 onwards did indeed generate a quite distinctive account of the political in Marx's later work. Perhaps the most influential of these later developments, in respect of Marx's political understanding, are the privileged status of the economic, (seen to be notoriously 'determinant in the last instance'), and the claim to have constituted socialism as a science. The ubiquitous claim that Marx's view of the political was vitiated by the belief that politics was 'finally' an expression of objectively-given economic conditions is too familiar to require discussion. The claim that his political analysis was further undermined by scientistic positivism – the uncritical adoption of the prevailing characterization of science as *the* exhaustive technique for the understanding of the (social) world – is almost as familiar. While it is probably mistaken to dismiss Marx's central works as crudely deterministic or positivistic, there are important elements of both economic determinism and scientistic positivism in his later work which clearly contributed to serious oversights in his political analysis. Thus many of the classic problems of socialist political practice – notably, the status of parliamentary institutions, the proper attitude to the (bourgeois) state and the nature of reformism – which we have already seen to have been 'resolved' in Marx's early writings were, for differing reasons, similarly neglected by the more mature Marx. His 'blindness' to these problems can be explained not only by reference to the particular historical circumstances under which he wrote but, perhaps above all, by those deterministic and positivistic elements in his general outline of historical materialism which eliminated the theoretical 'space' in which such problems might arise.

There are two key components in this analysis – first, Marx's theoretical model of capitalist development – especially, though not exclusively, in its summary form in, for example, 'The Communist Manifesto' and the 1859 'Preface' – in which socialism is seen to emerge from the internal development of capitalism, as its logical 'completion' and, secondly, in conjunction with this, his conception of the relation between ideology and the material conditions of production – that is, at its simplest, the subordination of the political and ideological super-structure to the economically determinant base. Both points are made in a very familiar passage from the 1859 'Preface':

> The mode of production of material life conditions the social, political and intellectual life process in general. It is not the consciousness of men that determines their being, but, on the contrary, their social being that determines their consciousness. At a certain stage of development, the material productive forces of society come in conflict with the existing relations of production . . . and] from forces of development of the productive forces these relations turn into their fetters.[30]

This is Marx at his most summary and deterministic. In his more substantive works he often showed himself to be keenly aware of the uncertain relationship between theory and practice. But it remains the case that, within this model, Marx's understanding of the political derives principally from this conjuncture of the political economy of necessarily antagonistic relations between capital and labour, (a relationship of exploitation), and the determination of politics and ideology by this economic reality. The envisaged revolutionary resolution of this antagonism is grounded in a further assumption about the innate and growing contradiction in capitalism between the relations of production, geared to private accumulation, and the increasingly social forces of production. The dynamic of capitalism – the unending pursuit of profit as an end in itself, the tendential fall in profit rate and attempts to counteract this – ensures that the workers come increasingly to be in the same position, which position is one of growing disparity between capital and labour. For Marx, the more excessive, apparent and shared this exploitation becomes, the more the working class will come to 'see' its position and accordingly to realize its historic mission. Having grounded his critique of political economy, the political activity of the working class is, for Marx, in some sense, unproblematic.

This did not lead Marx to neglect political action. He repeatedly stressed the need 'to raise the proletariat to the position of ruling class' and 'to conquer political power'. But it did on occasion, especially in those middle years in which the focus of his attention was upon the critique of political economy, lead him towards an over-simple identification of the universalization of the suffrage with the proletariat's elevation to ruling class and to a general neglect of those very limitations upon the effectiveness of purely political power, which he himself had exposed in the writings of 1843–4. While a quite 'minor' thesis for Marx himself, this claim that universal suffrage might be conterminous with the political rule of the proletariat was to assume very considerable importance as the bedrock of later attempts to derive a 'parliamentary democratic road to socialism' from Marx's own writings. This aside, the expectations generated by Marx's determinism were certainly to colour his evaluation of political democracy. For example, in 'The Communist Manifesto', in many ways the *'locus classicus'* of this deterministic model, Marx insists that 'the first step in the revolution by the working class is to raise the proletariat to the position of ruling class, to win the battle of democracy.'[31] Yet, making due allowance for the propagandist and polemical intent of the 'Manifesto', it is clear now, as perhaps it could not have been to Marx in the late 1840s, that 'winning the battle of democracy' is not, (unless by definitional fiat), synonymous with 'raising the proletariat to the position of ruling class'. Similarly, his further claim that, having secured such a victory, 'the proletariat will use its political supremacy to wrest by degrees, all capital from the bourgeoisie, to centralize all instruments of production in the hands of the state' remains generally unrealized and perhaps unrealizable. Again, the measures that Marx claimed would 'in the most advanced countries . . . be pretty generally applicable' to put this political supremacy into effect – the curiously modest 'Ten Regulations', including progressive income tax, extension of state ownership, free and universal education – have become central pillars of social democractic orthodoxy and have shown themselves to be not only consistent with but indeed a means of buttressing an (albeit amended) form of capitalism. Yet these measures were seemingly, for Marx, to be the means of realizing the supersession of politics, the elimination of classes and of class antagonism, and were to yield to that happy association 'in which the free development of each is the condition for the free development of all'.[32]

Some five years later he was to claim, in writing of the Chartists, that universal suffrage, (as conventionally understood), would in England have, 'as its inevitable result . . . the political supremacy of the working class'. But the six points of the Charter were, of course, to be substantially conceded, albeit hesitantly, over the next seventy years without this issuing in the political supremacy of the working class that Marx had envisaged. These errors were perhaps understandable in the mid-nineteenth century context in which Marx wrote. Indeed, it might even be argued that to have secured universal suffrage wholesale at this time would have been a far different, and more radical, achievement than it was to be, cumulatively conceded, some seventy years later.[33] But it seems clear that these were not simply errors of political judgement, rendered self-evident by the benefits of hindsight. They were just as much dictated by those assumptions – such as the primacy of the economic and the immanent development of revolutionary class consciousness – that were inscribed in the *theoretical* bases of Marxist explanation. Thus, working within the materialist conception of history and attempting to render socialism 'scientific', Marx tended to lapse into a latently positivistic account of politics, in which what were, in practice, the most vigorously contested social struggles were seen to proceed more or less unproblematically from a given material base.

Since the writings of the early Marx were generally unavailable until the 1930s, it was this deterministic model, especially as mediated through Engels' 'Anti-Dühring', which was to exercise the profoundest influence upon Marxist accounts of politics in the generation that followed Marx's death.[34]

Parliaments or Democracy?

So far, I have concentrated upon what I take to be the two major theoretical accounts of democracy in Marx's work. In this section, I want to turn to some of the more occasional political writings of the later Marx and to focus not only upon the extent to which they are consistent with earlier positions but, more especially, and anticipating the concerns of later chapters, upon the issue of Marx's attitude to the state and parliamentary institutions in the transition to socialism. This means, of necessity, drawing upon Marx's less systematic and journalistic writings. Though these are not to be dismissed as incidental or ephemeral – including, as they do, Marx's substantial contemporary histories of the rise and fall of the Second Empire in France – it is sometimes difficult to reconcile them with the broader theoretical apparatus of Marx's major writings and this is clearly important for those who draw upon these less systematic writings as evidence of a particular disposition within the mainstream of Marx's thought.

In fact, these 'secondary' texts are often drawn upon quite selectively and this is particularly clear among those who seek to enlist Marx as a supporter of an (albeit selective and quite radical) 'parliamentary road to socialism'. Revealingly, advocates of this position have their most frequent recourse not to Marx but to the late Engels, especially to the 'bowdlerized' version of his 1895 'Introduction to Marx's *Class Struggles in France*', in which he criticizes insurrectionary 'surprise attacks', as of 1848, as 'obsolete' and claims that the 'successful utilization of universal suffrage' makes 'the bourgeoisie and the government . . . much more afraid of the results of elections than those of rebellion'.[35] But seemingly similar claims can be found in Marx's own writings. His belief that the carrying of the Chartists' demand for universal suffrage would have, 'as its inevitable result, the political supremacy of the working class' or his expectation that in England, the United States and Holland it was possible that 'the workers might attain their goal by peaceful means' are perhaps the best known among a number of examples. But partisans of an 'anti-parliamentarist' reading of Marx are able to mobilize a perhaps still wider range of counter-examples in which universal suffrage is seen 'not to be a weapon for the proletariat but a trap', 'harmless' to the existing ruling class and a source of debilitating 'parliamentary cretinism'.[36]

These differences of interpretation are not exclusively attributable to the political dispositions and interests of their rival proponents. They reflect an ambiguity that clearly existed in Marx's own view. I have already stressed that whatever the contested nature of Marx's politics, he was firmly opposed to all species of abstentionism. Thus he argued, notably in 'The Communist Manifesto' and *Capital*, that through united action, exploiting divisions within the bourgeoisie, the working class is able to win substantial gains within the present system. In the enactment of the Ten Hours Bill he insisted that 'the political economy of the middle class succumbed to the political economy of the working class.' At times, it seemed that Marx saw in these concessions, won within the prevailing system, the presentiment of more systemic change. Thus, for example, writing in 1866 of legislation to reform children's labour, he insisted that 'in enforcing such a law, the working class do not fortify governmental power', rather 'they transform that power, now used against them into their own agency.'[37]

In itself this might seem to justify an explicitly reformist position; but the intent of Marx's recommendations here is tactical rather than strategic. While he consistently supported legislative action which he thought would benefit the working class, he never claimed that this exhausted the possibilities of struggle, nor should his suggestion – in opposition to the political abstentionists – that the working class should act politically to force the government into reforming legislation, be conflated with the claim that socialism could therefore be realized through legislative enactment. Certainly, Marx regarded the expansion of the franchise as a substantial gain for the working class and in his more sanguine moments his materialist premiss drove him to claim that, with the working class forming the majority of the population, universalization of the vote would necessarily lead to their political ascendancy. But even in these moments of optimism, he did not argue that parliamentary democracy is in itself an adequate expression of this political supremacy. He did not claim that the accession of working-class representatives to parliamentary institutions on a basis of equality with all other classes – and with a potentially 'majority constituency' – establishes the basis of socialism, but rather that the political power thus gained may assist the proletariat in its more general task of seizing political power.

This is made especially clear in Marx's commentary on events in France between 1848 and 1851. Here he writes of a 'comprehensive contradiction' in the 1848 Constitution – with its installation of universal suffrage – inasmuch as 'it gives political power to the classes [proletariat, peasantry and petty bourgeoisie] whose slavery it is intended to perpetuate', imposing upon the political rule of the bourgeoisie 'democratic conditions which constantly help its enemies towards victory and endanger the very basis of bourgeois society'. The bourgeoisie's abandonment of the democratic Constitution and its embracing of the Empire, is evidence that 'its political power must be broken in order to preserve its social power.'[38] But this incompatability of universal suffrage and bourgeois rule does not mean that the former can be the medium of the overthrow of the latter. Universal suffrage, Marx insisted, was 'not the miracle-working magic wand which the republican worthies had assumed'. Much more was it 'a school of development' for the popular classes – shaping and clarifying the clash of social forces – but one which would be superseded in a revolutionary period in which 'it had to be abolished . . . by revolution or by reaction.'[39] In fact, universal (male) suffrage was not even unambiguously a proletarian principle. For Marx, the election of Louis Bonaparte by the peasant vote showed that, without the necessary freedom of speech and assembly – and under the tutelage of 'the priest and the gendarme' – universal suffrage could be 'a farce'. To expect that universalization of the franchise could become a 'transformative principle' and to characterize 'parliamentary victories as real victories' – positions which Marx associated with the emerging social democratic parties – was to lapse into *'parliamentary cretinism'*.[40]

For Marx then, universal suffrage was ambiguous and his attitude to it remained ambivalent. Certainly he never afforded to it the kind of categorical status it has generally enjoyed within the social democratic tradition. The emphasis of both 'The Class Struggles in France' and, more particularly, 'The Eighteenth Brumaire of Louis Bonaparte' was much more upon the nature of the division between (civil) society and the state and the oppression, under Bonaparte, of the former by the latter. Echoing his earliest analysis of the state–civil society relation, Marx argued that the Bonapartist state – 'this frightful parasitic body' – is the one means of securing the rule of the (internally divided) bourgeoisie. It is thus a medium of class rule, as well as constituting a 'specific oppression' of society in general. The strategy of the proletariat, Marx insisted, must be to meet this bourgeois dictatorship with 'the *class dictatorship* of the proletariat as a necessary intermediate point on the path towards the abolition of class differences in general'.[41]

This transformation could not be effected by reform within the existing machinery of the state. The working-class movement had to learn from the (bitter) experience of all previous political upheavals – which had 'perfected this machinery instead of smashing it' – and replace the existing apparatus of the state with new and distinctively proletarian state institutions.[42]

The Paris Commune

In the period 1848-51, Marx concluded that the French proletariat, as the product of an immature French capitalism, was insufficiently developed to put into effect the kind of revolutionary practice for which he had called. Twenty years later, he found this immaturity overcome and a practical revolutionary strategy pioneered – albeit as the prologue to bloody defeat – in the practice of the Paris Commune.

Although Marx's account of the Paris Commune does limited justice to the actual experience of Paris in 1871 – he was, of course, writing a 'contemporary history' with a practical and polemical intent – it was decisive in providing Marx with a model of 'the political form . . . under which to work out the economic emancipation of labour'. The parallels with the early Marx – particularly his critique of the state–civil society division – are striking. The experience of the Commune, he insisted, showed that 'the working class cannot simply lay hold of the ready-made state machine and wield it for its own purposes.' By contrast, the Commune was 'a revolution against the state itself . . . a resumption by the people for the people of its own social life'.[43]

Also seen to be overcome, in the brief life of the Commune, was the division, of which Marx had made so much in his early writings, between the members of civil society and their political representatives. The Commune was to be made up of councillors elected by universal suffrage and subject to recall and revocation at short notice. Its members were to be ordinary working men, it was to be 'a working not a parliamentary body', combining executive and legislative functions, and its public service was to be performed 'at workmen's wages'. Though not, in itself, the realization of socialism, the Commune was to be the 'concrete form' through which transition might be realized, through which the reunification of political and civil society might be secured and the existence of specific and separate political institutions overcome. It was, above all, to be 'the political form of the social emancipation'.[44]

It was Engels who described the Paris Commune – for Marx 'a thoroughly expansive political form' to be contrasted with 'all previous forms of government [which] had been emphatically repressive' – as 'the dictatorship of the proletariat'.[45] Marx himself nowhere uses this designation in describing the Commune, though he was to write some five years later in 'The Critique of the Gotha Programme' that 'the period of revolutionary transformation between capitalist and communist society' was one in which 'the state can only take the form of a *revolutionary dictatorship of the proletariat*'.[46] This 'dictatorship of the proletariat' has been subject to the most diverse interpretation. For some it is an inconsequential aside, for others it describes an expansive and democratic form of government, as in the model of the Commune, while a number of commentators – both sympathetic and hostile – identify in the formula of dictatorship of the proletariat, the essence of Marx's commitment to a centralized state and coercive, class-based rule.[47] Disputes over the nature of this 'dictatorship of the proletariat' have come to define some of the very fiercest doctrinal differences within the Marxist political tradition and, where appropriate, corresponding weight will be given to these in later chapters. But such a concern must largely be read retrospectively into Marx's own work, which was much more concerned with the dictatorship of the bourgeoisie than with the dictatorship of the proletariat. Neither of the theoretical accounts of democracy I have outlined, nor Marx's less systematic writings on state, democracy and parliament, can be said to rely heavily upon dictatorship of the proletariat. Indeed, it will become increasingly clear that it is precisely the *absence* of a treatment of (the necessity of) continuing coercive state institutions – and the contrast this makes with the experience of subsequent revolutionary and proto-revolutionary movements – that is the most striking and revealing feature of Marx on the 'dictatorship of the proletariat'. Consideration of this 'absence' I shall defer to a more general evaluation of Marx's treatment of democracy.

Democracy and 'the End of Politics'

It should be clear from this review that Marx's writings on the relationship between democracy and socialism were anything but consistent and the unscrupulous and selective reader may find textual evidence to vindicate a wide range of quite opposing views of the relation between socialism and democracy as being Marx's own. But on the basis of the evidence marshalled here, it would seem fair to suggest that Marx generally adhered to his aphoristic claim that 'the working class is revolutionary or it is nothing.'[48] While he consistently agitated for the improvement of the immediate condition of the working class and for their 'political emancipation' within the prevailing system – and thus supported claims for the expansion of popular democracy in so far as these promoted such ends – he never maintained that the unilinear expansion of the popular element within existing institutions could, in and of itself, yield to socialism, without the necessity of a revolutionary break. But it is here that many of the real problems begin. For these strategic recommendations were, in fact, based upon a quite inadequate account of the nature of political democracy, which, if it did not wholly dismiss its effectiveness, tended to depict it as either a purely formal transformative principle or else as the (quasi-automatic) mechanism for effecting a necessary historical change. Many of what are often conceived to be in principle, if not always in practice, the most important features of a democratic polity – popular rights, legislative intervention in civil society, control of the government, protection from overweening authority – are systematically ignored in an account of democracy which presupposes circumstances *beyond* the necessity of these practices. In the chapters that follow, I shall argue that this insufficiency not only weakened Marx's own account of the political but was also to have a profound and continuing impact upon later socialist political strategy in so far as this drew upon the established Marxist canon. Here, I want to give rather fuller consideration to the nature of this weakness.

'True Democracy'

In the above outline of Marx's position, it is possible to isolate two distinct, though overlapping, accounts of democracy, both of which are seriously flawed. The first – the more detailed and explicit – is that which Marx established in his early philosophical writings, the influence of which can however still be seen in a number of later works – for example, in 'The Eighteenth Brumaire of Louis Bonaparte' and 'The Class Struggles in France'. Here, Marx's critique turns upon the somewhat abstract distinction between a 'complete' human emancipation and a 'partial' political emancipation. While arguing that 'political emancipation is certainly a big step forward', Marx was insistent that this is a *definitively* restricted form of emancipation. Nor should this restriction be understood simply as a matter of degree – so that the securing of political emancipation might mark some 'half-way house' on a unilinear road, further progress along which would yield to a higher and fully human emancipation.[49] Rather, Marx argued – most clearly in 'On the Jewish Question' – that where emancipation is primarily political, this, in itself, expresses the failure to overcome that division between civil and political society which is the barrier to 'true' democracy and 'truly human' emancipation. Political emancipation is indeed to be preferred to political slavedom but its achievement, which Marx tended to associate with the ascendancy of the bourgeoisie over feudalism, is typically associated with the severance of civil and political society – under which circumstances, he further insisted, the exercise of newly won rights does not and cannot constitute a threat to the prevailing bourgeois order.

We saw that Marx characterized the French Revolution as establishing 'juridical and political equality only upon the basis of a new and deeper inequality' and that in 'the contradiction between the democratic representative state and civil society' he located 'the perfection of the classic contradiction between the public commonwealth and slavedom'. Thus the 'citizen' can exist only where divided from and contrasted to the 'bourgeois'. Indeed, Marx insisted, in *Capital* and the *Grundrisse*, that the authentic realm of freedom and equality *as citizens* under the rule of the bourgeoisie is, in fact, indispensable to the operation of a market society and thus of the capitalist mode of production. However, at the same time, this 'authentic realm of freedom and equality', is seen to be definitively restricted – 'the right of man to freedom', Marx argued, is 'the right . . . of man to private property'. In this way, he came to identify the extension of civil and political emancipation with the juridical structure of capitalism. Thus, political rights have a progressive aspect, associated with the progressive role of the bourgeoisie in displacing formalized feudal inequalities, but at the same time they tend to be identified with the legal apparatus of enforceable rights of contract – itself the basis for the 'concealed' expropriation of surplus value – and thus cannot form the basis for the transformation to 'True Democracy' or socialism.

Fortunately, for Marx at least, these limitations within the exercise of existing political rights were not a barrier to the securing of democracy, for this was itself based upon the *supersession* of such rights. *Human* emancipation was more or less conterminous with 'true' democracy – 'the solution of the riddle of every constitution' – and this in turn was to be realized through the reunification of civil and political life. Still more fortunate was the expectation that this democracy was also, in some sense, 'the solution of every riddle of the constitution' – thus classic problems of the political authority of the state, the difficulties of representation, the limitations of parliamentarism simply ceased to exist where 'man' resumed his 'true self' to himself. The state, representation and democratic rights had been an expression of a divided individual and a divided society – where this division was overcome, these problems ceased to exist, yielding, in some sense, 'an end of politics'.

This Marxist critique of political emancipation is interesting and suggestive of very real limitations in those accounts of democracy which can see nothing in this principle beyond parliamentary institutions and universal suffrage. As Buchanan notes, in his early writings Marx had offered a 'forceful critique of political emancipation, which stops at equal citizenship rights, while ignoring vast inequalities in the effectiveness with which members of different social classes can exercise their rights', while Maguire draws attention to Marx's unmasking of 'the "suppressed ideological" function' of equal citizenship in political society that conceals the essential differences of class interest that predominate in civil society.[50] But the critical impact of these insights was vitiated by at least two substantial weaknesses. First, Marx tended to associate representative democratic institutions too closely with the rise of the bourgeoisie and with the juridical structure of capitalism – a position that is particularly clear in the *Grundrisse* and *Capital*. While there is strong historical evidence to associate the early development of civil and political freedoms with the emergence of a capitalist market economy, this cannot be held to justify the claim that the conception of representative democracy is unproblematically and irredeemably a feature of a 'bourgeois' polity. For the struggle for and securing of democratic rights has never been confined simply to the struggle to secure those freedoms essential to the operation of a market economy. While some such rights – free movement of labour and capital, freedom to enter into legally enforceable contracts – may indeed be indispensable in establishing such an economy, the winning of political rights also represents an authentic (if limited) popular conquest and, perhaps most importantly, a means of exercising (again, limited) constraint upon overweening political authority. Nor should this expansion of political 'citizenship' be too readily associated with an exclusively 'bourgeois' interest. Much of the history of the (international) labour movement could be written in terms of the attempt to generalize what are sometimes dismissively characterized as 'bourgeois' rights. Not only the universalization of the franchise but other, civil rights – for example, rights of association and combination – have all, at times, been fiercely contested by the representatives of the bourgeoisie and have shown themselves to be effective, if limited and defensive, instruments in the promotion of working-class interests. Similarly, any attempt to posit a straightforward identity of capitalism and formal freedoms – a claim which also finds widespread favour among the *defenders* of a 'free market society' – is bound to seem historically insecure. Capitalism has not always been associated with the fullest civil and political freedoms. In many parts of the world, there is no need to penetrate beneath a 'surface process' of free and equal exchange to reveal a 'hidden' mode of exploitation.

'The Overcoming of Rights'

Of course, a defender of Marx's position might be willing to concede some or all of these objections by insisting that they do not materially effect the force of his argument. Indeed, they only become critical when related to a second major weakness in Marx's account – that is his expectation that, whatever the particular nature of existing institutions, the whole problematic of political *institutions* would be overcome with the inception of ('True') democracy or communism. The precise historical and categorical status of democratic rights and representative institutions was in some sense unimportant because those differences of interest and problems of political authority which generated the necessity of such institutions would be 'resolved' in democracy based upon the reunification of civil and political society and with it the 'overcoming' of politics.

It seems then, that for Marx, political rights and formal democratic institutions may only be valuable and necessary under capitalism, because only here did there exist the 'potential for the serious infringement of the freedoms' these institutions were held to guarantee. This potential for infringement existed only where power was exercised over individuals, and such circumstances could only arise out of the differences of interest entailed in the division of civil and political society or, in later accounts, in the existence of classes. Where these circumstances no longer existed, there would be no need of guarantees against an exercise of power that would have become obsolete.

However, the grounds for accepting Marx's account of 'True Democracy' are extremely uncertain. To accept it, we should have to accept some, if not all, of the following propositions:

1 that 'all social conflicts can ultimately be derived from the institutions of private property and the class structures created by it', so that 'with the abolition of that institution social conflict loses its essential basis';[51]
2 that, correspondingly, all disputes over which it makes sense to appeal to democratic forms of conflict resolution would be eliminated with the transcendence of class society;
3 that under communism there would be no specifically political institutions over which it would be appropriate to seek to exercise constraint or control;
4 that under communism it would be possible to ensure such an abundance of production that all competition over scarce goods and resources would be rendered obsolete;
5 that the harmony engendered by the elimination of classes and the resumption by 'man' of his 'true self' would eliminate disputes over the allocation of resources and reveal 'man' as a naturally cooperative animal.

It is difficult to see how these several claims could be maintained. To take but one of these, it now seems that the expectation of abundance is extremely improbable, especially in a world perceived to have finite resources, and certainly the threshold of abundance that would eliminate all disputes over the allocation of resources is almost unimaginable. Indeed, as a number of commentators have observed, it is anyway extremely difficult to see how even hyperabundance could eliminate the making of politically contentious choices, (for example, over the trade-off between economic growth and its human and enviromental costs). Similarly, the expectation of 'a stateless society' – without any co-ordinating or conflict-resolving institutions – is open to increasing theoretical criticism, even among socialists.[52] Not only are claims for the overcoming of politics in a post-class society exaggerated, there is in fact good reason to suppose that the sanction of democratic rights might be still more important under a socialized economy. On the one hand, the 'constrained' but two-edged freedoms of the capitalist mode of production – for example, contractually free labour and the free movement of such labour – represent a very real means of restraint that could be lost after socialization. On the other, where the market principle ceased to operate, the allocation of resources might well represent a new seat of authority over which it might be appropriate to seek to exercise political control. These reservations are made still more acute when one recognizes the likelihood of socialization under other than optimal conditions.

Draper is among those who insist that Marx never abandoned his 'early naïve notions about political democracy'.[53] In fact, as I have suggested, a number of these earliest formulations on democracy can be seen to re-emerge in the later works as, for example, in the critique of representation in Marx's analysis of the Commune, itself an important source for Lenin's account of Soviet rule in *The State and Revolution*. But this later account is heavily overdetermined by Marx's general reliance upon the theoretical framework of historical materialism. I have indicated that I take this to be a theoretically questionable position and that its concomitant features of economic determinism and scientistic positivism seriously weaken the later Marx's account of politics. While rejecting the claim that these later analyses are crudely or consistently deterministic, it is clear that the general reliance upon capitalist development and some sort of primacy of the economic detracted from his ability to give a persuasive account of an 'autonomous' political sphere. Even if this fault were not very pronounced in Marx himself, as Gilbert has pointed out, his analysis, especially where filtered through the authoritative interpretation of Engels, does afford the basis for such an interpretation and this is an opportunity that has been amply exploited.[54] As I suggested above, Marx's more sanguine expectations for transformation through universal suffrage were in large part based upon an account of capitalist development which would necessarily yield an homogenous and majoritarian working class allied to a general anticipation that this economic position would be the principal determinant of political practice. The primary political objective lay in mobilizing an inherent majority interest in socialism, which was generated and in some sense guaranteed by capitalist development. While the Marxist claim that historical materialism afforded (such) 'guarantees of history' to the project of socialism can, of course, be overstated, it remains important. It was certainly influential among the generation of Marxists who wrote after Marx's death – perhaps, most notably, for Karl Kautsky.

Associated difficulties surround Marx's account of the state and of democracy. For he attributed to both state and democracy certain categorical qualities, as in the claim that the state necessarily acts in the interests of the ascendant class, and tends to define them in holistic terms, in which both are seen to define unified and society-wide categories. Relying upon the exclusivity of oppression by class (as the basis of the state) and the absence of problems of political authority (itself related to this class-state matrix) in a post-revolutionary order, Marx systematically evaded or 'bracketed out' what has been the most fiercely contested terrain of socialist political strategy and practice.

While it would be unfair to accuse Marx of a general neglect of or a contempt for democratic practices and representative institutions, there are severe limitations in his account which were to make it quite inadequate as the source of an anticipated socialist political strategy. For while Marx's view of the supersession of state and democracy may indeed be defended as coherent, even cogent, this is only possible if one recognizes Marx's argument to apply only where the circumstances for an 'end of politics' have already been realized. But it is also clear that just these circumstances (for a 'fully communist' society) are, in any envisageable future, almost certainly unattainable. This recognition demands, correspondingly, a distinctive and considered *socialist* political strategy, a politics for transitional circumstances where the state and democracy have not been surpassed. For whatever reason – whether it issues from the neo-Hegelianism of the early writings or the historical materialism of the later works – Marx systematically underestimated the problems of continuing political authority, the state and democratic practices which such a *socialist* political strategy would be obliged to address.

In itself, this weakness might warrant little more than a cursory footnote in the history of socialist ideas. But, of course, Marx's theory was to be profoundly influential and we shall see in the following chapters that these weaknesses inherent in the Marxist appraisal of the political were to resurface in the bitter and continuing disputes of subsequent generations attempting to establish a coherent socialist political strategy.

2
Democracy
Socialism's 'Best Possible Shell'?

Within a few years of Marx's death, the political institutions of
capitalist Europe and the circumstances under which socialists were
called upon to intervene within them, had radically altered. Thus, for a
number of commentators, the signal importance of the Gotha
Programme of 1875 – in which the merger of the Social-Democratic
Workers' Party (SDAP) and the General Association of German
Workers (ADAV) to form the German Social Democratic Party (SPD)
was secured – is to be found in the 'Critique' it elicited from Marx and
in the opportunity it thus afforded him for the authoritative renunciation of reformism, the advocacy of revolutionary dictatorship and the
sketching of the outlines of that transitional society which was to lie
between capitalism and communism. But quite as important is the
historic moment that it marks in the evolution of European social
democratic and labour parties. For, Marx's commentaries on the
earliest manifestations of social democratic reformism and his counterposed advocacy of the Paris Commune notwithstanding, these were
developments which largely post-dated Marx's own account of democracy, and within twenty years of his death they were to have radically
transformed the circumstances under which the labour movement in
Western Europe, and Marxists within it, were to operate. Even before
the nineteenth century had closed, with a widening of the franchise, the
expansion of trades unionism and the re-establishment of the legality of
the German SPD, the fiercely resisted struggle was on to 'revise'
Marx's teaching on democracy to meet the quite changed circumstances
of a mass, legal social democratic labour movement.

Bernstein and the Codification of Social Democracy

In the frontline of this attempt critically to revise Marx was the leading
German social democrat and sometime friend of Engels, Eduard
Bernstein. His revision of Marx's teaching on the state and democracy
was, in fact, grounded in a much more general attack upon the most

essential claims of Marx's 'scientific socialism' as this had been interpreted for German Social Democracy – both in the theoretical outline of the Party's Erfurt Programme, (1891) and in the accompanying commentary, *The Class Struggle* – by the Party's leading theoretician, Karl Kautsky. In this sense, Bernstein's criticisms may be seen to be directed not so much against Marx as against that particular determinist reading of Marx which Engels and Kautsky did so much to promote in the closing years of the nineteenth century. As Andrew Arato notes, Bernstein's criticism was always much more compelling against Kautsky and Engels than against Marx. Yet, as the newly codified Marxism was, at the turn of the century, very largely what Kautsky and Engels – as its most authoritative interpreters – held it to be, the importance of Bernstein's criticisms were little lessened by this distinction.[1]

Bernstein began from a rejection of the claim that capitalism was moving towards inevitable collapse and that, correspondingly, social democracy should orient its strategy around the anticipation of 'such an imminent, great social catastrophe'.[2] This rejection of the inevitable collapse of capitalism – which, despite Kautsky's disclaimer, was deeply embedded in the Marxist orthodoxy of the late nineteenth century and explicitly endorsed by Bernstein's other great opponent, Rosa Luxemburg – Bernstein grounded in a wholesale critique of 'The Fundamental Doctrines of Marxist Socialism'. This meant a breach with Hegelian dialectics, the materialist conception of history and the labour theory of value and, correspondingly, a breach with the main lines of the Marxist account of capitalist development, which Bernstein was one of the first, among many, to insist had been empirically refuted. In contrast to the anticipations of 'The Communist Manifesto', Bernstein insisted, the 'possessing classes' and the 'middle classes' were not diminishing, nor were wage-earners being reduced to a homogenized, impoverished mass and, while there was evidence of concentration and centralization of capital, there was at the same time evidence of an expansion of the numbers of 'small and medium-sized undertakings'.[3] Bernstein's culminating heresy was to insist that, 'with the enormous extension of the world market and rapid communications allied to the growth of credit and cartels, general commercial crises similar to the earlier ones were to be regarded as improbable.'[4] Had Marx's account of capitalist development been correct, Bernstein insisted, 'certainly the economic collapse would be only a question of a short span of time', but, in fact, 'far from society being simplified . . . it has been graduated and differentiated in respect of incomes and business activities', so that the expectation of collapse was materially unfounded.[5]

From this radical breach with the canons of Marxist economic orthodoxy, there necessarily flowed a similarly far-reaching re-evaluation of Marx's political teaching. For, while Bernstein accepted that the development of productive forces that Marx had anticipated might indeed, as *The German Ideology* had suggested, have yielded an 'outcast' class 'emanat[ing] the consciousness of the necessity of a fundamental revolution', capitalist development had not, in practice, accorded with Marx's expectations and, correspondingly, Marx's political recommendations had themselves to be revised to take account of actual social development.

Here again, Bernstein's onslaught on the Marxist edifice was direct and wholesale, premised upon a rejection of the Hegelian dialectic – for everything that Marx and Engels had achieved, he insisted, was 'in spite of, not because of, Hegel's dialectic' – in favour of evolutionism as the leading component of Marx's philosophy. Given the oft-cited insufficiencies of Bernstein's philosophical knowledge, it would perhaps be mistaken to attempt to identify his philosophical stance too rigorously. But it is clear that this position committed him to a model of evolution without revolution and of a natural development into socialism which, if not without conflict, would not be, as Marx had envisaged, the result of endemic class conflict. In fact, Bernstein's analysis here – showing that 'elective affinity' with Fabianism which he developed in twenty years of exile among the leading socialist intellectuals of late nineteenth century London – can be seen to be 'thoroughgoingly whiggish', affording a central position to 'the march of democracy through history' and to the extension of citizenship to the broad mass of the people.[6] Giving classical expression to the characteristic revisionist commitment to *Evolutionary Socialism*, Bernstein insisted that the expansion of democracy and the broadening of political rights, through both their concession and their subsequent usage, made possible, and were indeed effecting, a gradual alteration in the nature of society.

Where the working class was, as Marx had argued, 'a class with *radical chains*, a class of civil society which is not a class of civil society', the call to revolution might be both necessary and justifiable. But with the concession of democratic rights, it was not only the respective strengths of the two sides, but the very rules of the game, which were altered. For Bernstein, democracy was not the means by which the working class could the more effectively (and legitimately) subject society to its own rule; it was, rather, the 'absence of class government'. While the right to vote conceded to an uneducated and undeveloped working class might long appear as nothing more than 'the right to choose "the butcher"', he insisted that 'the right to vote in a democracy makes its members virtually partners in the community', and this 'virtual partnership' would inevitably lead, in the long run, to 'real partnership'.[7]

Indeed, Bernstein did not confine himself to the claim that this democracy – which de-emphasized class in favour of citizenship within a national community – was the most desirable or secure means to achieving socialism as an end. For, with respect to socialism, Bernstein insisted, democracy was 'not only the means but also the substance'. Nor is the characterization of democracy thus identified with socialism one of pure majoritarianism – as it was, most notably, for the pre-war Kautsky, who argued that the working class might use its ('inevitable') majority to exercise *class* power through formally democratic institutions. In fact, in Bernstein's account of democracy, majoritarianism and the advocacy of the 'economic progress' of the working class was to be tempered by a commitment to civil rights. For 'the idea of democracy', he argued, necessarily embraces 'a notion of justice' – an 'equality of rights for all members of the community', in which principle 'the rule of the majority finds its limits.'[8] For Bernstein, with the coming of democracy, the idea of an epochal division between capitalism and socialism is much diminished, as the transformation capitalist-socialist is subordinated to the anodyne 'transition (free from convulsive outbursts) of the modern social order into a higher one'.[9]

The strategic consequences of Bernstein's analysis of democracy are very clear. 'Universal franchise' is, he insisted, 'the alternative to violent revolution'. For, 'as soon as a nation has attained a position where the rights of the propertied minority have ceased to be a serious obstacle to social progress . . . the appeal to revolution by force becomes a meaningless phrase.' Though it is very far from clear that universalization of the franchise is conterminous with 'a position where the right of the propertied minority has ceased to be a serious obstacle to social progress', Bernstein clearly felt that this was sufficiently true to press upon the Social Democrats 'the necessity of dropping "dictatorship of the proletariat"', (which had been formalized as party orthodoxy in the Erfurt Programme), as outmoded 'political atavism'.[10]

Bernstein rejected that conventional wisdom which contrasted the slowness of legislative reform with the speedier and more radical remedy offered by revolutionary force. Which method would provide for the more effective transition to socialism, he insisted, depended entirely upon 'the nature of the measures and on their relation to different classes and customs of the people'. He was in little doubt that where democratization had made the legal method possible, this was much to be preferred to the uncertainties of revolutionary action.

Against the errors and violence entailed in a sudden proletarian seizure of power, Bernstein argued that 'the more experience the working class democracy has had in the school of self-government, the more certainly will it proceed.' By contrast, a working class without political rights and ill-educated would certainly conspire and, from time to time, revolt but it would lack the 'breadth of vision and a fairly well developed consciousness of rights' which Bernstein insisted is essential 'to make a socialist out of a workman who is accidentally a revolter'.[11]

Bernstein was happy to note that the prospects for this peaceful and gradual transition to socialism are made still more favourable by the convenient adaptability of existing capitalist institutions. While the institutions and practices of feudalism 'had to be destroyed nearly everywhere by violence', the 'liberal organs of modern society' – among which we must take Bernstein to have included the contemporary state – are 'flexible and capable of change and development'. They do not need to be destroyed, but rather 'further developed' – a transformation which required not a revolutionary dictatorship but simply 'organisation and energetic action'.[12]

At the turn of the century, this gradual transformation was already underway. In the 'Preface' to *Evolutionary Socialism*, Bernstein insisted that a 'social reaction has set in against the exploiting tendencies of capital' and that in all the 'advanced countries' it was possible to see 'the privileges of the capitalist bourgeoisie yielding step by step to democracy.' Under these circumstances, Bernstein's political recommendations were clear. Since so much could be achieved through the exercise of political power, and as 'the conquest of political power necessitates the possession of political *rights*', the priority of the German Social Democrats had to be 'to devise the best ways for the extension of the political and economic rights of the "German working class"'. His belief that this was the most effective way to secure the realization of socialism led to his famous disavowal of the (Utopian) 'final aim of socialism', in favour of a 'strong belief' in the socialist movement, 'in the march forward of the working class, who step by step must work out their emancipation by changing society . . . to a real democracy which in all its departments is guided by the interests of those who work and create'. Since, for Bernstein, the Social Democrats had already become 'a party that strives after the socialist transformation of society by the means of democratic and economic reform', he argued that it would be best served, and its support most reliably expanded, if it would abandon its 'outworn' revolutionary phraseology and 'make up its mind to appear what it is in reality today: a democratic, socialistic party of reform'.[13]

Kautsky and Luxemburg: Against Economic 'Revisionism'

In *The Social Democrats in Imperial Germany*, Guenther Roth has drawn attention to the exceptional importance of the deterministic interpretation of Marx to the isolated social democratic movement in Germany as it emerged from the period of anti-socialist repression.[14] It is to this late nineteenth century variant of Marxism – filtered through Engels and codified in the theoretical position of the Erfurt Programme – that Bernstein's 'revisionism' is principally addressed. Correspondingly, it was the leaders of social democratic orthodoxy, notably Rosa Luxemburg and, above all, Karl Kautsky, who felt Bernstein's criticism most stingingly and accordingly it was they who made the fiercest attempts to defend the orthodoxy of the Erfurt Programme against Bernstein's 'revisionism'. United in their hostility to Bernstein, though increasingly at odds over the properly Marxist view of democratic politics, their differing responses define what were probably the most important Marxist views on democratic politics down to the First World War, views which were to remain influential, particularly within Western communist parties, even after the success of the Russian Revolution had drastically recast the contours of Marxist political analysis.

The most immediate riposte to Bernstein's 'revisionism' came in Kautsky's '*Antikritik*'. Defending the account of Marx he had given in 'The Erfurt Programme' and *The Class Struggle*, Kautsky maintained both that Marx's account of capitalist development had, by and large, been historically vindicated and further that the defence of this claim was itself *indispensable* to the historical claims made for the project of socialism. For Kautsky, the very preservation of the socialist cause, and its claim to have 'history on its side', required the refutation of Bernstein's belief that the Marxist expectation of the concentration and centralization of capital and the polarization and homogenization of classes had failed to be realized. He insisted that Marx's theory, in fact, demonstrated not only that the proletariat was held in a subordinate position but further that the dynamics of capitalist development afforded this class an ever-decreasing share in the total social wealth that it produced. It was this additional characteristic of capitalist development that gave rise to the inevitability of class struggle and its necessary intensification.

While the challenge to the Marxist account of concentration and centralization appeared to be buttressed by quantitative evidence, Kautsky maintained that Bernstein was only able to sustain this appearance by neglecting the changed relationship between the various sectors of capitalist production, which ensured the growing hegemony of big industrial and finance capital. For, while the formal ownership of industry and agriculture might not seem to have been concentrated, as Marx had anticipated, in fact the transfer of effective control to a few major cartels and the banks vindicated the Marxist model. Similarly, he argued that the growth of joint-stock companies did not occasion a 'spread' of wealth among a growing army of small capitalists but rather a further example of concentration in which small capital was brought under the control of large stockholders. Under such circumstances the experience of the working class was one of continuing, though relative, impoverishment – that is, the working class received an ever-smaller proportion of a rapidly growing social wealth. Furthermore, the emergence of the middle classes – which had been called into being by the development of big capital – did not significantly alter the laws of capitalist development and they too would, under conditions of intensified class conflict, find themselves increasingly polarized in terms of Marx's two-class model. Finally, Kautsky rejected Bernstein's claims that the expansion of the market could postpone *sine die* a general crisis, insisting that the insufficiency of demand dictated by the class structure of capitalism made it unavoidably liable to 'chronic over-production'.

Luxemburg's 'anti-critique' – most comprehensively developed in *Reform or Revolution* – shares with Kautsky an overriding concern with the indispensability of Marx's account of capitalist development to the possibility of socialist transformation. For Luxemburg, either 'the socialist transformation of society is only a utopia' or 'the theory of "means of adaptation" is false.' Paralleling Kautsky's attack, she insisted that the extension of credit and cartelization cannot afford the means of averting systemic crises. Rather, by aggravating overproduction, underconsumption, speculation, and so on, 'credit reproduces all the fundamental antagonisms of the capitalist world. It accentuates them.'[15]

Cartels and trusts, she argued, were merely a short-term response to problems of accumulation and rather than attenuating the contradictions of capitalism, they could only exacerbate them. Nor could general crises be averted, as Bernstein had supposed, by an indefinite expansion of the capitalist market. For Luxemburg insisted – anticipating the position she was to develop at length in *The Accumulation of Capital* – the capitalist market was finite, and this finitude, which had been the source of imperialism, would eventually precipitate the inevitable collapse of global capitalism.

Similarly, while recognizing the continuation of small and medium-sized enterprises upon which Bernstein had placed such stress, she denied that this constituted a refutation of Marx's expectation of growing concentration. For even under the hegemony of big capital such smaller enterprises continued to have an innovative function – as the 'pioneers of technical change' – and their continued existence was, as Marx himself had recognized, consistent with the general process of concentration. Luxemburg raised similar objections to Bernstein's claim that the growth of joint-stock companies and the expansion of shareholding furnished further evidence of a refutation of Marx. For both developments, Luxemburg insisted, marked 'the growing socialization of production' and Bernstein was only deceived into seeing in them an expansion rather than a suppression of capitalist property by the 'simple economic error' of taking 'capitalist' to mean not 'a category of production but the right to property'. 'Revisionism', she insisted, was simply 'a theory of socialist standstill justified through a vulgar economic theory of capitalist standstill'.[16]

In this defence of the orthodox Marxist account of capitalist development against Bernstein's 'revisionism', Kautsky and Luxemburg spoke with one voice. Though they were again united in their hostility to his 'political' revisionism, there were important differences in their counter-proposals which were, in the years that followed, to give rise to two mutually irreconcilable accounts of Marxist politics. In the remainder of this chapter I trace the circumstances in which unity of opposition to Bernstein was to give way to violent division between Kautsky and Luxemburg, a division which Luxemburg's biographer, Nettl, describes as having 'greater historical significance than the entire revisionist debate'.[17]

Kautsky and Luxemburg: The Divided Opposition to Political 'Revisionism'

Although, as we have already seen, Kautsky and Bernstein defended mutually exclusive accounts of capitalist development, in their recommendations for political practice they shared both an advocacy of the indispensability of parliamentary democracy and the claim that such democracy was not only the means to, but also in some sense an expression of, the realization of socialism. While Kautsky, in distinguishing his position from that of the revisionists, was keen to stress their differences, throughout a long and prolific career – and especially in his polemics with Bolshevism – he moved ever closer to Bernstein's account. By the time that he wrote Bernstein's obituary, (in 1932), he was to insist that their violent disagreement during the revisionist dispute had been 'only an episode' and that generally he and Bernstein had 'always adopted the same point of view'.[18] While this may have represented a fair, if overstated, assessment of the 'end-state' of

Kautsky's relationship with Bernstein, it is certainly historically inaccurate. In fact, a careful consideration of Kautsky's development will show how, principally in his disputes with Luxemburg and later with Bolshevism, Kautsky was to move from one-time trenchant opposition to near unanimity with Bernstein.

Kautsky and 'the Parliamentary Road to Socialism'

While Kautsky's early writings indicate support for what was subsequently to become the 'leftist' position on parliamentarism, (its use solely for organizational and tactical purposes), by the early 1890s, before his major encounter with revisionism, he had adopted what was to remain a life-long advocacy of 'the parliamentary road to socialism'. This espousal of parliamentarism was, in turn, grounded in a belief in the profound importance to the working class of its attainment of a broad range of political and civil rights. Echoing 'The Communist Manifesto','The Erfurt Programme' insisted that the struggle of the working class against capitalism was necessarily 'a political battle' and its economic interests could not be secured 'without political rights'. The most important of these rights – freedoms of association, assembly, the press and the vote – were the '*vital conditions of existence* without which the class itself cannot develop'. These freedoms were 'light and air for the proletariat' and whomsoever detracted or diverted from these rights was, 'whatever great love for the proletariat he may feel or feign', to be numbered 'among the worst enemies of the working class'.[19]

It was upon this claim for the indispensable centrality of the securing of civil and political rights that Kautsky proceeded to defend his claims for the efficacy of parliamentarism. As early as 1892 , he argued that once 'the proletariat engages in parliamentary activity as a self-conscious class, *parliamentarism begins to change its character*' (my emphasis). It is no longer 'a tool in the hands of the bourgeoisie'. Participation, of itself, has an uplifting effect upon the morale and organization of the working class. It is 'the most powerful lever that can be used to raise the proletariat out of its economic, social and moral degradation'. Accordingly, the working class must resist the siren calls of those who draw it away from the parliamentary arena and must seek rather to maximize its own parliamentary representation and to strengthen the power of parliaments over and against other less popular departments of government.[20]

It is in his evaluation of the way in which this parliamentarism must necessarily yield socialism that the decisive difference between Kautsky and Bernstein arises. For the Kautskyan account of the 'parliamentary road to socialism' is very heavily reliant upon his (deterministic) model of capitalist development. Universal franchise – for Kautsky, 'prerequisite to a sound development of the proletariat', – at first allows the working class to secure only limited, if valuable, concessions from the ruling bourgeoisie. But capitalist development, in which for Kautsky, class struggle necessarily becomes more polarized and intense, just as inevitably throws up an independent labour party. This party, in its turn, 'must sooner or later exhibit socialist tendencies' and, acting under the compulsion of historical materialism, 'must have for its purpose the conquest of the government in the interest of the class which it represents'. Fortunately, 'economic development will lead naturally to the accomplishment of this purpose.'[21] Quite as unproblematic as this victory of the independent labour party is the necessity of that party's instituting socialism. Again echoing 'The Communist Manifesto', Kautsky argued that the proletariat cannot, as have all previous ascendant classes, use its newly won power to shift the burden of exploitation upon others – for the abolition of exploitation for the proletariat means the abolition of exploitation generally. But this overcoming of exploitation is only possible through the elimination of commodity production and private property. Just as, for Marx, the proletarians could not 'become masters of the productive forces of society, except by abolishing their own previous mode of appropriation', so, for Kautsky, was 'socialist production . . . the natural result of a victory of the proletariat . . . Its victory will have become inevitable as soon as that of the proletariat has become inevitable'. Happily, Kautsky concluded, 'there can be no doubt as to the final victory of the proletariat.'[22]

Accompanying this optimistic anticipation of the 'forward march to socialism' was an insistence upon the indispensability of the parliamentary form, not only as the means to but, quite as importantly, as the institutional form of, socialism. Opposing the claims of some form of direct democracy, Kautsky argued that 'in a great modern state' the proletariat, like the bourgeoisie, could acquire influence on the administration of the state 'only through the vehicle of an elected parliament'. He insisted that 'so long as the great modern state exists the central point of political activity will always remain in its parliament.'[23]

In opposition to Karl Bürkli, who had contrasted the representative republic, as political instrument of the bourgeoisie, with 'direct legislation' as the typical form of proletarian rule, Kautsky insisted that not only was the parliamentary form adequate for the struggle of the proletariat within bourgeois society, it was, in fact, also the only effective means of securing political revolution and the transfer of power. The appeal to direct legislation and anti-centralism was inappropriate to the developed state of contemporary capitalism. Control over necessarily centralized power could only be effectively exercised by the development of representative institutions. Since parliament was the 'technically indispensable means' of governing within any 'great modern state' and since parliament was transformed by the accession to it of social democracy it was clear to Kautsky that 'parliament was not merely an essential avenue for socialists under bourgeois rule, but also the necessary instrument for the exercise of their power.'[24]

However, Kautsky was quite as insistent that this proletarian power would not be compromised by its parliamentary form. For the combination of the majoritarianism inherent in parliamentarism and the 'built-in' majority which capitalism secured for the working class necessarily generated the requisite conditions for the unmediated rule of the proletariat, ensuring that 'a genuine parliamentary regime can be as much an implement of the dictatorship of the proletariat as an instrument of the dictatorship of the bourgeoisie.'[25] It was, again, this inevitability of the victory of socialism, guaranteed in the Kautskyan model of capitalist development, which generated his optimism for peaceful transition. In 'A Social Democratic Catechism', he urged the labour movement to reject violence and conspiracy in favour of a parliamentary transition, in which violence would arise only out of the despair of the usurped bourgeoisie. Even this might be avoided, he argued, since a further advantage of democratic politics was that it reflected accurately the relative class forces in the wider society and might thus dissuade premature proletarian assaults upon the seizure of power, encourage the ruling class to recognize the inevitability of its decline and persuade it, accordingly, to 'accept the verdict of history, peacefully'. Democracy could, then, minimize the social costs of transition but, Kautsky insisted, it could not lead to the integration of the working class under the prevailing system, and a dissipation of its strength in a reformed capitalism, because democracy 'could not abolish the class contradicitons of capitalist society and prevent their necessary result, namely the overthrow of society'.[26]

This then constitutes the essential Kautskyan view of the 'parliamentary road to socialism'. Although it was to be amended and give rise to differing political recommendations, this account, which relied so heavily upon 'the guarantees of history' that Kautsky had identified in capitalist development, was to underpin his position from the attacks upon revisionism to the polemics against Bolshevism.

Forward from 'Anti-revisionism'

While this analysis suggests a measure of common ground in Kautsky's and Bernstein's evaluation of political rights and parliamentary democracy, there were important divergences in their respective positions – differences largely founded in their counterposed accounts of capitalist development – and it was these which Kautsky held to distinguish his position from revisionism and which were to form the basis of his later theoretical 'centrism'.

Of all the differences that emerged from these opposed accounts of capitalist development perhaps the single most important was Kautsky's rejection of Bernstein's de-emphasis of class struggle. While Bernstein had defined democracy as 'the absence of class government', Kautsky insisted that democracy was merely a 'form of rule by majority' and as such not incompatible with the class rule of either bourgeoisie or proletariat.[27] Democracy might indeed 'constitute the indispensable condition for the elimination of class rule' but this end to class rule could only be realized where the proletariat had first been raised to the position of the ruling class. It was indeed the historic mission of the proletariat to 'use democracy to put an end to all class differences', but 'without the class rule of the proletariat there can be no end to classes.' Nor should democracy be described as 'class-neutral', for, Kautsky insisted, democracy was increasingly being abandoned by the bourgeoisie and 'a progressive democracy in a modern industrial state is henceforth possible only in the form of a proletarian democracy.'[28]

Kautsky similarly rejected Bernstein's insistence upon the 'necessity of dropping "dictatorship of the proletariat"' as 'political atavism'. While Kautsky's own understanding of 'dictatorship of the proletariat' was not uniform throughout his career, his characterization of its essential features was clear and largely consistent. Crucially, this proletarian dictatorship was *not* to be understood as the exercise of arbitrary power and the suspension of democratic procedures. Rather it was held, by Kautsky, to be the normal form of government occasioned by first, a general extension of political democracy and secondly, the emergence of that 'built-in' working class majority which capitalist development itself created. Kautsky anticipated that this dictatorship might be called upon to use force against recalcitrant reactionaries and 'slave-holders' rebellions' but this would not be undemocratic where carried out with the support of, and with the authority deriving from, a majority consensus for socialism. This 'dictatorship as a condition', where democratic procedures themselves gave rise to the unmediated rule of the working class, Kautsky was later to distinguish from 'dictatorship as a form of government', which he was to condemn as a Bolshevist usurpation of democracy. Marx, he insisted, had identified with the former position, hailing proletarian dictatorship as an expansive and democratic form, as in the Paris Commune – as 'a condition which necessarily arose in a real democracy, because of the overwhelming numbers of the proletariat'.[29]

Kautsky also vigorously opposed Bernstein's recommendations that the German SPD should recognize itself as 'a democratic, socialistic party of reform' and rejected the claim that the commitment to parliamentarism and legal reforms must necessarily give rise to reformism. In *The Class Struggle*, he condemned the continuing advocacy of the 'primitive socialist' argument that any piecemeal advance for the working class would merely postpone a revolutionary overthrow and that therefore any 'struggle for the gradual elevation of the working class [was] not only hopeless, but harmful'. This absence of an awareness of 'gradualist class struggle' Kautsky saw as 'a children's disease', typical of an immature labour movement which had not yet outgrown 'the maximalist spirit of utopianism'. While defending the growth of trades unions and their attempt to improve the immediate condition of labour, he insisted that it was 'a profound error to imagine that such reforms could delay the social revolution'. But 'equally mistaken' was the claim that it was impossible to admit the usefulness of winning reforms without insisting upon the preservation of society on its present basis. Rather, Kautsky favoured what he understood to be the *revolutionary advocacy of reforms*, which reforms 'so far from doing away with the suicidal tendencies of the capitalist system, rather strengthen them'. In this way, Kautsky was able to endorse the pursuit of reforms and the prosecution of the 'gradualist class struggle', while rejecting the further claims that this negated the necessity of revolution or that socialism might itself be introduced incrementally by an accumulation of such reforms.[30]

There were anyway, he insisted, important tactical reasons for preserving the revolutionary orientation – to drop it would damage the morale of the working class, mean the loss of a lever over the ruling class and encourage anarchistic adventurism – but, for Kautsky, the essential point was that no reform based upon the existing system of property could resolve the ever-intensifying contradictions of capitalism. Reforms that proposed overcoming the growing contradiction between the forces of production and the existing forms of property, while upholding the latter, he declared to be 'inoperative'. For it was only through 'the transformation of capitalistic ownership . . . into social ownership' that the rapidly growing productive capacity of modern industry could be transformed for the working classes from 'a source of misery and oppression to a source of the highest welfare and all-round harmonious perfection'. There was, he conceded, a 'kernel of truth' in reformist accounts, inasmuch as capitalism was indeed developing towards socialism through the concentration and centralization of capital, the growth of the proletariat and of its organization. But what presented itself to these reformers as 'a peaceable growth into Socialism' was, in reality, 'only the growth in power of two antagonistic classes, standing in irreconcilable hostility to each other'.[31]

'Transforming' the State

This divergence over the status of the class struggle and of the necessity of revolution led to further important differences between Kautsky and Bernstein over the possibility of class alliances and the nature of the (capitalist) state. Even before his major dispute with Bernstein, Kautsky had taken issue with the reformist trades union leader von Vollmar and those of his Southern German supporters who had endorsed his call for an alliance with the small and middling peasantry, rapprochement with a Bismarckian 'state socialism' and a reformulation of the Erfurt Programme. Kautsky did not subscribe to the Lassallean belief that all opponents of social democracy constituted 'a single reactionary mass' and was willing to contemplate short-term tactical alliances with certain elements in the liberal bourgeoisie. However, he insisted that such an alliance could not be allowed to interfere with 'the full organizational, ideological and parliamentary independence of the SPD', and certainly he refused to entertain the possibility of entering into a long-standing alliance with what he regarded as a retrogressive and obsolete class whose disappearance was guaranteed by further capitalist development.

A similar proviso informed his attitude to ministerialism or 'Millerandism' – that is, the participation of individual socialists in bourgeois, albeit bourgeois-reformist, governments. While this might be possible under 'transitory and exceptional' circumstances – for example, in alliance against a reactionary *coup d'état* – it should only be temporary, contingent and strictly under the control of a party mandate. Any formulation which claimed that such participation could allow the socialists a gradual acquisition of power, Kautsky rejected. It was only possible to win such power 'not *through* a coalition but *against* a coalition'. Generally, the presence of a socialist minister in a bourgeois government would merely give ideological cover to what would remain essentially bourgeois measures. Fortunately, Kautsky argued, such long-term strategic alliances were not only damaging but also unnecessary. For once social democracy had united in a 'bloc' the industrial

proletariat and all those seemingly independent industrial and agri-
cultural workers 'who are in fact only wage workers for capital . . . no
force will be able to offer any resistance to it'. Accordingly,

> The principal task of Social Democracy is and will remain to win over the
> mass, to organise it politically and economically, to raise its intellectual
> and moral level, and to bring it to the point at which it will inherit the
> legacy of the capitalist mode of production.[32]

Kautsky was also hostile to von Vollmar's assertion that the workers'
movement and bourgeois reformism were converging and finding
common expression in economic and social reforms carried through by
the state and that therefore 'Social Democracy had no reason to
combat the viewpoints of *Staatssozialismus* with any particular zeal.'
This position Kautsky vigorously opposed insisting that nationalization
within the prevailing state would always be a reform in the interest of
the property-holding ruling class. He insisted that 'the modern state is
pre-eminently an instrument intended to guard the interests of the
ruling class.' In so far as it intervened to secure measures of general
utility of interest not only to the ruling class but to the whole of 'the
body politic', this was only because 'otherwise the interests of the ruling
class would be endangered with those of society as a whole'. Indeed,
nationalization might even form the basis of a more effective
exploitation of labour – the economic power of capital being reinforced
by the political power of the state – a claim which was to be echoed in
Kautsky's later condemnation of the Bolsheviks. Certainly, state-
sponsored reforms could never be pursued 'in such a manner as to
endanger the overlordship of the capitalist class'. The state, Kautsky
concluded, 'will not cease to be a capitalist institution until the
proletariat becomes the ruling class' and this, in turn, conditions social
democratic strategy, which is 'to call the working class to conquer the
political power to the end that they may change the state *into a
self-sufficing co-operative commonwealth*'.[33]

It is important to note, however, that while Kautsky was clearly and
consistently opposed to the revisionist claim that it was possible to
effect a gradual transition to socialism through reforms carried out by
the presently constituted (and capitalist) state, he did not suggest that
the alternative to this incrementalism was violently to overhaul or
'smash' the existing state apparatus. The functions of the state and the
bureaucracy, he insisted, were *technically indispensable* to a modern
society. In *The Dictatorship of the Proletariat*, he maintained that
exercising control over the government is 'the most important duty of
parliament and in that it can be replaced by no other institution', for

'the executive can only be supervised by another central body, and not by an unorganized and formless mass of the people.' A socialist government might make the institutions of representative government more accountable but it could not dissolve them in favour of some form of direct democracy. This was to be a major point of division between Kautsky and those to his 'left'.[34]

These then were the essential features of Kautsky's critique of Bernstein's political revisionism – emphasis upon the continuing necessity of class struggle and 'the dictatorship of the proletariat', insistence upon the political independence of the working class and upon the revolutionary status of its party – as 'a revolutionary party that does not make revolutions' – and opposition to compromise with 'state socialism'. But while maintaining his distance from the revisionists, Kautsky did place a growing emphasis upon the centrality of the democratic-parliamentary struggle and this, especially after 1905 and the impact of the first Russian Revolution, was to lead him increasingly to distinguish his position from that of Luxemburg and the insurrectionary left. Increasingly, Kautsky was to present himself as holding 'the middle ground' between the 'statesman's impatience' of the reformist right and the 'rebel's impatience' of the revolutionary left.[35] To locate this centrism, we must return to Luxemburg's own critique of revisionism and the quite different political conclusions to which she was driven.

Luxemburg: The Split with Kautsky

Although the split between Luxemburg and Kautsky only became explicit in the polemics of 1909–10, fundamental differences in their political strategy and especially in their evaluations of the possibilities inherent in parliamentarism can be traced all the way back to their differing critiques of Bernstein.[36]

The first point to note, however, is one of similarity – that is, Luxemburg's consistent endorsement of the importance to the working class of the acquisition and exercise of political rights. In the 'Introduction' to *Reform or Revolution*, she recognized that the 'daily struggle for reforms' – the fight to secure democratic institutions and to ameliorate the immediate circumstances of the working population within the prevailing order – is 'the only means of engaging in the proletarian class war and working in the direction of the final goal – the conquest of political power and the suppression of wage labour'. Again, in *The Mass Strike*, she wrote of the 'immense importance' of a reactionary threat against what is for 'the wide masses of the people the most important political right – universal suffrage', and it was indeed the defence of democratic rights which was to be the main point at issue in her later polemics with Lenin and Trotsky.[37] But while she was repeatedly to stress these rights, the account she gave of their purpose differed decisively from that offered by either Bernstein or Kautsky. We have seen that the essence of the latter's critique of Bernstein's political revisionism turned upon the defence of the continuing necessity of class struggle, revolution and proletarian dictatorship but that, at the same time, Kautsky was insistent that these could all be adequately realized through parliamentary-democratic struggle. It was the latter position that Luxemburg so violently opposed. While parliament constituted an important arena of class struggle it was not conterminous with democracy and did not furnish an adequate vehicle for the transition to socialism. Indeed, for Luxemburg, parliamentary democracy was an *essentially* bourgeois form.

She first developed this position in her anti-revisionist polemic *Reform or Revolution*. Bernstein, she argued, had abandoned the Marxist account of the emergence of socialism, grounded in the intensification of the contradictions of capitalism in favour of an account of 'the adaptation of capitalism' in which the activity of trades unions, social reforms and the political democratization of the state were to issue in the progressive realization of socialism. She rejected this anticipation on all three counts. Firstly, trades unions were necessarily limited to struggles over the pay and conditions of wage labour, that is 'to efforts at regulating capitalist exploitation within the market relations'. They were 'nothing more than the organized *defense* of labor power against the attacks of profit' and, as such, they had not 'the power to suppress exploitation itself, not even gradually'.[38] With capitalism moving into its 'descending phase' of intensifying crises of profitability, it became 'doubly difficult' for the trades union movement not only to secure piecemeal gains but even to hold its present ground.

She similarly rejected the revisionists' claim that 'social reforms' represented the encroachment of a transformative socialist interest upon the terrain of capital. For factory acts, labour legislation, the control of industrial organizations through shareholding and so on, were not 'a threat' to capitalist exploitation but 'simply the regulation of this exploitation'. Echoing Marx's account of the equivocal consequences of labour legislation, Luxemburg insisted that this was enacted 'as much in the interest of the capitalist class as in the interests of society in general'.[39]

But Luxemburg's most extended and interesting criticisms were reserved for the third plank in the revisionist platform – that is, the growing democratization of the state. In contradistinction to Bernstein's unilinear account of 'the evolution of the state in society',

Luxemburg insisted upon the increasingly contradictory nature of the capitalist state. On the one hand, capitalist development led the state increasingly to intervene in society, to exercise 'social control' and take upon itself new functions. In this limited sense, capitalist development was preparing 'little by little the future fusion of the state and society', preparing for 'the return of the function of the state to society'. But, on the other hand, Luxemburg insisted, the present state was 'first of all, an organization of the ruling class'. While in capitalism's ascendant phase, state action in the interests of the ruling class had accorded with the more general social interest, once capitalism and the bourgeoisie had ceased to be progressive – and Luxemburg argued that 'this phase has already begun' – the state, in continuing to support the particularist bourgeois interest, was now acting against the broader interests of general social development. It lost 'more and more it's character as a representative of the whole of society' and descended, at the same rate, 'into a pure *class* state'. Thus, on the one hand, Luxemburg identified a 'growth of the function of a general interest on the part of the state', but, at the same time, this was increasingly outweighed by its class character which led it into activities which were useful only to the bourgeoisie and which had 'for society as a whole only a negative importance'.[40]

For Luxemburg, the extension of democracy, which Bernstein had heralded as the means to a gradual realization of socialism, 'does not contradict but, on the contrary, corresponds to [this] transformation realized in the nature of the state'. Indeed, the contradiction which Luxemburg had identified within the capitalist state 'manifests itself even more emphatically in modern parliamentarism'. For, while Luxemburg endorsed the claim that 'democratic forms of life [express] clearly the evolution of the state in society' and that they were, in this sense, 'a move towards a socialist transformation', she insisted that this democratic form was vitiated by its increasingly capitalist content. Parliamentarism does indeed express the interests of the whole society – but those of 'a society in which capitalist interests predominate'. Correspondingly, she argued that, under these circumstances, representative institutions, while 'democratic in form, are in content the instruments of the ruling class'. At first sight, it is not entirely clear why these formally democratic institutions should be suffused with a capitalist content. It is possible that this claim could be interpreted as an advocacy of Marx's supposition that 'the ideas of the ruling class are in every epoch the ruling ideas.' But Luxemburg seemed rather to have in mind her own model of trades union activity – that is of the expression of opposed interests, contained within the limits set by the prevailing social order.[41]

The parliamentary struggle, she made clear in *The Mass Strike*, is 'a fight conducted exclusively on the basis of the bourgeois social order'. This is 'by its very nature, political reform work', paralleling trades unions' 'economic reform work', and, as such, it is merely one (passing) phase in the evolution of 'the complete process of the proletarian struggle', the 'ultimate goal' of which lies 'as far beyond the parliamentarian struggle as it is beyond the trades union struggle'. Parliamentarism is not then 'a directly socialist element impregnating gradually the whole capitalist society'. Rather is it 'a specific form of the bourgeois class state, helping to ripen and develop the existing antagonisms of capitalism'.[42]

This opposition between socializing/progressive form and capitalist/ regressive content, Luxemburg was to apply much more generally as proof of the impossibility of a gradual introduction of socialism. For, as the process of production comes to be increasingly socialized, the state – as the political organization of capitalism – and property relations – as juridical organization of capitalism – become more capitalist rather than more socialist, thus posing 'two insurmountable difficulties' to the advocates of a progressive introduction of socialism. For these juridical and political relations establish between capitalist and socialist society 'a steadily rising wall' which, far from being overthrown, is in fact, 'strengthened and consolidated by the development of social reform and the course of democracy'. Luxemburg is insistent that 'only the hammer blow of revolution . . . the conquest of political power by the proletariat, can break down this wall.'[43]

Luxemburg: Socialist Democracy v. Parliamentary Democracy

There is thus far in Luxemburg's reply to revisionism much which Kautsky would have been willing to endorse. Both insisted that trades union activity is essentially confined to protecting the immediate economic-corporate concerns of wage labour and should be subordinated to the wider political interests of the working class. They both argued the necessity of retaining a commitment to the 'hammer blow of revolution', the conquest of political power and the exercise of proletarian dictatorship. They were united in condemning ministerialism, the dissolution of the revolutionary end in the parliamentarian means, and the belief that socialism could be won gradually by an accretion of particular reforms. Both insisted that the inevitable upshot of such ministerialism and opportunism is a disarming and demoralization of the labour movement, issuing in a 'reversion to anarchism' which they both condemned. The decisive breach between them arises over their quite differing evaluations of the potency of parliamentary democracy. Thus Kautsky held that, with the requisite extra-parliamentary support from the mass of the population, parliamentary democracy is an adequate vehicle for what is still a revolutionary transformation to socialism. Indeed, except under quite exceptional circumstances, it was for him the only adequate form for the transition from capitalism to socialism – a claim which he was vigorously to defend against the practice of the Bolsheviks. Luxemburg, by contrast, insisted that the institutions of parliamentary democracy could *never* pose the issue of socialist revolution and that to claim that they could was, whatever one's revolutionary protestations, to give aid and succour to the revisionists.

To understand how Kautsky and Luxemburg, seemingly united in their hostility to revisionism, came to be so bitterly divided over the nature of socialist transformation, it will prove necessary to consider in further detail Luxemburg's own account of democracy. Luxemburg began by condemning that Whiggish account of democracy which, she argued, Bernstein had borrowed from bourgeois liberalism, in which democracy is characterized as 'a general law of historic development', a general feature of the evolution of modern society. Parliamentarism, she wrote in 1904, was not just such 'a product of democratic development, of the progress of the human species, and of such nice things'. Rather was it 'the historically determined form of the class rule of the bourgeoisie and . . . of its struggle against feudalism'. Correspondingly, bourgeois parliamentarism would remain 'only so long as the conflict between the bourgeoisie and feudalism lasts'. By the turn of the twentieth century, the epoch of the (progressive) historical struggle of the bourgeoisie against feudalism had largely passsed and democratic institutions had, she argued in *Reform or Revolution*, completely exhausted their function as aid in the development of bourgeois society, and correspondingly the bourgeoisie were increasingly abandoning the democratic form in favour of 'world politics and militarism'.[44]

This did not however mean that the working class should itself simply abandon the democratic terrain. For while democracy had become redundant for the bourgeoisie, it remained 'indispensable' to the working class, for 'only through the struggle for democracy, can the proletariat become aware of its class interests and its historic task.' Democracy is indispensable not because it makes the proletarian conquest of power superfluous but rather because it renders this conquest 'both necessary and possible'.[45]

This again sounds remarkably similar to the Kautskyan position but there are, in fact, quite decisive differences. Firstly, Luxemburg argued that trades union and parliamentary struggles are important in raising the consciousness of the proletariat precisely because they induce a recognition that such activity *cannot* in itself yield fundamental change and thus in fuelling the conviction that the revolutionary seizure of power is unavoidable. But once it is argued that trades union or, as in Kautsky's case, parliamentary struggles can themselves become the vehicles of socialist transformation, 'as instruments of the direct socialization of capitalist economy', they entirely 'cease being means of preparing the working class for the conquest of power'. These two positions, Luxemburg insisted, are 'diametrically opposed' and this opposition led Luxemburg to stress the problem of trades union and party bureaucratization and to a corresponding advocacy of the necessity of 'premature' mass attempts at the seizure of state power which were quite alien not only to Bernstein but also to Kautsky.[46]

The second major difference with Kautsky lay in Luxemburg's claim that, while democracy in itself was not specific to any particular social formation, *parliamentary democracy is an essentially bourgeois form.* Accordingly, parliamentary democracy, which was for Kautsky not only the revolutionary means but also the desired post-revolutionary form, could not be the means to a revolutionary transformation. Luxemburg's simplest objection to 'the parliamentary road to social-ism', one which pre-echoes Lenin, is that in elections conducted under the rule of the bourgeoisie, capital would always be able to secure its interests through its control of the media, resources, employment and so on. Thus, writing of plebiscites, she argued that the ruling class would always know how to prevent them or to influence their results in the same ways 'which make it impossible to introduce socialism by a popular vote'. Even the securing of a popular majority in parliament would not herald a socialist transformation, Luxemburg claimed, for such an anticipation failed to take account of her counterposition, within the capitalist state, of democratic form and capitalist content. Thus she argued that while democracy could bring a measure of popular participation and 'some sort of "peoples' state"', such partici-pation is limited to 'bourgeois parliamentarism . . . in which class antagonism and class domination are not done away with'.[47]

The idea of the conquest of a parliamentary reformist majority is then, for Luxemburg, illusory, relying solely, in 'the spirit of bourgeois liberalism', upon the formal aspects of democracy to the neglect of its 'real' content. For she argued that as soon as democracy appears to deny its (bourgeois) class character and to become an instrument of the real interests of the mass of the population, it is 'sacrificed by the bourgeois and its state representatives'. This parliamentarism rested, in turn, upon a criticism of the supposed potency of democratic institutions within the capitalist state, of that 'parliamentary cretinism' which sees parliament as the locus of effective power. Such 'parliamentary cretinism', she proclaimed, was unable to see beyond 'the complacent speechifications of a few hundred parliamentary deputies in a bourgeois legislative chamber' to 'the gigantic forces of world history' which continue to operate outside the precincts of the parliamentary assemblies and are 'unconcerned with . . . parliamentary law making'. It is this 'play of the blind elementary forces of social development' which leads to 'the inexorable undermining not only of the imagined, but also of the real significance of bourgeois parliamentarism'. This arises, on the one hand, out of the growth of 'global politics' in which 'bourgeois parliaments are tossed about powerlessly like logs in a stormy sea' and, on the other hand, by internal changes in the relations of classes and parties which 'brings to nought the pliancy and impotence of the bourgeois parliament'. Indeed a feudal-bourgeois compromise, which Luxemburg insisted had 'for the past quarter-century [been] the universal feature of political development in the capitalist countries', meant that the bourgeoisie had not even fulfilled its historically progressive role against feudalism. This class compromise had reduced parliament to 'a rudiment, an organ deprived of all function' and brought with it 'all the striking features of parliamentary decline'.[48]

The Necessity of a 'Revolutionary Break'

These might, in some sense, be styled Luxemburg's contingent criticisms of parliamentarism but they were supplemented by a number of further structural criticisms which were, if anything, still more damning of the supporters of parliamentary socialism. For, even if it were possible to secure a popular majority in parliament and both to pass and put into effect radical legislation, Luxemburg maintained that the parliamentary machinery could not be used to effect a revolutionary transformation since legal enactments and revolution are *qualitatively* different. Revolution is 'the act of political creation', of which the legal constitution is simply 'the product'. Social transformation and legislative reform 'condition and complement each other', but they are 'at the same time reciprocally exclusive'. It was upon this contrast between periods of gradualist normalcy and revolutionary exceptionalism as distinct – indeed as mutually exclusive – phases of the class struggle that Luxemburg based her later distinction between the 'stagnant waters of the bourgeois-parliamentary period' and the 'revolutionary periods of the mass strike'. It was upon this basis that she made her claim that the inevitable fruit of revisionism would be 'not the realization of *socialism*, but the reform of *capitalism* . . . the suppression of the abuses of capitalism instead of the suppression of capitalism itself'.[49]

Of course, it might be argued that in this counterposition of revolution and legislative action, (as in that between democratic form and capitalist content), Luxemburg draws a purely *formal* distinction – that she has simply eliminated the possibility of revolutionary transformation through legal enactments by definitional fiat. Luxemburg might, in turn, seek to counter this criticism in two ways. The first counter-objection would be to cite 'the evidence of history'. Thus in a speech to the Hanover Congress of the German SPD, (in 1899), Luxemburg advised her audience that, in all previous class struggles the rising class had exploited legal reforms within the old society only until it was sufficiently strong to throw off the shackles of the old order 'by means of a social and political catastrophe'. Those who believed that it might be possible to lead society into socialism peacefully, she insisted, had 'no historical basis in fact'.[50]

But it was possible to argue, as Bernstein had in *Evolutionary Socialism* and as indeed did Kautsky in *The Road to Power*, that while this claim against the effectiveness of legislative reform was generally valid for the revolutionary struggle of the bourgeoisie against feudalism, the concession of political rights to the working class had changed the rules of the revolutionary 'game', enabling the proletariat to seize power through a parliamentary-democratic victory. Against Bernstein, Kautsky and those others who argued that, while insurrection had been essential in the past, 'the development of the bourgeois juridical system' makes a legislative and gradual transformation possible, she insisted that 'the very opposite is true.' For what distinguished capitalism from earlier class societies is precisely that 'class domination does not rest on "acquired rights" but on real economic relations' – that wage labour is not a juridical but an economic relation. In fact, Luxemburg argued, it would be possible to imagine a legal passage in the transition from feudal to bourgeois society, since feudalism was grounded on formal juridical inequalities which were, in some measure, capable of redress within the old framework. But, in practice, even here, legal reforms did not obviate the necessity of the ascendant class, the bourgeoisie, seizing power. If under these conditions which were more suited to a legal transition, the rising class was still obliged to proceed by means of 'a social and political catastrophe' how much more must this be the case for the ascendant proletariat, whose oppression is not expressed in inequalities open to legal redress. For, she argued, it is not laws but economic necessity that obliges the proletariat to sell itself to the bourgeoisie and she argued that the proletarians cannot hope to seek a purely legal redress where 'not laws but economic development have torn the means of production from [their] possession'. From this, Luxemburg concluded that 'the fundamental relations of the domination of the capitalist class cannot be transformed by means of legislative reforms . . . because these relations have not been introduced by bourgeois laws.'[51]

It would certainly be mistaken to suggest that this argument of Luxemburg incontestably carries the day against the proponents of legislative transition. The fact that bourgeois domination is seen to be essentially extra-legal is insufficient to demonstrate that it is incapable of legislative redress. However, Luxemburg's account did expose an important structural feature of capitalism, as opposed to feudalism, namely the existence of formal equality and freedom alongside systematic inequalities. In this, she echoed the account given by Marx of the relation between civil and political society, discussed in the opening chapter, and this is only one of a number of significant parallels between the analyses of Marx and Luxemburg. For she went on to argue that one of the characteristic weaknesses of bourgeois democracy is that it is a *representative* form – which Marx, as we saw, had criticized as a usurpation of democracy. In the 'normal' course of bourgeois society, Luxemburg insisted, the masses were not typically involved directly on the political stage, but were present – 'in correspondence with the forms of the bourgeois state' – only 'in a representative fashion'. But 'as soon as a period of revolutionary struggle commences . . . the indirect parliamentary form of the political struggle ceases', giving way to a 'revolutionary mass action', in which 'the political and the economic struggle are one.'[52] This, in its turn, points towards a third area of common ground shared by Marx and Luxemburg. For, at the same time, Luxemburg insisted that 'the separation of the political and the economic struggle . . . is nothing but an artificial product of the parliamentarian period' and she, like Marx, sought to develop an analysis which would reveal bourgeois democracy's 'hard kernel of social inequality and lack of freedom hidden under the sweet shell of formal freedom and equality'.[53]

Kautsky's Centrism: A 'Tough-minded Democracy'?

Starting out from a common hostility to Bernstein, it should be clear that Luxemburg had developed from her critique of revisionism an account of parliaments and democracy which – whatever its parallels with (the early) Marx – was quite clearly at variance with the position established by Kautsky. Increasingly in the pre-war decade, especially after the Russian Revolution of 1905 had emboldened Luxemburg to produce her advocacy of *The Mass Strike*, Kautsky was to define his position not only in terms of hostility to revisionism but also around his opposition to the 'insurrectionism' represented by Luxemburg. It was around this opposition to both 'revisionism' and 'ultra-leftism' that Kautsky was to establish his 'centrism' and it was in this, rather than as 'the Pope' of Marxist orthodoxy, that Kautsky was to make his most lasting impact upon West European communism.

In *The Mass Strike*, Luxemburg, drawing upon the evidence of spontaneous, mass intervention in the revolutionary events of 1905 in Russia, insisted upon applying these 'lessons of 1905' to Germany, in the form of extra-parliamentary insurrection, street actions and mass political strikes. The adoption of such a 'strategy of annihilation', as Kautsky characterized it, in which everything was to be staked upon all-or-nothing confrontation with the ruling class had been, and indeed remained, the appropriate, because the only possible, form of class struggle where the working class had not yet won for itself political and organizational rights. It had thus been the appropriate form of struggle in the Russia of 1905. However, where these rights had been secured, as in Germany, it was senseless to risk all in an uncertain confrontation with the ruling class, especially where this class would be supported by the vastly superior repressive forces the rulers of an advanced nation always have at their command. In this democratic phase of the class struggle, Kautsky argued that the working class must rather pursue a 'strategy of attrition'. The struggle against capital must be waged in such a way as to 'constantly strengthen the proletariat and weaken its enemies, without allowing the decisive battle to be provoked so long as we are the weakest'. Such a strategy did not eliminate the possibility of 'battles', but it did assume that social democracy would only willingly enter upon such a conflict where it was likely to succeed. Indeed, Kautsky maintained that the 'only' difference between the 'strategy of annihilation' and the 'strategy of attrition' was that the latter 'does not aim at the decisive battle directly, but prepares it long in advance and is only inclined to engage such a battle when it considers the enemy to have been sufficiently weakened'.[54]

The appropriate form for this 'strategy of attrition', Kautsky argued, was parliamentary democracy. But he was still keen to distinguish this advocacy of parliamentarism from that of the revisionists. The securing of political rights by the working class did, in some sense, change 'the rules of the game' of class struggle, increasing the prospects of a peaceful transition to socialism, but it did not vitiate the need for a revolutionary seizure of power. Thus, Kautsky firmly distinguished his own 'strategy of attrition' from the politics of revisionism, which expected an attenuation of class struggle, by continuing to stress 'the irreconcilability and constant aggravation of class conflict'. In *The*

Road to Power, he was quite explicit: '[we] are revolutionists . . . The social transformation for which we are striving can be attained only through a political revolution, by means of the conquest of political power by the fighting proletariat.'[55]

Of course, the 'radical left' would have been happy to endorse this general Kautskyan insistence upon the continuing importance of the class struggle, but it would certainly not have endorsed his further claim that 'the only form of the state in which Socialism can be realized is that of a republic and a thoroughly democratic republic at that.' For Kautsky, democratic rights did not eliminate the *need* for revolutionary transformation but they did radically alter the *form* that revolution might take and the circumstances under which it might be effected. He argued that democracy 'cannot do away with the class antagonisms of capitalist society. Neither can it avoid the final outcome of these antagonisms – the overthrow of present society.' But this did not mean that democratic institutions could be discounted as capitalism's 'safety valves'. The expectation that in a democracy the proletariat ceases to be a revolutionary force and renounces political and social revolution was quite false. Rather, every victory secured by the proletariat in pursuit of, or through the exercise of, its democratic rights marks 'a mighty increase in the effective strength of the proletariat'. Such victories do not lead it towards an accommodating reformism but 'mightily arouse its feeling of strength and thereby the energy of its volition for the class struggle'. Thus, for Kautsky, with the winning of democracy, 'the direction of development is not changed' but in a number of ways 'its course becomes steadier and more peaceful.'[56]

These changes were best seen in the contrast between the methods of the anticipated proletarian revolution and its bourgeois forerunner. Thus, he argued, it is probable that the revolutionary battles of the proletariat will see much less reliance upon the use of military force and a much greater dependence upon 'economic, legislative and moral methods'. While echoing Engels' argument that the overwhelming military superiority of the modern state made a physical confrontation or street action more perilous, Kautsky pointed out that contemporary revolutionaries have 'better weapons for economic, political and moral resistance' than were available to the insurgents of the eighteenth century. Nor is the securing of democratic political institutions – including freedom of organization, of the press and universal suffrage – useful only in that they equip the proletariat with weapons that were unavailable in the revolutionary battles of the bourgeoisie. An important by-product of democracy is that 'it creates clearness regarding the relative strengths of the different parties and classes' – an indicator wholly lacking in the struggle of the bourgeoisie against absolutism.[57]

Democracy, then, while 'it cannot abolish the revolution . . . can avert many premature, hopeless revolutionary attempts and render superfluous many revolutionary uprisings'. While the 'democratic-proletarian method of battle' may be 'more monotonous . . . less dramatic and striking than the revolutionary struggle of the bourgeoisie, 'it calls for fewer sacrifices.' The essence of the Kautskyan position is that, under modern democratic conditions, the proletariat 'can well afford to try as long as possible to progress through strictly "legal" methods alone', and that the limitations upon such a legal and peaceful path will be found not in its insufficiency to the realization of the proletariat's historical mission but in the 'nervous attitude of the ruling class'.[58]

On the basis of this 'centrist' account of the relation between socialism and democracy, Kautsky himself presented, in *The Road to Power*, a summary of the necessary conditions under which the proletariat, under a democratic constitution, would be able to press for 'a great transfer of political power' and the 'destruction of a tyranical regime'. These were:

1 that the great mass of the people should be opposed to the existing regime.
2 that there should be a great organized party in opposition to such a regime.
3 that this party must represent the interests of the great majority of the population and enjoy their confidence.
4 that confidence in the ruling regime should have been destroyed internally – both in the army and the bureaucracy.[59]

Under such circumstances, the Social Democrats might effect the revolutionary transfer of power through the institutions of parliamentary democracy and with a minimum of violence and furthermore, such circumstances would *inevitably* arise in the course of capitalist development, as the German proletariat came increasingly to constitute not only a majority of the population, but also a majority of the *enfranchised*.

3
State, Power, Socialism?

In the last chapter, I traced the evolution of the (disintegrating) Marxist view of democracy and the transition to socialism in the early years of the twentieth century through the competing accounts of Bernstein, Kautsky and Luxemburg. The world-historical events of 1917 were radically to change the terms of reference of this debate and it is to the sharply drawn divisions on democracy, socialism and dictatorship which arose in the wake of the Russian Revolution that I turn in this chapter.

Kautsky against Bolshevism

Once again Kautsky was at the heart of these disputes and his critique of the Bolsheviks – vigorously resisted by Lenin and Trotsky – remains the definitive social democratic account of post-revolutionary Russia. Kautsky's criticism, prompted by the Bolshevik seizure of power in October 1917 and reinforced by the dissolution of the Constituent Assembly in January 1918, finds its most celebrated expression in *The Dictatorship of the Proletariat*. Here, Kautsky defined the most important issue of the Russian experience as 'the clash of two distinct methods, that of democracy and that of dictatorship'. Having set up the issue in this way, Kautsky's own preference was unequivocal. 'Modern Socialism', he claimed, was not to be identified simply with the socialization of production, for it entailed 'not merely . . . the social organization of production, but the democratic organization of society as well'. Correspondingly, he insisted that 'Socialism as a means to the emancipation of the proletariat, without democracy, is unthinkable.'[1]

Although, as Salvadori suggests, Kautsky may have grown to be increasingly uncertain as to the 'guarantees of history' afforded the project of socialism, his account of democracy and countervailing critique of Bolshevik practice is still firmly grounded in that Marxist orthodoxy – which Kautsky had done so much to propagate – in which the conditions for the emergence of socialism were to be generated by the course of capitalist development. This was clear in his enumeration of the 'prerequisites for the establishment of socialism' with which he was to reproach the adventurist Bolsheviks. He isolated five 'objective' conditions as being of particular importance: first, 'the will to Socialism', which was to be found increasingly among the masses as small production gave way to large-scale production; secondly, 'the material conditions to realise Socialism', which also 'increase with the growth of the large industry'; thirdly, that 'those who want Socialism must become stronger than those who do not want it'; fourth, that the proletariat must have the capacity to *retain* power once it is seized; and fifth, the *sine qua non* of these several 'objective conditions', 'the maturity of the proletariat'.[2]

Early and primitive forms of working-class protest – Utopianism, Blanquism, Millenialism, and so on – had proven to be inadequate as a means of achieving this 'maturity of the proletariat'. Such maturation only became possible through the labour movement's struggle to attain its democratic rights. The working classes of the whole of Europe, Kautsky argued, in numerous – often bloody – struggles had fought for and secured 'one instalment of democracy after the other' and through these struggles 'to use, maintain and extend democracy, and by constantly making use of each instalment for organization, for propaganda, and for wresting social reforms, have they grown in maturity from year to year'.[3]

Kautsky felt that the *objective* conditions for socialization, those grounded in the development of capitalist production, had been largely fulfilled. There was 'no reason for believing that the organisation of the largest part of production for social ends . . . [was] not already possible in modern industrial states'. He insisted that 'the decisive factor' was, indeed, 'no longer the material, but the personal one' and this led him naturally to consider 'had the proletariat already attained the maturity which Socialism postulated?' This decisive question, Kautsky argued, was not easily answered, for 'adequate maturity' is an uncertain and comparative concept, the powers required varying in different states and under different circumstances. But democracy, Kautsky concluded, was the most reliable guide to this maturity of the working class. It is not possible, he argued, to be sure that when the proletariat constitutes the majority of the people and when the majority declares its support for socialism, that the socialization of the economy has become unproblematic. On the other hand, it is certain that when such majority support for socialism cannot be found, circumstances are not yet 'ripe' for its implementation.[4]

For Kautsky, then, the democratic struggle was both the most effective means of raising the maturity of the working class to a level at which it would be competent to take and to *retain* power and also the best way of gauging proletarian development towards this goal. He argued that it 'not only matures the proletariat soonest, but gives the quickest indications of this process'. But this did not exhaust the importance of democracy in the Kautskyan account. For, recalling his own prognostications in *The Road to Power*, he insisted that it was possible to carry out the social revolution 'by peaceful, economic, legal and moral means, instead of by physical force, in all places where democracy had been established'.[5] For democracy transformed class struggle from 'a hand to hand fight' into 'a battle of intelligence'. Furthermore, the most important institutions of democracy – parliamentary bodies, civil rights and the formalized protection of minorities, were indispensable as the means of exercising effective surveillance over, and control of, the state bureaucracy. Echoing his earlier stress upon the importance of parliamentary democracy as the appropriate form of government in a *post*-revolutionary society and upon the continuing necessity of representative institutions as a means of popular surveillance over state and government, he insisted that it was

> urgently necessary for the executive to be subjected to public criticism, for free organisations of citizens to counterbalance the power of the state, for self-government in municipalities and provinces to be established, for the power of law-making to be taken from the bureaucracy, and put under the control of a central assembly, freely chosen by the people, that is a Parliament.[6]

Democracy, Kautsky insisted in *Terrorism and Communism*, 'is the one and only method through which the higher forms of life can be realised, and which Socialism declares is the right of civilised men'.[7]

Democracy versus Dictatorship

In this way, Kautsky denied the very possibility of a realization of socialism where democracy was displaced by dictatorship, and indeed for each of the strengths he had identified in democracy, he found a corresponding weakness in the practice of dictatorship. In essence, Kautsky argued that 'wherever Socialism does not appear to be possible upon a democratic basis and where the majority of the population rejects it, its time has not yet fully come.' Marx, he recalled, had taught in *Capital* that a society could not 'clear by bold leaps, nor reverse by legal enactments the obstacles offered by the successive phases of its normal development'. At best, it could 'shorten and lessen the birth-pangs'. But it was precisely this lesson that the Bolsheviks had ignored in forging a dictatorship which was itself just such 'a grandiose attempt to clear by bold leaps . . . the successive phases of normal development'. The result was not to lessen the birth-pangs of a new society but to induce abortion, to give issue to 'a child incapable of life'. A majoritarian proletariat invested with the 'maturity' to attain self-government, a disintegrating peasantry, a highly developed indust-rial base – all these were the necessary prerequisites of a socialist transformation. The Bolsheviks, having seized power, found these material conditions for the realization of socialism absent and were increasingly obliged to rely upon force to coerce their ever more disenfranchised subjects. Indeed, of the dissolution of the Constituent Assembly Kautsky argued, 'the less the material and intellectual conditions existed for all that they aspired to, the more they felt obliged to replace what was lacking by the exercise of naked power, by dictatorship.'[8]

But had not Marx himself argued that in the period of transition between capitalist and communist society 'the state can only take the form of a *revolutionary dictatorship of the proletariat*'? This, Kautsky conceded, was true, but what Marx had understood by dictatorship of the proletariat was quite different from its Bolshevik interpretation. He argued, as we have seen in the previous chapter, that, for Marx, the *locus classicus* of such a dictatorship had been the Paris Commune – an expansive and democratic form. This was because for Marx, as for Kautsky, 'the dictatorship of the proletariat . . . was a condition which necessarily arose in a real democracy, because of the overwhelming numbers of the proletariat.' It was 'a state of sovereignty' – the unmediated, though not arbitrary, dominance of the working class which obtained where, under fully democratic conditions, the prole-tariat constituted a majority of the population, (a circumstance itself 'guaranteed' by capitalist development).[9]

For Kautsky, the dictatorship of the proletariat meant nothing other than 'its rule on the basis of democracy'. This 'dictatorship as a condition', issuing from proletarian majoritarianism, was to be vigorously distinguished from the Bolshevik 'dictatorship as a form of government'.[10] The latter meant disarming its opponents, by taking from them the franchise, and liberty of the press and of combination, thus eliminating the many indispensable strengths of democratic struggle to which we have seen Kautsky to be indissolubly wedded. Furthermore, this dictatorship as 'a form of government' – grounded in ever-contracting support at the base – would be inexorably driven towards '*personal* dictatorship'. Starting out with the idea of estab-lishing the dictatorship of the proletariat, the Bolshevik regime was bound to become the dictatorship of the party within the proletariat. The inevitable outcome was the fermentation of civil war.

This contrast of democracy and dictatorship was to find its bitterest expression in Kautsky's *Terrorism and Communism*. The 'hereditary sin of Bolshevism', Kautsky protested, was 'its suppression of democracy, through a form of government, namely the dictatorship, which represents the unlimited and despotic power either of one single person, or of a small organisation.' He was adamant that Bolshevism was 'incompatible with the higher forms of existence for which pioneer work had already been done in Western Europe'. His maxim remained that 'Socialism will only acquire for itself state power when it is strong enough, within the framework of democracy, to gain the balance over the other parties.'[11]

Meanwhile, in splitting the working-class parties of the West and in threatening the long-entrenched rights of the mass of the population, Bolshevism was positively damaging the cause of socialism in Western Europe. Here, he insisted, it was 'absolutely impossible to deprive all society of all political rights . . . to introduce a real, permanent and active form of dictatorship'. He rejected the Bolshevik claim that 'parliamentarism and democracy in their very essentials are bourgeois institutions' and that 'the working class could not win a parliamentary majority within the prevailing order.' In fact, he argued that, in the West, democracy afforded 'the one means of avoiding despotism, and of coming to some calm and positive construction'. By contrast, the Bolshevik dictatorship was nothing more than a primitive 'Tartar socialism', still more oppressive for the working class than the open and democratic institutions of West European capitalist societies.[12]

Lenin: Countering 'The Renegade Kautsky'

It is hardly surprising that Kautsky's scathing criticisms of the Bolsheviks were vigorously and vitriolically resisted by Lenin and Trotsky.[13] Against them, Lenin passionately defended that account of the socialist revolution and its relation to democratic institutions which, at least from his wartime insistence that imperialism was 'the eve of the socialist revolution' onwards, he was to maintain consistently throughout Russia's revolutionary period. The tragic history of the Soviet Union after Lenin – particularly the rise of Stalinism, the experience of the forced collectivization of agriculture and 'the Gulag' – has meant that these texts have continued to be received as polemically as they were written. Even today, it is possible for an author to claim of 'The State and Revolution' that 'the text . . . is guilty of subsequent developments.' For the present, I want to renounce, in so far as is possible, the uncertain benefits of such hindsight and to seek to reconstruct Lenin's account of democracy in this period around his substantial objections to Kautsky and his rejection of 'the parliamentary road to socialism'.[14]

It is worth noting that Lenin's attacks upon 'the renegade Kautsky' substantially pre-date their polemical exchanges over the Bolshevik seizure of power. Although he had once been inclined to recommend Kautsky to the Russian workers as 'one of the most outstanding representatives of German Social Democracy', following the outbreak of war and the 'betrayal of internationalism' of the Second International, Lenin was much more disposed to see in him 'the high priest of social chauvinism' than 'the Pope of Marxist orthodoxy'. Correspondingly, the authoritative 'The State and Revolution', replete with condemnations of Kautsky's apostasy, was largely intended to furnish a settling of accounts with what Lenin styled the 'miserable bankruptcy' of (the prevailing) Kautskyism. What Lenin regarded as this 'bankruptcy' of the Kautskyan account of democracy, he isolated with particular clarity in his polemic 'The Proletarian Revolution and the Renegade Kautsky'. Replying to the criticisms Kautsky had voiced in *The Dictatorship of the Proletariat*, Lenin rejected the counterposition of democracy and dictatorship – 'the essence of Kautsky's pamphlet' – as 'a complete renunciation of Marxism'. To talk, as did Kautsky, of 'democracy in general' and of 'dictatorship in general', was to argue 'like the liberals'. For while it was natural for a liberal to speak of democracy as a general principle, a Marxist, Lenin insisted, should never fail to establish 'for what class' democracy was established. For, he argued, 'as long as different *classes* exist, we can only speak of *class* democracy.' Correspondingly, it was imperative to distinguish between bourgeois and proletarian democracy. To speak, under the prevailing circumstances, as did Kautsky, of 'pure' or, at least, of undifferentiated democracy, was merely to shield the exercise of bourgeois dictatorship under the form of bourgeois democracy. At the First Congress of the Comintern, Lenin insisted that 'in no civilised capitalist country does "democracy in general" exist; all that exists is bourgeois democracy.'[15]

For Lenin, Kautsky's inability to recognize the importance of the class specificity of democracy derived, in turn, from a more general and still graver weakness – his 'complete misunderstanding and misrepresentation of Marx and Engels' writings on the state'. It is in Lenin's own account of what constitutes this fundamental Marxist teaching on the state – classically outlined in 'The State and Revolution' – that his own counterposed understanding of democracy and dictatorship is to be found.

Lenin proceeded from a number of categorical Marxist claims about
the essential nature of the state. He maintained that, for Marx, the
state is irreducibly 'a product and manifestation of the irreconcilability
of class contradictions'. It arises 'where, when and to the extent that
class contradictions objectively *cannot* be reconciled'. It is 'an organ of
class *rule*, an organ for the *oppression* of one class by another'. These
are the 'unavoidable truths' of the Marxist account of the state, and as
such, hold good no less for democracy than for any other form of the
state. For Lenin, 'Democracy is a state' and thus 'like every other state
it represents the organised systematic use of violence against persons.'
Democracy is always democracy *for* a particular class secured through
its exercise of dictatorship *over* another class. Even 'the most advanced
type of bourgeois state . . . the parliamentary democratic republic' was
'no more than a machine for the suppression of the working class by the
bourgeoisie'.[16]

The Impassability of 'the Parliamentary Road to Socialism'

Although, as Hindess is perhaps only the most recent commentator to
point out, there is an element of 'essentialism' in this analysis of
democratic form, Lenin did attempt to show how the institutions of
parliamentarism – as the most typical form of the contemporary
democratic state – necessarily articulated the political rule of the
bourgeoisie. Bourgeois parliaments, he argued, were not the *locus* of
real power. Because of the crucial division between legislature and
executive, they were rather 'hollow talking shops', 'the real business of
state' being carried out 'behind the scenes [in] the departments,
chancelleries and general staffs'.[17] Indeed, the isolation of parliaments
and the bureaucracy, of legislative and executive functions – characteristic of the institutional structure of bourgeois democracy – was one
which would have to be overcome in the inception of proletarian
democracy. Furthermore, existing democratic rights – freedom of the
press, of assembly, of association – in practice, favoured the
bourgeoisie because of the latter's greater control over the levers of the
electoral machine – money, media, meeting places and so on. Lenin
drew attention to the corresponding systematic limitations upon the
exercise of these rights by the masses. He identified in the 'petty'
restrictions of the suffrage, in the 'techniques' of the representative
institutions, in actual obstacles to free assembly and in the capitalist
organization of the press, a series of restrictions which, if seemingly
slight in themselves, in their sum total effectively 'squeeze out the poor
from politics, from active participation in democracy'. He took issue
with Kautsky's characterization of bourgeois democracy as one which

generally protects the rights of minorities since, Lenin insisted, such tolerance was extended only to other bourgeois parties, while 'the proletariat, on all *serious, profound and fundamental* issues, gets martial law or pogroms.' 'The equality of citizens', Lenin concluded, 'bourgeois democracy everywhere has always promised but never effected'.[18]

A still more damaging claim was that an equality of rights was necessarily chimeric where the greater economic inequalities inherent in the system of wage labour remained untouched. For, 'under bourgeois democracy, "freedom and equality" remain purely formal, signifying in practice *wage-slavery* for the workers (who are formally free and equal) and *the individual rule of capital*, the oppression of labour by capital.' Drawing directly on Marx, Lenin concluded that 'to decide once every few years which member of the ruling class is to repress and crush the people in parliament – such is the real essence of parliamentarism.'[19]

This did not, of course, mean that Lenin considered the winning of bourgeois parliamentary democracy unimportant. He adopted the 'orthodox' Marxist view that democracy was generally an historically progressive principle and that bourgeois democracy was much to be preferred to the feudal arrangements that preceded it. Indeed, he had spent much of the period between 1895 and 1910 advocating mobilization behind just such a democratic revolution in Russia.[20] He even insisted in 'The State and Revolution' that 'the democratic republic is the nearest approach to the dictatorship of the proletariat.' But this was not, as the advocates of the 'peaceful development of democracy' supposed, because it afforded the possibility of the peaceful transfer of power to the proletariat. Indeed, Lenin argued that the democratic republic was a particularly entrenched form of the bourgeois state – 'the best possible shell for capitalism' – under which capital is established 'so securely, that *no* change, either of persons, of institutions or of parties in the bourgeois-democratic republic, can shake this power'. Rather did the democratic republic sponsor a 'wider, freer and more open *form* of the class struggle and of class oppression [which] enormously assists the proletariat in its struggle for the abolition of classes in general'.[21]

'Smashing the State'

The bourgeois democratic republic was not then a 'special case'. It was but one form of the bourgeois state and thus of the dictatorship of the bourgeoisie, and its particular entrenchment of the rule of capital made it all the more important that it should be subjected to the full rigour of

Marxist teaching on the state. Drawing upon Marx's insistence that 'the working class cannot simply lay hold of the ready-made state machinery and wield it for its own purposes', Lenin identified as 'the chief and fundamental point' of this teaching, the necessity of 'smashing' the state. Marx's idea, Lenin stressed, was that 'the working class must *break up*, smash the "ready-made state machinery" and not confine itself simply to seizing it.' He repeatedly insisted that 'the supersession of the bourgeois state by the proletarian state is impossible without a violent revolution.' It is precisely this central tenet of Marxism that Kautsky sought to avoid in speaking only of 'the conquest of state power' and thus avoiding recognition of the imperative of 'destroying the state machine'. Such a circumlocution Lenin condemned as 'the complete *wreck* of Marxism' in which 'all the lessons and teachings of Marx and Engels of 1852-1892 are *forgotten* and distorted.' Over against this, Lenin insisted that 'the liberation of the oppressed class is impossible not only without a violent revolution, *but also without the destruction* of the apparatus of state power which was created by the ruling class.'[22]

The proletariat was thus compelled to 'crush, smash to smithereens, wipe off the face of the earth the bourgeois, even the republican-bourgeois, state machine'. But the state, as 'a special organization of force . . . an organ of violence for the suppression of some class', would not disappear with the overthrow of the bourgeois state. Indeed, it is the advocacy of just this view that led Lenin to berate anarchism as 'utopian'.[23] For the state, as we have seen, was held to be conterminous with the existence of classes, and indeed, on the morrow of revolution, class struggle is at its most intense, and the proletariat, correspondingly, must seize and exercise state power 'both to crush the exploiters and to *head* the enormous mass of the population . . . in the work of organizing socialist economy'. To this new proletarian state – embodying the 'dictatorship of the proletariat' – there corresponded a new form of proletarian democracy. This proletarian democracy was indeed a far more 'expansive' form than bourgeois democracy – 'a million times more democratic', Lenin claimed – but it did not represent the attainment of 'pure' democracy, a condition that was conterminous with the disappearance of the state and its own dissolution. Thus, while it represented 'an immense expansion of democracy', it entailed at the same time 'the *forcible* suppression of the exploiters as a *class*, and, consequently, the *infringement* of "pure democracy", i.e. of equality and freedom, *in regard to* that class'. Still, Lenin compared very favourably this proletarian democracy – 'democracy for the vast majority of the people, and suppression by force, i.e. exclusion from democracy, of the exploiters and oppressors of the people' – with its bourgeois forerunner which, 'curtailed, wretched, false', secured democracy 'only for the rich, for the minority.'[24]

Although bitterly critical of the anarchists' expectation of dissolving the state on the morning of the revolution, Lenin agreed with them in insisting that 'destruction of state power is the aim set by all socialists, including Marx above all.' It was imperative that the bourgeois state should be replaced by the dictatorship of the proletariat but, given the latter's expansive democratic basis and its historic task of destroying the very bases of class division, this was a state which, from its very inception, was already tending towards its own self-suppression. Thus, the transition 'from bourgeois into proletarian democracy' was, at the same time, a move 'from the state (= a special force for the suppression of a particular class) into something which is no longer, properly speaking the state', 'from the state as a *"special force"* for the suppression of a particular class to the suppression of the oppressors by the *general force* of the majority of the people'. Thus, 'proletarian democracy . . . by enlisting the mass organizations of the working people in constant and unfinishing participation in the administration of the state . . . immediately begins to prepare *the complete withering away of the state*.' Indeed, with the accession of 'the state that is no longer properly a state' – that is already officiating over the transition from capitalism towards communism – the role of the state, independent of society, is drastically reduced.[25]

Democratic Dictatorship: Commune and State

For Lenin, the definitive model of this 'state that is no longer properly a state' is the Paris Commune, or, more properly, Marx's model of the Commune outlined in 'The Civil War in France', as 'the political form at last discovered under which to work out the economic emancipation of labour'. The Commune, Lenin insisted, was 'the first attempt of proletarian revolution to *smash* the bourgeois state machine' and though it was defeated, in part because of its failure to pursue its revolutionary mission with sufficient vigour, it set the programme, 'in different circumstances and under different conditions', for the Soviets of 1905 and 1917 to 'continue the work of the Commune and confirm the brilliant historical analysis given by Marx'.[26]

I have already discussed the nature and content of the commune-model which Marx sought to derive from the Parisian experience of 1871. This account reappears, more or less verbatim, not only in 'The State and Revolution' but in a number of the most important texts of the immediate revolutionary period – for example, in the 'April Theses', 'Dual Power' and 'The Tasks of the Proletariat in our

Revolution', (all dating from 1917). In 'The "Dictatorship of the Proletariat"' 'the *essence* of the Paris Commune as a special type of state' is exhaustively defined around:

> 1 Abolition of the police and the standing army and their replacement by the arming of the whole people, ('the very essence of the Commune');
> 2 Abolition of parliamentarism 'as a special system' and its replacement by *more* democratic institutions, of short-term recallable delegates paid at average workers' wages; conversion of representative institutions from talking shops into 'working bodies', executive and legislative at the same time;
> 3 Abolition of the bureaucracy as the 'bossing' of the workers by a privileged staff, independent of the working population. The smashed bureaucratic state machine to be replaced by mandated, elective employees of the people, paid at average wages, whose functions will be gradually eliminated by 'the direct rule of the people themselves'.[27]

For Lenin, the existence of a massive state apparatus is substantially to be attributed to the 'parasitism' and division of state and society which are specific features of a degenerate capitalism which is called upon to repress the vast majority of the population in the interests of a small, exploiting minority. The repressive needs of the state are vastly reduced when it is the overwhelming majority who must restrain this expropriated minority. The purely administrative functions of the bureaucracy, Lenin insisted, have been radically simplified by the development of capitalism so that, under socialism, 'the function of control and accounting, becoming more and more simple, will be performed by each in turn, will then become a habit and will finally die out as the *special* function of a special section of the population.' The immediate abolition of the bureaucracy is indeed 'utopian' but the programme for the gradual 'withering away' of all bureaucracy is 'the direct and immediate task of the revolutionary proletariat'.[28]

Thus, the revolutionary overthrow of capitalism cannot yield immediately to the abolition of state, class and systematic violence. But it gives way to a proletarian state and proletarian democracy which, because of the changed relation of the working majority and the exploiting minority, is so radically different from what went before that it is no longer 'a state in the proper sense of the word,' but 'a state which from its inception, is beginning to wither away'. Lenin himself explained the historical evolution thus:

> Under capitalism we have the state in the proper sense of the word, that is, a special machine for the suppression of one class by another . . . during the *transition* from capitalism to communism suppression is still

necessary . . . but this is already a transitional state, . . . compatible with the extension of democracy to such an overwhelming majority of the population that the need for a *special machine* of suppression will begin to disappear . . . only communism makes the state unnecessary, for there is *nobody* [as a class] to be *suppressed*.[29]

Correspondingly, 'the state withers away in so far as there are no longer any capitalists, any classes, and consequently, no *class* can be suppressed.'[30]

Democracy, as we saw, was but one form of the state – 'a state which recognizes the subordination of the minority to the majority' – and correspondingly it too tends to 'wither away' with the state. Here again, Lenin presents a development through three successive phases:

In capitalist society we have a democracy that is curtailed, wretched, false, a democracy only for the rich, for the minority. The dictatorship of the proletariat, the period of transition to Communism, will for the first time create democracy for the people, for the majority, only with the necessary suppression of the minority – the exploiters. Communism alone is capable of giving really complete democracy, and the more complete it is the more quickly will it become unnecessary and wither away of itself.[31]

The case is still more summarily put in *Marxism on the State*. Here Lenin insisted that 'democracy precludes freedom', tracing a dialectical historical development 'from absolutism to bourgeois democracy; from bourgeois democracy to proletarian democracy; from proletarian democracy to none at all'. Democracy withers away because, freed from the exigencies of capitalist exploitation, people 'gradually *become accustomed* to observing the elementary rules of community life . . . without the special apparatus of coercion which is called the state'. Under the higher phase of communism – beyond the state and beyond democracy – 'the necessity of observing the simple, fundamental rules of all human community life will very soon become a habit.'[32]

Luxemburg on the Russian Revolution

It would be improper to move on to a discussion of these opposing accounts of socialism and democracy surrounding the revolutionary events of 1917 without considering what Poulantzas called 'the first correct and fundamental critique of Lenin and the Bolshevik Revolution'. This he retraced to Luxemburg's short critical essay on *The Russian Revolution*. Her criticisms, as one would anticipate, are quite different from those of Kautsky and the Mensheviks. 'Whatever a party could offer of courage, revolutionary far-sightedness and consistency in a historic hour', she insisted, the Bolsheviks had shown 'in good measure'. This heroism she contrasted contemptuously with the 'home-made wisdom derived from parliamentary battles between frogs and mice' spun by 'the bred-in-the-bone disciples of parliamentary cretinism' who dominated German Social Democracy. The latter, she complained, had 'forgotten that the bourgeoisie is not a parliamentary party but a ruling class in possession of all the means of economic and social power'. Nor did she condemn the Bolsheviks for seizing power without first achieving a parliamentary majority. The true dialectic of revolutions, she argued, echoing Lenin, was not through 'a majority to revolutionary tactics, but through revolutionary tactics to a majority'.[33]

However, she did deny that the Russian Revolution, made under 'conditions of bitter compulsion and necessity in the midst of the roaring whirlpool of events', set 'a shining example of socialist policy toward which only mutual admiration and zealous imitation are in order'. Seeking to avoid a 'revolutionary hurrah-spirit', she condemned both the policies of land distribution to the peasantry and the commitment to national self-determination as developments which, though in part arising from the desperate situation in which the emergent Bolshevik government found itself, led away from socialism. But her most severe criticism was reserved for Lenin and Trotsky's 'suppression of democracy'. She suggested that they had indeed been right to criticize 'the special inadequacy' of the Constituent Assembly which had been elected in the first few weeks of the revolution and which soon failed to represent social forces which were changing rapidly under the radicalizing impact of revolutionary events. (Though Luxemburg insisted that, in fact, in a revolutionary period even the existing representative bodies were galvanized and radicalized by the dominant spirit of insurgency.) But instead of calling new elections and quite properly convoking 'an assembly that would issue forth out of the renewed Russia that had advanced further', Trotsky mistakenly drew 'a general conclusion concerning the inadequacy of any popular representation whatsoever which might come from universal popular elections during the revolution', expressing a general dissatisfaction with 'the cumbersome mechanism of democratic institutions'.[34] Conceding that every democratic institution – in common with 'all other human institutions' – has its limitations and shortcomings, Luxemburg insisted that the drastic remedy proposed by Lenin and Trotsky – 'the elimination of democracy as such' – was 'worse than the disease it is supposed to cure':

For it stops up the living source from which alone can come the correction of all the innate shortcomings of social institutions. That source is the active, untramelled, energetic political life of the broadest masses of the people.[35]

This was particularly evident in the Bolsheviks' attitude to the rights of suffrage. Here again, she did not attack them on the same grounds as Kautsky, for whom universal suffrage was indivisible and indispensable, (though she rather wickedly questions the Bolsheviks' need of a general principle of suffrage since they were unwilling to hold popular elections in which this suffrage might be exercised). Indeed, she denied the coherence of deriving the franchise from some general and abstract conception of 'justice' – from an equality of the right to representation – insisting that the suffrage had to be restricted to 'the social and economic relationships for which it is designed'. But she did complain that the Bolshevik circumscription of the right to vote – granted only to those who lived by their own labour and denied to everybody else – meant, in the war-torn circumstances of post-revolutionary Russia, disenfranchising not only the former ruling class but also 'broad and growing sections of the bourgeoisie and proletariat', to whom the disrupted economy afforded no opportunity of exercising the obligation to work. While it was legitimate to exercise socialist dictatorship over the dispossessed bourgeoisie and its class allies, 'the general disenfranchisement of broad sections of society . . . a deprivation of rights not as a concrete measure for a concrete purpose but as a general rule' was 'not a necessity of dictatorship but a makeshift'. Nor were these reservations confined to the Bolshevik positions on the Constituent Assembly and the suffrage. For Trotsky's unsatisfactory account of the cumbersome nature of democratic electoral bodies had been used to justify a curtailment of all 'the guarantees of a healthy public life and of the political activity of the labouring masses' – freedom of the press, association and assembly. She insisted that 'without these rights, the rule of the broad mass of the people is entirely unthinkable.'[36]

Democracy and Dictatorship Reconsidered

This brings us to the very heart of Luxemburg's critique which focuses on the Bolshevik definition of dictatorship and its relation to democracy. Luxemburg argued that while it had sufficed to bourgeois class rule to be able to exercise constraint over the ruled mass of the people, the building of socialism was directly dependent upon 'the political training and education of the entire mass of the people'. The great strength of Marxism over against Utopian socialism was that it recognized that there was no infallible blueprint for socialism that could be put into effect on the morning after the revolution and that, correspondingly, 'the socialist system of society should only be, and can only be, an historical product, born out of the school of its own experiences, born in the course of its realisation.' This self-realization of socialism is dependent upon the masses – at present, 'degraded by centuries of bourgeois class rule' – aspiring to spiritual and intellectual self-regeneration. This, in turn, is dependent upon the fullest possible expansion of public life and, concomitantly, of democracy. For, Luxemburg insisted, 'the public life of countries with limited freedoms is so poverty-stricken, so miserable, so rigid, so unfruitful, precisely because, through the exclusion of democracy, it cuts off the living sources of all spiritual riches and progress.' If the whole mass of the people are not actively involved in its development, 'socialism will be decreed from behind a few official desks by a dozen intellectuals.' Correspondingly, the only way to achieve socialist development is through 'the school of public life itself, the most unlimited, the broadest democratic and public opinion'.[37]

But it is precisely this possibility that Lenin and Trotsky foreclose in their exclusive reliance upon the soviets. For, 'with the repression of political life in the land as a whole, life in the soviets must also become more and more crippled.' Without general elections, freedom of opinion, of expression and of assembly, 'life dies out in every public institution.' Public life 'falls asleep', the bureaucracy remains the only active branch of the constitution and increasingly 'a few dozen party leaders of inexhaustible energy and boundless experience direct and rule.' This is certainly a rigorous dictatorship – 'not the dictatorship of the proletariat, however, but only the dictatorship of a handful of politicians . . . dictatorship in the bourgeois sense, in the sense of the rule of the Jacobins'. Its inevitable outcome is the 'brutalization of public life'.[38]

Indeed, Lenin and Trotsky are seen to be at the opposing pole of the same mistaken opposition that Kautsky had posed – that between dictatorship and democracy. While Luxemburg argues that the proletariat should not demobilize the socialist revolution by tying itself to Kautsky's advocacy of an exclusively parliamentary democracy, she insisted that the socialist dictatorship that it should seek to promote has to be 'a dictatorship of the *class* not of a party or clique – that is, a dictatorship in the broadest public form on the basis of the most active, unlimited participation of the mass of the people, of unlimited democracy'.[39] Citing Trotsky's insistence that 'as Marxists, we have never been idol worshippers of formal democracy', she insists:

All that really means is: We have always distinguished the social kernel from the political form of *bourgeois* democracy; we have always revealed the hard kernel of social inequality and lack of freedom hidden under the sweet shell of formal equality and freedom – not in order to reject the latter but to spur the working class into not being satisfied with the shell, but rather, by conquering political power, to create a socialist democracy to replace bourgeois democracy altogether.[40]

This socialist democracy is 'not something which begins only in the promised land after the foundations of a socialist economy are created'. Indeed, it is 'the same thing as the dictatorship of the proletariat'. But this dictatorship consists 'in the *manner of applying democracy*, not in its elimination, in energetic, resolute attacks upon the well-entrenched rights and economic relationships of bourgeois society, without which a socialist transformation cannot be accomplished'. It must ever be the dictatorship of a class and 'arise out of the growing political training of the mass of the people'. She insisted that, but for the appalling circumstances which faced the Bolsheviks – the cumulative effects of war-exhaustion, civil war and encirclement – this was the pattern of socialist revolution they would undoubtedly have followed. Unlike Kautsky, she was inclined to lay a greater portion of blame for the circumstances of the Bolsheviks in Russia upon the failure of the leaders of the German proletariat to respond to the initiative in the east, than to a 'premature' seizure of power by Lenin and Trotsky. The real danger in Bolshevik practice, as she perceived it, was not so much in the exceptional measures Lenin and Trotsky were forced to undertake in the face of the backward circumstances of Russia, but rather in their making 'a virtue of necessity', 'seeking to freeze into a theoretical system all the tactics forced upon them by these fatal circumstances' and recommending these 'to the international proletariat as a model of socialist tactics'.[41] Of course, just such a codification of Bolshevik experience as *the* model for proletarian revolution and the continuing failure of the German proletariat 'to realize its historic mission', were to have the profoundest impact not only upon the development of socialism, but, indeed, upon the entire course of twentieth century world history.

Marxism in the Golden Age: Conclusion

In Kolakowski's manichean *Main Currents of Marxism*, all the writings discussed in this and the previous chapter are seen to fall within 'the Golden Age' of Marxism. Whatever reservations one may have about Kolakowski's general schematization, it is clear that within this period – from the late 1890s to the early 1920s – many of what have remained the most influential parameters of the Marxist account of democracy and its relation to socialism were established. For the period prior to party 'Bolshevization', first in Russia and subsequently in Western Europe, saw a series of wide-ranging, open and heterodox debates about the strategic possibilities afforded to socialism by the development of (varying forms of) mass democracy. If Marx's discussions seem sometimes to be at a distance from any recognizable contemporary democratic practice, with the coming of the Second International we enter an era of mass democracies and mass parties which, if not quite our own, is recognizably modern. Correspondingly, the agenda-setting account of Marxism and democracy from the epoch of the Second International is of particular importance.

Kautsky against Lenin

Of course, those who claim to speak for Marx in this period are far from univocal and we may begin our evaluation of the Marxist view of democracy, parliaments and the state in 'the Golden Age' by mobilizing the strengths and weaknesses of the historically dominant accounts of this epoch – 'Kautskyism' and 'Leninism' – against each other.

We have seen that the critical weight of the early writings of Kautsky, those published around the turn of the century, was directed against revisionism in general, and Bernstein in particular. However, what was quite evidently not at issue between Bernstein and Kautsky was the strategic importance to the working class of the winning of political rights and it became clear that throughout a long and prolific career, Kautsky, in fact, drew ever closer to Bernstein's advocacy of a gradual and parliamentary transition to socialism. Corresponding to this growing commitment to the parliamentary road to socialism, and apparent from the criticism of Luxemburg's 'revolutionary impatience' onwards, was Kautsky's ever-sharpening hostility to the characteristically Leninist supposition that there were inherent limitations in any political practice premised upon the exercise of democratic rights – an hostility which was to reach its most acute and outraged expression in Kautsky's extended polemic with Bolshevism.

The Leninist position – so Kautsky argued – was dependent upon the misapplication of a number of schematic and purely formal generalizations. Among the most pernicious of these, he insisted, was the Leninist claim that democracy is a state form which, like any other, unalterably embodies the unmediated rule of a single dominant class. Against this, he asserted that, while the winning of democratic rights did not dissolve the class struggle and could not correspondingly eliminate the necessity of revolutionary change, it did decisively alter the forms of both class struggle and revolutionary transformation. It allowed both the continuing class struggle and revolutionary transition to socialism to be effected through the exercise of generalized democratic rights within parliamentary institutions.

These quite decisive historical changes, Kautsky insisted, were systematically ignored by Lenin and his supporters. Neglecting the epochal changes that democracy brings, they continued to advocate 'smashing the state' – a strategy which might have been appropriate where the workers were political pariahs but which was radically inappropriate where the exercise of its democratic rights afforded the working class the opportunity of transforming the state into 'a self-sufficing commonwealth'. At the same time, they aspired to the exercise of political dictatorship – not as a 'condition of government', as an expression of the resolute enforcement of that majority will for socialism which capitalist development necessarily generated, but rather as a coercive 'form of government', secured through the suspension of democratic procedures and imposed upon a disenfranchised majority. This brings us to the core of the Kautskyan critique – that is, the insistence that the Leninist theses on smashing the state and instituting a 'dictatorship of the proletariat' were not, in fact, the necessary conditions of transition to socialism but simply the necessities of a premature attempt to enforce socialization where the objective conditions for transition had not yet developed. The claim to greater 'Marxist authenticity' of the Leninist slogans was but a cover for what was, in fact, a quite un-Marxist political strategy.

Marx's great achievement, Kautsky argued, was to have demonstrated that the move to socialism was not simply an act of political will but rather was entailed in, and of necessity required, a certain stage of historical development. Among the requisite historical conditions for such a transition, Kautsky insisted, was that socialization should attract majority support. It was in attempting to defy this historical logic, (which Marx himself had revealed), and in trying to effect a voluntarist 'short-cut' to socialism that the Leninists had been obliged to resort to the strategies of 'smashing the state' and of dictatorship as 'a form of government'. But the laws of history were not so easily to be defied. In effecting socialization where the historical conditions were not 'ripe', the Leninists had been obliged to suspend general democratic institutions – thus eliminating what was for Kautsky the only effective means of exercising constraint over political authority and the bureaucracy – and to have ever greater resort to political coercion and terror.

Kautsky concluded that, in attempting to circumvent 'the laws of history', evading the recognition that socialism could only arise from the freely expressed and democratic will of a majority of the population, the Leninists did a grave disservice to the socialist movement, splitting the working-class parties of the West and instituting in Russia circumstances more oppressive than those 'suffered' by the Western working class under capitalism.

Lenin against Kautsky

Turning to the Leninist counter-critique, it is clear that this was, in part, reliant upon an appeal to a set of 'unavoidable truths' – that the state is always an instrument of class dictatorship, that the democratic republic is but one form of the dictatorship of the bourgeoisie and so on – upon which Kautsky had 'reneged'. However, this largely formal renunciation was buttressed by a number of substantive objections to the Kautskyan model. Among the most important of these was the insistence that representation, far from being the one sure means of guaranteeing democracy in a large-scale society, is an intrinsically anti-democratic principle. Rather than affording the possibility of new forms of self-administration, representation, is depicted as a means by which to ensure that government is kept at a distance from the influence of the mass of the population over whom political authority is exercised. This general criticism of representative institutions is seen to be particularly true of parliamentary institutions, in which elections are infrequent, the franchise is subject to curtailment and in which representatives are largely unaccountable to their electors. Furthermore, Lenin insists, these parliamentary institutions are not anyway the locus of real power. Through the division of legislature and executive, effective power comes to be located outside the legislative assemblies – 'the hollow talking shops' – and is vested in the unaccountable and inaccessible organs of executive power.

Both these points were held to be systematically ignored by those, like Kautsky, who advocated a parliamentary road to socialism. Their anticipation of such a transition, Lenin argued, rested upon the illegitimate tendency to identify parliament with government and government with the state, in such a way that the election of working-class representatives to parliament was seen to afford the possibility of a working-class 'take-over' of the state. But the division between executive and legislature ensured that government is something other than a committee of parliament – and that the state itself is something quite different again. The state, for example, has powerful bureaucratic and military apparatuses which are not simply the neutral instruments of the elected government and it is these bureaucratic and military apparatuses which are most resistant to revolutionary change and which the working class must dismantle if it is ever to take power.

Nor can the working class simply 'win over' these bureaucratic and military arms of the state. For the existing state, whose institutions and apparatuses rely upon maintaining a distance from, and exercising power over, the mass of the population, can never be the means of effecting real self-government. Such authentic self-government Lenin insisted, could only be achieved under the form of direct conciliar democracy in which the exercise of the authority of the state is beginning to wither away. Such a conciliar democracy could, in turn, only be established through the dissolution of the bureaucracy as an institution independent of the lay organization of day to day life and through the elimination of specialized armed forces and a standing army in favour of a militia of the armed people.

But perhaps the single most decisive point of the Leninist critique – and one that was also forcefully made by Luxemburg – is that the Kautskyan model of a gradual transition to socialism ignores the systematic division under capitalism between the economic and the political, confining its recommendations for a strategy of democratization exclusively to the latter. Against this, both Lenin and Luxemburg insisted that the decisive power of the bourgeoisie is economic rather than political and that this power is largely untouched by the democratization of political life. Since the dictatorship of the bourgeoisie is not secured through a curtailment of political rights, they insisted that it cannot be overcome by even the most expansive political emancipation. This dictatorship, they insisted, is in fact embodied in the institutional form of the bourgeois state and the systematic division between the economic and the political – which circumstances lie beyond the domain of political emancipation. These very real barriers to socialization and the inauguration of conciliar self-government, they asserted, could only be overcome through insurrection. Kautsky's infamy, for Lenin, resided precisely in his willingness to 'recognize in Marxism *everything except* revolutionary means of struggle'.[42]

Kautsky and Lenin: The Marxist Heritage

Although setting these Kautskyan and Leninist positions against each other does give some indication of where their respective strengths and weaknesses lie, it gives rather less evidence of the weaknesses which are common to both, and which are symptomatic of the more general limitations of the Marxist framework for the analysis of democracy, which they both work within and help to define. Here, I want to indicate the ways in which these accounts either reproduce or extend upon the analytical weaknesses I have already isolated in Marx's own account of democracy and socialism.

The most important theoretical weaknesses of the Marxist account that I sought to isolate in chapter 1 may be summarized under the following heads: first, *determinism/derivationism* – in which state and democracy are seen to be determined by or derived from other (principally economic) aspects of Marx's analysis; secondly, *essentialism* – in which categories such as the state and democracy are reduced to a pre-given categorical quality, as in the claim that the state necessarily acts in the interests of the ascendant class; and thirdly, *holism* – in which the state and democracy are seen to define unified and society-wide categories and/or practices.

An intermingling of many of these same weaknesses can be seen to underlie criticisms of both the Kautskyan and Leninist variants of the Marxist account of socialism and democracy. Thus Kautsky was able to avoid a consideration of the particular question of the state under capitalism, and the strategic issue of how the institutions of this state would need to be altered in order to enable it to operate under socialism, only by his reliance upon the historically determined evolution of a majority class destined to introduce socialism, the form of the state being 'read off' from this ascendancy of a new dominant class. Since the state was but the mechanism of centralized power of the dominant class, its transformation was as unproblematic as the historically necessary transition from capitalism to socialism. If, as Salvadori suggests, Kautsky came increasingly to doubt 'the guarantees of history' which are so strongly associated with his 'pre-heretical' writings as 'the Pope of Marxism', there is little indication that this led him to reconsider the problem of the transitional state.

Lenin, by contrast, was, of course, massively concerned with the problem of the capitalist state and its 'transformation'. But he showed, as we have seen, a still more rigorous commitment to a series of categorical imperatives on the state – the state as the undivided and unmediated dictatorship of a single class – a commitment which largely precluded consideration of the internal transformation of the state, divisions within the state or the inclusion under the aegis of the state of interests other than those of the ascendant class and its allies.

Similar problems surround their accounts of democracy. While democracy – substantially identified with existing parliamentary democratic practice – was afforded by Kautsky, in a classically social democratic manner, something approaching canonical status, he gave precious little consideration to democratic principles in and of themselves. In addition to its indispensable function as a check upon bureaucracy, the world-historical significance of democracy is largely confined to its accuracy as a barometer of social changes, which it records rather than promotes. Though it helps to educate and instruct the workers and signals to the declining bourgeoisie the 'inevitability' of its historical overhaul, the single greatest strength of democracy is that it gives unequivocal expression to the emergence of that immense majority in favour of socialism which is itself inscribed in the very processes of historical development. Certainly, Kautsky values the securing of parliamentary democracy, attributing Leninist criticisms of it to their dissatisfaction with its unwelcome, though historically valid, verdict upon the Bolshevik seizure of power. But Kautsky's recognition of the importance of parliamentary democracy does not entail a corresponding recognition of an authentic and independent sphere of political discourse. While pluralist in form, the laws of historical development determine its necessarily socialist content, allowing Kautsky, at least down to the mid-1920s, to see in parliamentary democracy an expectation of 'the dictatorship of the proletariat'.

Here again, this Kautskyan position must be sharply contrasted with Lenin's hostility to parliamentary democracy and his reliance upon the scathing criticism of it to be derived from the essential categories of Marxist explanation. For Lenin, democracy was simply one form of the state, and as such subject to the full rigour of Marxist criticism of the state. Democracy was always democracy for a class whose rule was secured though dictatorship over other classes. Parliamentary democracy may have certain tactical advantages – promoting clarity as to the 'real' and irreconcilable difference of class interest – but it had to be displaced by, rather than developing into, a materially different conciliar democracy, which was itself destined to 'wither away' once the circumstances of class contradiction which had called the state into being were overcome.

Misapprehending Democracy and Socialism

It is clear that neither Kautsky nor Lenin were uninfluenced by the quite differing practical experiences of their indigenous labour movements, but, at the same time, both were heavily indebted to the *theoretical* heritage of Marxism, of which, in their turn, they were to be such influential exponents. Thus Harding, in his painstaking reconstruction of *Lenin's Political Thought*, rejecting the conventional characterization of Lenin as opportunist and pragmatist, depicts Lenin as 'an extraordinarily doctrinaire politician . . . [whose] theoretical findings distorted his practical activity', while Paul Mattick rather neatly summarizes Kautsky's life's work as 'the retreat of theory before practice'.[43] At this point, I want to consider the ways in which the respective theoretical debts of Kautsky and Lenin led both of them to misappraise, in differing though not quite discrete ways, the significance of democracy in its relation to socialism.

1 On history

Under this first head, I want to consider the neglect, by both Kautsky and Lenin, of the extent to which the securing of local and central democratic institutions is an *historical* achievement – not in the sense of the unfolding of an immanent historical purpose but as the winning of sets of limited institutions and practices secured through protracted and often quite violent struggle. In part, this neglect can be retraced to Marx's supposition that the representative democratic state, complemented by a full range of civil and political liberties, is the characteristic form of polity under capitalism. This claim is, of course, far from self-evidently true. Outside of a limited (and privileged) range of metropolitan capitalist countries, possibly those wealthy enough to co-opt or contain significant sections of its working population, capitalism has not been universally associated with this full range of civil and political freedoms and open democratic institutions. Nor should the double-edged significance of Macpherson's simple point, that the liberal democratic state was liberal long before it was democratic, be readily neglected.[44] For this tells us something not only about the struggle to democratize the state, but also about the state upon which such democratization was to be brought to bear. It is though, within the rubric of historical materialism itself, that history is perhaps most effectively suppressed. The teleology which historical materialism affords both Lenin and Kautsky's histories of democratic form not only suppresses the recognition that democracy was only won through popular, (or at least anti-oligarchic), struggles, it also encourages a mistaken confidence that such gains are either irreversible and/or that they have a particular 'class-belongingness'. The latter is perhaps more evident in Lenin – as, for example, in his claim that parliamentary democracy is bourgeois, while conciliar democracy is proletarian – though Kautsky tends to identify continuing democracy with the interests of the necessarily majoritarian working class. The former is, of course, one of the central planks of the Kautskyan platform for pursuing 'the parliamentary road to socialism'. Both can be seen to be historically suspect. Indeed, the categories of historical materialism applied to parliamentary democracy tend to lead towards both an 'overvaluing' – sufficient means of socialist transformation (Kautsky) – and an 'undervaluing' – necessarily confined to bourgeois 'politicking' (Lenin) – of institutions which are neither unalterably given nor necessarily identified with any particular class. The tendency of both Kautskyan and Leninist accounts is to treat existing democratic institutions as essences rather than as capacities. As Laclau and, following him, Jessop have argued, the class-specificity of democratic institutions is not pre-given but is intimately connected to the effectiveness with which competing classes – and other potential social actors – intervene within the 'contested terrain' of democratic politics to secure their interests.[45]

At the same time, an exclusive emphasis upon the 'world-historical' and transformative significance of the concept of democracy can lead to an undervaluing of other achievements of democratic and emancipatory struggle which have, historically, been quite as important as the winning of parliamentary institutions. E. P. Thompson, for example, lays considerable stress upon the importance, in radical and early working-class agitation of the appeal to the rights of 'the Free-Born Englishman', rights which were understood to be 'not so much democratic as anti-absolutist'.[46] Nor can these claims be properly seen as simply an early form of protest, articulated, like the call for certain freedoms under the rule of law, within a 'bourgeois frame of reference' but symptomatic of, and 'speaking for', quite other and distinctively proletarian claims and institutions. For any group of ordinary citizens, freedom from arbitrary arrest, freedom of assembly and association can be seen to be quite as important as the right to vote, every fourth or fifth year, in parliamentary elections. Indeed, within capitalist democracies, it has often been the former, civil and daily exercised freedoms which have come under much fiercer attack than the periodic right to vote.

Both Lenin and Kautsky recognized democracy to be a progressive principle. However, my reading of them suggests that, through the imposition of a particular theoretical apparatus upon the lived experience of democratic struggles, they both propagated a quite mistaken view of the nature of democratic advances and (mis)appropriated 'democracy' for a progressivist account of social development which was quite unable to meet their expectations. Thus much of what is most valuable in the historical development of democratic politics is jettisoned in an account in which democracy is seen as the medium through which an immanent historical development towards socialism is enacted.

2 On politics

This sublimation of political *action* to seemingly predetermined and objectively given political interests is nowhere more readily apparent than in the Marxists' unwillingness to afford any autonomy to political struggles within, and the institutions of, *civil society*. Once again, this is a hostility which can be traced back to Marx's own (unwarranted) anticipation of 'True Democracy' as the recombination of state and civil society. It is perhaps easy to see how this 'denial of politics' reappears – in an acutely pronounced form – in Lenin's expectations of an 'end of democracy'. For this is at the end of a chain of reasoning which identifies the end of democracy with an end of the state, which itself expresses the end of class contradictions that, in their turn, are defined around the formal ownership and non-ownership of private property. But it is also present in the Kautskyan expectation that open democratic form will necessarily give expression to an immanent socialist content. Both thinkers tend to conflate socialization with emancipation and deny the existence of a politics, autonomous of the mobilization of particular economically defined interests. Yet, as I indicated in the opening chapter, this 'collapse' is unjustified in several respects. First, socialism if it is to represent at least a potential political practice, cannot be identified with the (Utopian) expectation of general human emancipation, nor can it be synonymous with passing beyond systematic social contradictions and 'the circumstances of politics'. This is particularly clear where socialism is identified with nothing more than the social ownership of the means of production. These claims should be abandoned along with the expectation that socialism is necessarily inscribed in the processes of historical development.

Again, it is difficult to see how and why, except by definitional fiat, socialism should be defined as *the* sole or overriding emancipatory historical project. The Marxist tendency – of which both Kautsky and Lenin are leading exponents – to reduce all forms of struggle for liberation to mediated forms of class struggle betrays an incapacity to comprehend the full range of emancipatory struggles and the open-ended nature of any historical emancipatory project. This is, in turn, symptomatic of a general tendency to collapse politics back into economics or, more properly, discursive will-formation into some form of materialist determinism. At the institutional level, this has expressed itself in the traditional poverty of Marxist analyses of the state – a collapsing of the *locus* of 'allocative' and 'authoritative' powers, which has furnished a drastically impoverished account of both the effectiveness of, and the internal divisions within, political power.

Despite Lenin's timely recognition that socialism – as that form transitional between capitalism and communism – might constitute 'an entire historical epoch', this weakness is made still more severe by that failure, which I have already sought to isolate in Marx, to provide a satisfactory account of politics, the state and democracy *under socialism* which, given the improbabilities associated with the early emergence of a communist order, looms, even upon the most optimistic reading, as an extended if not indefinite historical period.[47]

Some of these weaknesses, most particularly the continuing importance of democratic politics and a public sphere after socialization, were raised in Luxemburg's critical analysis of *The Russian Revolution* – an appraisal which, it should be recalled, was directed not only at Lenin and Trotsky but still more critically against the inactivity of Kautsky and other leaders of the German labour movement. The difficulty is that Luxemburg's strategic alternative to both Kautskyism and Leninism shares much with the historical experience, as opposed to the Marxist and Leninist appropriation, of the Paris Commune. Democratic and expansive, this carries the hallmarks of revolution as a 'festival of the people' – a joyous, semi-anarchic interlude destined to pass through bloody reprisal to 'business as usual'. What it fails to do is to provide a satisfactory alternative strategy to the (unattractive) programmes of either Kautskyan or Leninist socialism. The very weaknesses of these traditions as the means of comprehending democratic socialist politics in advanced Western capitalist societies, in which mass democracy and the institutions of civil society are highly developed, have generated chronic difficulties for those who have subsequently tried to develop a Marxist political strategy under the circumstances of advanced capitalism. It is to two differing manifestations of these difficulties that I turn in the next two chapters.

Part Two
Destinations

4
Italy
A Third Road to Socialism?

In the first part of this study, I have set out what I understand to be the most important and often quite opposing views that underlie the 'classical' Marxist view of the state, democracy and the transition to socialism. Despite its undoubted historical interest, I have been principally concerned with the way in which this classical tradition has bestowed upon its inheritors what is, in many ways, a profoundly inadequate account of a democratic and socialist political practice. I suggested that, through its deterministic and categorical oversights, this was a tradition which gave precious little consideration to the kinds of political practice that might be appropriate under the circumstances of a more 'advanced' capitalism. In this and the following chapter, I consider two contrasting examples of the way in which this tradition has been reinterpreted to achieve some sort of consonance with a viable contemporary political programme and assess the extent to which the consequent strategies and practices are themselves able to generate a more compelling basis for a democratic socialist politics. I go on to offer an assessment of the ways in which the success or failure of these strategies may be related to their contested Marxist inheritance.

The two contrasting and complementary strategies I have chosen to consider are drawn from the Communist Party in Italy, (PCI), and the left wing of the Social Democratic Party in Sweden, (SAP). Both examples are taken from Western European advanced capitalist societies, with a comparatively long, if, in the Italian case, interrupted, experience of 'bourgeois' democracy. They are both societies with powerfully entrenched trades union movements and well-supported parties of the left. Both have a considerable record of Marxist scholarship and, perhaps most importantly, both have advocated differing Marxisant strategies for the transformation of advanced capitalism, strategies which have attracted widespread interest and support in other Western European parties of the left. Though addressing quite differing social forces and to rather differing effects, both strategies can be seen to be based upon a 'creatively interpreted'

Marxism. In considering the strengths and weaknesses of these two strategies, I venture some suggestions as to the general capacity of the Marxist tradition to offer a satisfactory basis for a contemporary democratic socialist politics.

In chapter 5, I consider recent initiatives on the left of Swedish social democracy. Here, I begin by considering the widely influential and much advocated strategy of the Italian Communist Party, (PCI).[1]

Italy: A Third Way?

For many commentators, the PCI is most closely associated with the emergence during the 1970s of a distinctive 'Eurocommunist' politics. However, the grasp of 'Eurocommunism' upon the informed public and academic imagination proved to be brief. The advances of the French, Spanish and Italian Communist Parties during the mid-1970s aroused the interest (and concern) of both academic commentators and practising politicians but by the early 1980s – with the communists eclipsed by the socialists in France and Spain and withdrawing from their brief and rather unhappy association with the 'governmental arena' in Italy – such interest had largely evaporated. But such an episodic account of the rise and fall of Eurocommunism tends to mask the much more extended historical development of a distinctively West European communist theory and practice. For the Italian Communists, above all, the tenets of Eurocommunism marked no decisive breach with previous theory and practice and its popularly assumed demise has occasioned no radical change in party policy. At the same time, while the French Communist Party, (PCF), and the Spanish Communist Party, (PCE), have been increasingly marginalized, the Italian Communists emerged from the 1984 elections to the European Parliament as Italy's single largest party.

For the PCI, this continuing advocacy of Eurocommunist strategy may be seen as a phase in their long-standing quest to define and pursue a distinctive *'terza via al socialismo'* – a 'third road to socialism', grounded in national institutions (and experience) and distinct from the (much-criticized) practices of either Soviet Leninism or traditional social democracy. In this chapter, I consider the PCI's claim that the *'terza via'* constitutes just such a distinctive (though still Marxist) political theory, strategy and practice, appropriate to the circumstances of contemporary Western Europe, and assess the extent to which this 'third road' has effectively overcome those weaknesses and oversights that I have identified in the 'classical' Marxist approach to democratic politics.

Gramsci as Theorist of 'Leninism in the West'

Given his authoritative status as the father of Italian communism and as the architect of a distinctive 'Leninism in the West', any consideration, whether historical or theoretical, of the PCI's development of the *'terza via'* is bound to begin with Antonio Gramsci.[2] Gramsci himself was keenly aware of the particular and peculiar historical circumstances under which the Communists in Italy, and to a lesser extent in Western Europe generally, were called to act. Though a committed supporter of the Bolshevik Revolution, under the tutelage of the council experience, of the *'Biennio Rosso'* and the rise of fascism, he came ever more firmly to believe that the strategy of immediate confrontation with state power which had been so spectacularly successful in the Russia of 1917 was inappropriate under the radically different conditions which existed in Italy and more generally in the West.

The most essential difference between East and West Gramsci located in the nature of the relation between 'civil society' – 'the ensemble of organisms commonly called "private"' – and 'political society', (the state). 'Civil society' corresponded to hegemony, exercised throughout society by a dominant group, 'political society' to 'direct domination' exercised through the State and 'juridical' government.[3] In Russia, where 'the state was everything', it had been possible and indeed essential, to mount a direct attack upon the repressive apparatuses of the state, to pose frontally the issue of state power. Here, the reliance of state power upon its repressive apparatus was not a sign of strength, but of brittleness. But such a seizure of state power could not be straightforwardly reproduced in the West, for here the state was buttressed by 'the sturdy structure of civil society'. Before the issue of state power could be posed in the West, it was first essential to win over control of civil society. The medium of the exercise of this control within civil society, Gramsci styled *hegemony*. Hegemony – in its Gramscian usage – was seen to entail the twin ideas of leadership and direction as the means of securing and the method of exercising a strategy of class alliance. It placed particular emphasis upon struggle at the ideological-cultural level. Although, in his later writings, Gramsci turned to the discussion of hegemony as a bourgeois strategy related to 'transformism' and 'passive revolution' – a perspective which the PCI has taken up in its analysis of the other major political parties and social forces in Italy – the Party's more recent leadership has been predominantly concerned with hegemony as a working-class strategy.

This Gramscian account of working-class hegemony discounts the (maximalist) claim that all elements outside the working class constitute 'a single reactionary mass'. Rather, Gramsci held it to be essential to distinguish between the implacable class enemy of the workers – the bourgeoisie – and those other subordinate classes – such as the peasantry and the petty bourgeoisie – with whom the working class, which by merit of its more 'fundamental' position within the class relations of the capitalist mode of production would retain its leading role, might enter into alliance. For Gramsci, this did not entail the abandonment of dictatorship of the proletariat – for it would still prove necessary to exercise coercion over the expropriated class – but it did imply the expansion of its popular base through its non-exercise over other subaltern classes with whom authentic compromises could be struck and to whom (within certain limits) genuine concessions could be made.

War of Position: A New Strategy for the West

Just as the institutional and societal differences between East and West implied different forms of the exercise of power and differing types of class rule so, correspondingly, did the possibility of revolutionary overthrow depend upon two differing strategies. Where the state, coercion and dictatorship were dominant it was necessary to wage a 'war of movement', where civil society, consent and hegemony were uppermost it was essential to resort to a 'war of position'.

The differences between war of movement and war of position Gramsci illustrated by the use of a military analogy drawn from the then comparatively novel experience of the First World War. Where, as in Russia, the fabric of civil society was undeveloped and the ruling class relied solely upon the coercive power of the repressive state apparatus, it was possible for the revolutionary to prosecute a war of movement – that is a direct assault upon the state in the hope of securing victory in a single decisive encounter. But this war of movement, which had scored such spectacular success in the Russia of 1917, was radically unsuited to the developed capitalist nations of the West. Here, where the state was 'more complex and massive' and where bourgeois rule was largely mediated through the exercise of hegemony in civil society, the ruling class could not be unseated by a frontal assault. To ensure proletarian rule it was *first* necessary to displace bourgeois hegemony within civil society by proletarian hegemony – and this was only possible through a period of sustained and protracted mass struggle. In the West, the workers' interests were themselves often organized within bourgeois hegemonic institutions – notably, in social democratic parties and reformist trades unions – and it was necessary to win workers away from these to genuinely proletarian organizations before the issue of state power could be posed. This required of the revolutionary party in the West 'a strategy and tactics altogether more complex and long-term than those which were necessary for the Bolsheviks'.[4]

This change in 'the art and science of politics' was analagous to the development of the attritional struggles of the trench-system of modern warfare. Gramsci insisted that in the West 'civil society' had become a complex structure 'resistant to the catastrophic "incursions" of the immediate economic element'. A frontal assault, either military or political, might appear to have overrun the enemy when, in fact, it had only breached its outermost defences and just as military technique had to be adjusted to meet the development of new attritional forms of struggle so, analogously, had the art of politics to be amended to meet the new circumstances of its own trench-warfare. This dictated that 'war of movement increasingly becomes war of position.' The revolutionary party in the West had to dedicate itself to the arduous and gradual labour of raising the proletariat to the role of hegemonic class for, he insisted, 'in politics, war of position is hegemony.'[5]

Togliatti on Gramsci: The Genesis of the '*Terza Via*'

On the basis of even this brief summary, it is possible to see that Gramsci's own position was informed by reflection upon the contingent elements of the Italian situation – the 'incomplete' political revolution of the Risorgimento, the division of north and south, the defeat of the factory councils and, perhaps above all, the victory of fascism. It is also possible to identify in the tactical requirements issuing from Gramsci's emphasis upon the 'war of position' – the necessity of broad alliance/united front, gradualism, revolution as process, opposition to abstentionism, to maximalism, to sectarianism and insurrectionism, as well as the emphasis upon ideological-cultural struggle – a number of the most prominent and recurrent themes of the '*terza via*'. But, in so far as the further theoretical development of the '*terza via*' is indebted to Gramsci, it is, in fact, reliant upon a quite partial reading of the latter, and to understand this partiality it will be necessary to consider the authoritative interpretation of Gramsci given to the PCI by Palmiro Togliatti, who succeeded Gramsci as general secretary of the PCI in 1927 and who was to continue to lead the Party until his death in 1964.[6]

Three Gramscian formulations are of particular importance in Togliatti's interpretation – the advocacy of class alliance, the emphasis upon differing roads to socialism and the characterization of revolution in the West as an attritional struggle for (civil) hegemony. Like Gramsci, Togliatti was a reluctant subscriber to the 'ultra-leftism' of the

Comintern's 'third period' after 1928, and reflecting on the twin Italian experience of the defeat of the labour movement and the victory of fascism, he came increasingly to insist, in opposition to the Comintern orthodoxy, that fascism had a mass basis and that its victory had only been made possible by the failure of the post-war working class and its leadership to secure an alliance with the middle strata. In 1935, Togliatti was restored to the mainstream of orthodoxy when the Comintern's Seventh Congress called for the introduction of a new line – the strategy of the Popular Front. Rejecting the sectarianism of the period of 'social fascism', the strategy of the Popular Front posited a firm distinction between bourgeois democracy and fascism. Its aim was to mobilize as broad as possible a bloc of 'popular', anti-fascist forces which were to be rallied around the 'intermediate' goal of the overthrow of fascism and the restoration of a more or less 'bourgeois' democracy.

Although the immediate circumstances of the adoption of the Popular Front in 1935 were closely related to the contingent requirements of Soviet foreign policy, its consequences for Italian communism were both profound and lasting. It represented a far more radical departure from Leninist orthodoxy than the United Front strategy of the previous decade both in the anticipated breadth of its alliances and in the limitation of its objective – that is, the restoration of democracy rather than the institution of socialism. In it are contained both significant divergences from Gramsci and important anticipations of what was eventually to become Eurocommunism. For the appeal to 'the overwhelming majority of the population', *including* sections of the bourgeoisie, against the tiny minority of the monopoly section of capital which came to be characteristic of the *'terza via'* can, in fact, be traced back to the Popular Front's advocacy of the broadest possible popular alliance against fascism. Under this Popular Front strategy, the appeal to class and to militant working class activity were to be de-emphasized in favour of a non-sectarian popular-democratic struggle within an alliance which was to reach into the bourgeoisie, excluding only the representatives of finance and monopoly capital, who were held to constitute 'the principal social basis of fascism.'

This advocacy of a much-expanded popular alliance demanded, in turn, a much-revised strategy for the transition to socialism. The priority accorded to the mobilization of a majority against fascism and for the restoration of democracy required that the specific, militant demands of the (minoritarian) working class for a transition to socialism be, at least temporarily, suspended. In the struggle against fascism, it was first essential to re-establish democracy before the issue of the transition to socialism could be posed. In a suitably amended form this 'two-stage' strategy – first, restoration of democracy; then, transition to socialism – became entrenched as a part of the orthodoxy of post-war European communist practice. While the fear of fascism remained a major point of reference even after 1945, the 'frontist' strategy became increasingly oriented around the struggle of 'the great majority of the population' against the usurpation of democracy by the power of monopoly capital. At the same time, the status of the democratic stage was raised beyond that of a mere restoration of 'bourgeois' democracy to the possibility of a 'progressive' democracy. It was argued that important changes could be effected and certain 'elements of socialism' introduced within the democratic stage. There was a tendency to draw ever more 'transitional' elements into the democratic stage and correspondingly to de-emphasize the socialist stage.

Just as the victory of fascism and the necessity of unseating it had been a decisive influence in shaping Gramsci's 'Leninism for the West', so the victory *over* fascism and the need to eliminate its 'social basis' were a formative influence on Togliatti's (post-war) account of the Italian road to socialism. As was the case in many parts of Europe, the record of communists within the Resistance movement had earned the PCI a measure of popular legitimacy and, even before victory over the fascists was complete Togliatti sought, in the celebrated 'Svolta di Salerno', to redefine the PCI as a new and mass-based party. Sassoon is right to insist that 'this mass party was born out of a specific situation: the Second World War' and Togliatti, indeed, set out to define the programme of the Italian Communists as an expansion/extension of the frontist struggle against fascism. 'The defence against fascist and reactionary threats', he wrote, 'becomes a positive action of social change'.[7]

The 'Svolta di Salerno', the new party it defined and the changes it both instituted and formalized, was to be a decisive influence in the shaping of the *'terza via'*. If Togliatti's new programme was still communist, it was, at first sight, far from conventional Leninism and Togliatti sought to explain this distance and justify his position by reference to the Gramscian distinction between East and West, a distinction he equated with the doctrine of *'differing roads to socialism'*. Thus, Togliatti argued, on the eve of the defeat of fascism, that the nationally and historically specific conditions of Italian communism allied to the differing international circumstances that had resulted, in part, from the very success of the Bolsheviks in 1917 meant that the Italian road to socialism would be quite different to that trodden by the Communist Party of the Soviet Union, (CPSU). In the circumstances of 1944, Togliatti insisted, the Italian Communists were confronted with 'completely new conditions' – principally, 'the special character' and 'national stamp' of the Party, the possibility of governmental participation and 'the popular and mass character' of the Party.[8]

This problematic of 'differing roads' – authority for which Togliatti sought not only in Gramsci but also in Lenin – enabled him to deny the exemplary status of the Russian Revolution and the leading role of the CPSU in favour of *'polycentrism'*. In the communist movement, he insisted, it was no longer possible to speak of 'a single guide'. Every party should be influenced by its 'own objective and subjective conditions, traditions, forms of organization'. This, in turn, enabled him to establish a distance and, at times, a critical distance from the practices of eastern bloc communism and was eventually to lead to the claim that there might be not only differing roads to socialism but also differing forms of socialism at the end of these roads. Thus in his testamentary 'Yalta Memorandum', Togliatti insisted that the circumstances of the further advance of socialism would be 'very different from what they had been in the past' and the differences between countries would be 'very great'.[9]

Togliatti on 'Progressive Democracy': The Gradual Revolution

Togliatti's strategic recommendations for the 'Italian road to socialism' follow a third neo-Gramscian premiss – that is the characterization of revolution in the West as an attritional struggle for hegemony. Most immediately, this led Togliatti towards a rejection of insurrectionary tactics in favour of a recognition of the revolution in the West as a gradual process. It also led him, in conformity with the faith in 'progressive democracy' that he had expressed in developing the strategy of frontist alliance, towards a rejection of the Leninist practice of a dictatorship of the proletariat in favour of struggle for the hegemony of the proletariat largely within the existing democratic framework. This rested in turn, upon Togliatti's belief that within the prevailing institutional structure it would be possible to advance beyond an 'illusory' bourgeois democracy to an 'advanced' or 'progressive' democracy which would be able to instigate measures that would take Italian society beyond capitalism towards the threshold of socialism. He insisted that the restoration of democracy in Italy was a great popular-democratic achievement and had opened up the possibility of 'a peaceful development towards Socialism' through a 'struggle to extend democracy and give it a new content'.[10]

Although Togliatti alluded to workers' control and the extension of direct democracy, the 'new content' of this 'extended democracy' was to be found not so much in a transformation of (existing) democratic *institutions* as in the introduction of what Togliatti called 'structural reforms', what were later to be styled 'elements of socialism' which would 'democratize' the economy, begin to transform the state 'in a socialist direction' and secure the hegemony of the working class in alliance with the 'anti-monopolist forces'. These transformations were to be achieved within the prevailing order but were held to be capable of profoundly changing the nature of this order from within. This possibility of profound reform meant, in its turn, the elimination of all maximalist sympathy for abstentionism and economic catastrophism. Economic crisis brought with it the danger of a reversion to fascism, and it thus fell to the Communist Party and the labour movement to intervene *positively* to attempt to resolve economic crisis, to raise efficiency and improve productivity, while attempting to direct this process of renewal in a 'socialist direction'.

Leading the Party for nearly forty years, Togliatti was clearly decisively influential in the development of '*la terza via*'. Characteristically, judgements of his leadership have tended to concentrate upon the 'authenticity' of his derivation of Party strategy from Gramsci, admirers applauding his 'creative interpretation' of the latter, in which his critics identify a continual betrayal of the original and radical content of Gramsci's 'Leninism for the West'. Given the paucity of Togliatti's appeal to the Marxist 'classics' and his constant involvement in the 'immediate' tasks of the Party, it is perhaps surprising that so little attention is generally given to the practical and situational determinants of the Togliattian position.[11] Paul Piccone is exceptional in recognizing that Togliatti, inheriting the leadership of the Party in the wake of the victory of fascism and on the eve of the emergence of Stalinism, led the Party through a period in which 'PCI development can be understood only in terms of the politics of survival.' 'The politics of survival' meant, at times, alliances of convenience at home and accommodation with Stalinism abroad; it also entailed a recognition of American hegemony within Western Europe at the end of the Second World War. 'Far from leaving the general philosophical and cultural framework unaffected', as Piccone notes, this period 'left an indelible mark on the party'.[12] Of Togliatti, it required an ability to reconcile 'the party line' with the imperatives of 'the immediate situation'.

This he managed with considerable skill and dexterity. Identification with Leninism and the defence of 1917 as an authentically socialist revolution were seemingly a political and ideological *sine qua non* of the PCI, helping to distinguish the Party from its social democratic opponents, defining the 'fraternal' relationship with the Soviet Union, securing the morale of 'Utopian' workers and justifying the Party's democratic centralism. At the same time, it was considered essential to demonstrate the democratic pedigree of the PCI, to make an appeal beyond the traditional working class, to reach a rapprochement with the Catholic world and to maintain a critical distance from the social and political experience of the Soviet Union. This Togliatti was adeptly able to achieve by presenting peaceful revolution through broad-based alliance and 'polycentrism' as classically Leninist tenets and arguing that the October Revolution, made under conditions of unparalleled difficulty for the inauguration of socialism – the now familiar litany of economic backwardness, civil war and imperialist intervention – led to the inclusion in Leninist practice of certain 'contingent' and anti-democratic elements, which were alien to socialism but necessitated by the pressing demands of a far from ideal immediate situation. Togliatti was thus able skilfully to combine arguments concerning the unique-ness of the Bolshevik Revolution with the advocacy of 'different roads to socialism', insisting that the success of the former was itself the necessary condition for the pursuit of the latter. In this way, a critical distance from the USSR was reconciled with a 'triumphalist' account of the October Revolution.

'Terza Via' and Eurocommunism

Whether one calls Togliatti's contribution 'creative Marxism' or 'political opportunism' is largely a matter of political taste. What is clear is that his authoritative account of the Italian road to socialism has set the agenda for the development of the Party in the twenty years since his death. There have, of course, been changes and developments – perhaps most innovatively some breach with the long-standing tenets of democratic centralism – but these have tended to proceed from the nature of the PCI as a mass-based party in an advanced industrial society, a character it assumed under Togliatti. Perhaps the most celebrated of these innovations – and, to date, the most evolved account of the 'terza via' – is the emergence of an explicitly codified Eurocommunism.[13] Whatever its European-wide fate, for the Italian Communists this marked a quite natural development of the 'terza via', embodying the programmatic intent of 'Salerno' – participation of a mass-based, popular communist party in a democratically elected government. Though less circumspect, its debt to Togliatti is clear.

Thus, for example, contemporary leaders of the PCI set out to resolve the thorny issue of their relation to the USSR along lines broadly similar to Togliatti. Characteristically, they have argued that while both the Revolution and the post-revolutionary society are socialist, the Russian experience represents an historically limited form of socialism. More recent statements, however, show a less ambivalent hostility towards the Soviet Union. In the wake of Soviet intervention in Afghanistan and Poland, Berlinguer claimed that 'the Soviet model of socialism has proved inappropriate to Eastern Europe' and that 'the Soviet October revolution has proved itself to be a spent force.'[14] The Italian Communists still stop short of the Kautskyan claim that the Bolshevik Revolution was unjustified Blanquism, but they argue that under more favourable circumstances, where such difficulties as had confronted the Russians did not exist, it would be possible to introduce a more authentic socialism, less conditioned by the non-socialist elements that issued from Russian adversity and less subject to the 'degenerations' which had characterized the development of the Soviet Union.

These 'more favourable circumstances', the Italian Communists believe, are to be found in contemporary Western Europe. Following the doctrine of 'different roads to socialism', they isolate two structural changes – the supposed development of state monopoly capitalism and the popular conquest of democracy – and the further developments and possibilities that issue from them, as forming the basis of the contemporary advocacy of the *'terza via'* to socialism in the West.

There is a marked continuity between the strategic recommendations of the contemporary Italian Communists and those of the Popular Front period. While the enemy is no longer the fascists but rather the representatives of big monopoly capital, the means of overcoming that enemy remain substantially unaltered. In essence this requires the pursuit of 'great powerful struggles and mass movements, uniting the majority of the people around the working class' – a policy made possible by the concentration of capitalist class rule within the big monopolies.[15] Just as the Popular Front had been envisaged as an alliance which would go beyond the confines of the subaltern classes, so the strategy of alliance in the era of monopoly capital seeks to embrace the lower reaches of the bourgeoisie itself.

This quest for the broadest possible alliance found its most pronounced expression in Berlinguer's advocacy of the *'Compromesso Storico'* with the Christian Democrats, (DC). Although Berlinguer resisted the claim that this 'Historic Compromise' was primarily a parliamentary arrangement with the DC – seeking to present it as a much more popular-hegemonic strategy – it was widely interpreted in this sense and working with the DC clearly meant working with the representatives of at least a portion of monopoly capital. But launching this strategy in the mid-1970s Berlinguer and the leadership of the PCI, mindful of the recent victory of reaction in Chile, seemed to be primarily concerned with the threat of dividing Italian society and sponsoring a renewal of fascism that might follow from continuing economic crisis. They were seen to stress the need to intervene 'positively' to resolve the economic crisis, to urge cooperation with all (remotely) democratic forces to this end and, concomitantly, to play down their criticism of big monopoly capital as enemy of the broad alliance in favour of an attack upon the parasitic/non-productive elements of monopoly capital who were held to be largely responsible for the crisis-ridden state of the Italian economy.

Of course, this advocacy of 'broad alliance' makes only limited sense unless it is harnessed to a second and equally essential component of the frontist heritage – that is the commitment to democracy as popular conquest and means of social transformation/renewal. It is in this advocacy of democracy that the Italian Communists move furthest away from classical Leninism and have been seen to come closest to embracing conventional social democracy. For the identity of socialism and democracy, which is a characteristic supposition of this social democractic orthodoxy, is repeatedly stressed in their accounts. Thus, for example, the PCI-PCF joint declaration of 1975 maintains that 'Socialism will constitute a higher phase of democracy and freedom: democracy realized in the most complete manner' and corresponding stress is laid upon the securing of 'social pluralism, in politics and ideas'.[16]

I have already drawn attention to the introduction under the Popular Front of a two-stage strategy in the advance to socialism. In its Togliattian interpretation, the distinction between these two phases became blurred, greater emphasis being placed upon the first, popular-democratic phase and its transitional possibilities, while the second, strictly socialist phase was increasingly marginalized. In the developed Eurocommunist account these two stages became further fused – ever more elements of the socialist phase are held to be comprehended within what was to be an intermediary, democratic phase, while the socialist stage as an independent entity largely disappears. Through this development of the frontist strategy the Eurocommunist leadership is able to pose as communist or socialist a strategy which appears to be remarkably close to social democracy.

Of course, the PCI vigorously contest this claim that theirs is essentially a social democratic strategy. Certainly they reject both insurrection and the dictatorship of the proletariat as socialist strategies in advanced capitalist societies, but they argue that under the conditions of developed democracy in the West, it is essential to recognize the generic form of socialist revolution as a 'gradual process'. This advocacy of revolution as 'gradual process' rests, in turn, upon the Eurocommunists' particular understanding of democratization as the medium through which the working class is able to establish its hegemony within the various institutions of civil and political society. Accordingly, it is not held to be confined to the most immediately political sphere but is applicable wherever the working class struggles for hegemony. Through their day to day work on the influential and legislating parliamentary committees, through their promotion of regional autonomy, *'piani d'impresa'*, (company planning agreements), a national health service, neighbourhood councils, institutional reform and so on, the PCI seeks to elaborate a process of democratization as 'the gradual affirmation of working class hegemony' through the securing of a series of 'structural reforms'. Giuseppe Vacca, for example, insists that the pursuit of 'structural reforms' within the existing state defines 'an original process of democratic and socialist transformation in Italy . . . the framework of the Italian road to socialism'.[17] In this way it is argued that it is possible for the working class to pursue an incremental advance towards socialism through an ever growing hegemony within the many apparatuses of civil and political society, allowing it gradually to raise itself to the status of ruling class.[18]

'Terza Via' Today: The 'Democratic Alternative'

Under the Historic Compromise, the Communists suffered 'the worst of both worlds' – associated with the failures of a government over which they were unable to exercise effective power – and this was reflected in the electoral reverse of 1979, (to 30.4 per cent from 34.4 per cent in 1976), the first decline in the Communist vote since the War. In the face of these reversals, the 1980s have seen the development of a 'new' strategy – the Democratic Alternative – formally endorsed at the Party's 16th Congress in 1983 and forming the basis of its electoral programme in that year.

In a number of tactical respects the Democratic Alternative is quite distinctive. Its central feature is that the Communists, in a strongly prioritized alliance with the Italian Socialist Party, (PSI), should form a governmental alternative to Christian Democracy. Thus, for the first time as a mass party, the PCI presents itself as being capable of ruling Italy to the exclusion of the Christian Democrats. Though it remains an alliance strategy, there are changes in its perception of alliance, with a greater emphasis upon 'new movements' and groups, outside the traditional parameters of communist politics, and with political alliances being based upon programmatic agreements rather than agreements being derived from given political alliances. Recognizing that 'Italian society has changed deeply', it seeks support beyond the traditional working class among technical and intellectual workers, 'the masses of the unemployed, the marginalized and the young', as well as a 'positive dialogue' with progressive and productive elements of 'the entrepreneurial middle class' and 'executives'. It also seeks support among the 'new movements' – most notably, the women's movement – which it recognizes as having interests which cross class boundaries and which are not comprehended by the traditional categories of working class politics nor reducible to marginal activities of mainstream Party activity. At the same time, the PCI repeats its openness to 'progressive' elements within the Catholic world and continues to seek to clarify the distinction between Catholicism and Christian Democracy.[19] Institutionally, this 'updated alliance strategy' is addressed principally to the PSI, which is exhorted to abandon its centre-left arrangement with Christian Democracy in favour of 'a democratic, alternative government to the DC and to its system of power, based on the left wing parties and strong in the contribution from other democratic currents'.[20] However, the Democratic Alternative is marked much more by its continuity than its innovation. Despite the changes, the PCI retains its traditional commitment to alliance, the Italian road to socialism, the EEC, independence of the CPSU and the pursuit of revolutionary change as a 'gradual process of the affirmation of working class hegemony'.

Leninism: Opposing 'The Third Way'

At this point, having outlined the development of '*la terza via*' from Gramsci to the Democratic Alternative, I want to raise the two interwoven issues of, first, the extent to which PCI strategy does indeed constitute a distinctive Western European socialist strategy and, secondly, in so far as it does, the degree to which it has overcome those limitations which I have identified in the classical Marxist tradition. One classical (and essentially Leninist) response is to deny the possibility of pursuing such 'a third way'. To Togliatti's appropriation of Lenin as proponent of the '*terza via*', it is possible to oppose the latter's assertion that 'dreams of some third way are reactionary, petty-bourgeois lamentations.'[21] Although this Leninist criticism is substantially weakened by its largely formal character, and while this vitiates the Leninists' own counterposed account of socialist transition, it does not prevent them making a number of telling criticisms of the (Eurocommunist) 'third way'.

Summarily, these criticisms fall under two heads. The first is of the account of 'Stamocap', (state monopoly capitalism), through which, it is argued, it is possible to give an unwarranted breadth to the strategy of alliance. By seeking to define the 'class enemy' as monopoly capital or even as the parasitic element of monopoly capital, advocates of a third way are seen to promote a popular alliance which reaches into the bourgeoisie, spiriting away the problem of its relation to small or medium capital – a strategy which is seen to find its typical expression in Berlinguer's Historic Compromise. Similar criticisms are made of the perspective of 'two states within the state', which, it is argued, allows for the anticipatory suppression of the oppressive 'class function' of the state while further developing its universal 'technico-administrative function', thus embracing the danger of 'statism' and evading the Marxist imperative of 'smashing the state'.

A second set of criticisms is focused upon the Italian Communists' account of democracy. Such criticism is focused less upon their advocacy of the securing of democracy as 'strategic popular conquest' than upon their (supposed) willingness to confine their understanding of popular democracy to the presently existing institutions of representative parliamentary democracy and their further claim that through the development of these institutions towards a 'progressive' or 'advanced' democracy it is possible to secure an incremental advance towards socialism. This perspective is only attained, it is argued, through the initial separation and subsequent fusing of democratic and socialist stages of transition generating the claim that the transition to socialism can be effected through an expansion of popular-democratic struggle. This perspective of democracy as 'strategic popular conquest' is held to be insufficiently discriminating, failing to distinguish between genuine 'proletarian imposed' democratic conquests – universal suffrage, rights to free association and to strike – and other elements of contemporary democratic practice – notably, parliamentary-representative institutions – which are seen to be 'of typically bourgeois origin'.

Gramscianism: Towards an 'Authentic' Third Way?

Of course, not every critic of contemporary Italian Communist strategy calls for a return to a more traditionally Leninist practice. Indeed some, identifying the Italian advocacy of Eurocommunism with social democratization of the Party, have sought to isolate a distinctive *'terza via'* lying between Eurocommunism, on the one hand, and Leninism, on the other. Perhaps the most influential source of this alternative 'third way' – based upon a 'dual critique' of both Leninism and Eurocommunism – is to be found among those who advocate a 'return to the authentic Gramsci' as the basis for a critique of contemporary Party practice.

Jonas Pontusson, for example, insists that the advocacy of 'two states within the state', of the perspective of state monopoly capitalism and the corresponding strategy of alliances, which he holds to be characteristic of the PCI under Eurocommunism, is inconsistent with Gramsci's own position. To this effect, he cites Gramsci's claim that 'the socialist State must be a fundamentally new creation' and 'cannot be embodied in the institutions of the capitalist state'.[22] Similarly, he argues that Gramsci's conception of the state as 'a mechanism unifying the different fractions of the ruling class into a hegemonic bloc' vitiates the Eurocommunist account of state monopoly capitalism, while his account of alliance strategy, to be secured between the industrial working class in the north and the rural classes of the south in 'the immediate *pursuit* of socialist objectives', is irreconcilable with the PCI's advocacy of an 'electoralist and parliamentary' alliance with the non-monopolist bourgeoisie.

Gramsci recognized, Pontusson argues, that the socialist objectives of such an alliance 'cannot be accomplished by parliamentary democracy' and, correspondingly, called for the replacement of the democratic-parliamentary state by a new type of state, 'one that is generated by the associative experience of the proletarian class.'[23] For Gramsci, the real difficulty lay in:

> Constructing a state apparatus which internally will function democratically, i.e. will guarantee freedom to all anti-capitalist tendencies and offer them the possibility of forming a proletarian government, and externally will operate as an implacable machine crushing the organs of capitalist industrial and political power.[24]

A criticism of conventional Leninist practice is clearly implied.

Of course, the single most important and original aspect of the Gramscian heritage still endorsed by the contemporary Eurocommunist leadership of the PCI is his strategy of hegemony. Here again, Pontusson isolates three substantial differences between Gramscian and Eurocommunist accounts of the relation between war of position and war of manoeuvre with which the problematic of hegemony is centrally concerned. First, Gramsci did not understand the war of position as essentially 'electoralist and parliamentary'. Secondly, he insisted that the war of position is imposed by the strength of bourgeois rule rather than arising out of the strength of the labour movement. Thirdly, Gramsci did not generally suggest that the war of position is an alternative to the war of manoeuvre, rendering the latter, and the frontal assault upon the state, obsolete. However Pontusson argues that 'Gramsci continuously slips away from the centrality of state power' – particularly in the emphasis he placed upon struggles in civil society for

ideological-cultural hegemony – and this, in turn, allows his Eurocommunist interpreters to concentrate all their energies upon the mobilization of hegemonic consent to the neglect of state coercion.

'Passive Revolution' and 'Democratic Socialism'

This 'slippage' on the question of state power is itself seen to conceal
the 'statism' inherent in the Italian Communist strategy – enabling its
advocates to disguise the fact that theirs is a strategy for transition
which fails to redefine the relationship between the state and the
popular forces and which will therefore continue to embody the
domination of the state over the masses. Though fiercely contested by
the PCI, this is, in fact, a frequent complaint of left critics of
Eurocommunism, several of whom identify in the Gramscian formulation of 'passive revolution' an anticipatory critique of this emergent
statism. But this is a criticism levelled not only against Eurocommunism but also against traditional Leninism, in so far as both are seen to
be informed by an instrumental conception of the state. Against this
Buci-Glucksmann calls for a *'strategy of anti-passive revolution'*: that is
'an anti-passive democratic transition . . . based on non-bureaucratic
expansion of the forms of political life within the totality of structures
encompassed by the "enlarged state"'.[25]

Very similar concerns inform the 'dual critique' of Poulantzas, whose
State, Power, Socialism constitutes perhaps the most important recent
attempt to forge an independent socialist strategy out of the critique of
both Eurocommunism and (contemporary) Leninism.[26] For Poulantzas,
both positions are vitiated by a radically inadequate (and instrumentalist account of the state. By contrast, Poulantzas insists, the
state 'is always by nature a relation', expressing 'the condensation
of the balance of forces between the classes'.[27] While this 'relational'
account of the state is evident from Poulantzas' earliest writings, it is
only in his later work that he comes to break decisively with the
Leninist orthodoxy of the unitary power of the state. Thus, in *State,
Power, Socialism*, he insists that the state is 'a strategic field ploughed
from one end to the other by working-class and popular struggle and
resistance'. It is no longer sufficient simply to suggest that 'contradictions and struggles traverse the State', rather it is essential to recognize
that class contradictions are 'the very stuff of the State: they are present
in its material framework and pattern its organization'.[28] So long as the
Eurocommunist parties persist in an inadequate and instrumentalist
account of the state, they will be incapable of generating a viable
strategy for the transition to socialism. The belief that the state is
sufficiently independent of the dominant class to permit of a transition

to socialism without the state apparatus being broken by the seizure of class power, Poulantzas rejects as 'undoubtedly radically wrong'. It can only lead to 'state socialism'.[29]

This distinctive account of the state – particularly the importance of struggle *within* the state – led Poulantzas away from an endorsement of the countervailing Leninist orthodoxy. Indeed, in the traditional Leninist account of the transition to socialism, he identifies the same tendency towards statism that had been at the heart of his criticism of Eurocommunism. In fact, despite everything that distinguishes the recommendations of social democracy and the experience of 'real Socialism', they show 'a fundamental complicity': 'Both are characterized by *statism* and profound distrust of mass initiatives, in short by suspicion of democratic demands.'[30]

Poulantzas draws attention to the essentialism of Lenin's critique of the institutions of representative democracy and political freedoms, to the schematic assertion that 'representative democracy = bourgeois democracy = dictatorship of the bourgeoisie', which generates the claim that these institutions 'have to be completely uprooted and replaced by direct, rank-and-file democracy and mandated, recallable delegates – in other words, by the genuine proletarian democracy of soviets'.[31] Lenin's analysis was not initially premised upon an overweening centralism but rather upon the replacement of social democratic parliamentarism and 'formal' representative democracy by the 'real' direct democracy of workers' councils. But, Poulantzas argues, it was this very commitment to the 'sweeping substitution of rank-and-file democracy for representative democracy' which was to give rise to 'the centralizing and statist Lenin whose posterity is well enough known'. As we have seen, it was Rosa Luxemburg who had first reproached Lenin for this '*exclusive* reliance on council democracy and complete elimination of representative democracy'. She had insisted that without free elections, freedom of assembly and of the press, 'life dies out in every institution' leaving only the bureaucracy as an active element.[32] Poulantzas insists that the many 'degenerations' of Soviet life both during and more especially after Lenin's own lifetime – the single party, bureaucratization of the party, statism – were 'already inscribed in the situation criticized by Luxemburg'.

In this Leninist account, Poulantzas maintains, the state is conceived as 'a monolithic bloc without any cracks of any kind' and as an instrument of the bourgeoisie. Class struggle is thus external to the state – a struggle '*between* the State and the popular masses standing outside the State' – and the corresponding strategy for the transition to socialism is thus typified by instrumentalism and externality. The popular struggle for state power is located outside the 'fortress-state' and aims, principally, at establishing a situation of *dual power*, ('the *leitmotif* of Lenin's analysis'). Such a strategy eliminates the perspective of transition as process stressing the need to establish dual power and then 'to seize state power' – to transfer state power from the bourgeois state to the soviets. The perspective of rank-and-file democracy as alternative to the bourgeois state is replaced by the soviets as 'parallel state'. 'Distrust of the possibility of mass intervention within the bourgeois State' degenerates into 'mistrust of the popular movement as such' and this yields the perspective of a strengthening of the state/soviets, the better to make them subsequently wither away – a perspective that is seen inevitably to degenerate into 'Stalinist statism'.[33]

Poulantzas and the '*Terza Via*'

For Poulantzas, the Eurocommunism of the official communist parties of Western Europe, does not constitute a distinctive 'third road to socialism'. It is but a particular form of social democracy and as such is vulnerable to his criticism that both social democratic and Leninist accounts of the transition to socialism tend to collapse into 'the techno-bureaucratic statism of the experts'. The problem of the transition to socialism, Poulantzas argues, has been mistakenly posed in terms of this traditional dilemma:

> *Either* maintain the existing State and stick exclusively to a modified form of representative democracy – a road that ends up in social-democratic statism and so-called liberal parliamentarism; *or* base everything on direct, rank-and-file democracy or the movement for self-management – a path which, sooner or later, inevitably leads to statist despotism or the dictatorship of experts.[34]

Poulantzas insists that it is essential to go beyond this double-bind and to develop a distinct strategy for pursuing 'the democratic road to socialism'. Echoing Gramsci, he asks:

> How is it possible to transform the State in such a manner that the extension and deepening of political freedoms and the institutions of representative democracy (*which were also a conquest of the popular masses*) are combined with the unfurling of forms of direct democracy and the mushrooming of self-management bodies?[35]

It is to the outline of such a 'democratic road' that the closing pages of *State, Power, Socialism* are devoted.

The essential premiss of Poulantzas' 'democratic road' which enables him to escape the dilemma of the social democratic-Leninist opposition is his own radically different account of the state as the expression of a relationship of forces and his corresponding claim that this 'state is through and through constituted-divided by class contradictions'. His account of the taking of state power is correspondingly based upon struggles *within* the state. Drawing upon his analysis in *Political Power and Social Classes*, Poulantzas rejects the characterization of power as 'quantifiable substance' in favour of power as 'a series of relations among the various social classes'. Thus, for state power to be taken, there must have been a change in the relation of class forces *within* the state apparatus – a change which can only be the result of 'mass struggle'. Along the democratic road to socialism, the 'long process' of acquiring state power entails the development of the 'diffuse centres of resistance which the masses always possess within the state networks' so as to secure 'real centres of power on the strategic terrain of the state'.[36]

This radically different account of the taking of state power calls forth a concomitant strategy of transformation to be effected in the state. The perspective of 'smashing the state', which is a part of the strategy of dual power, is rejected in favour of a '*sweeping transformation*' of the state apparatus. The 'smashing of the state', Poulantzas insists, corresponds with the instrumentalist anticipation of replacing the bourgeois state with a parallel state in a situation of dual power, and is historically associated with the suppression of representative democracy and formal liberties. Sweeping transformation – 'combining the transformation of representative democracy with the development of forms of direct, rank-and-file democracy' – summarizes Poulantzas' alternative strategy which accords with the process of transition through the exploitation of the internal contradictions of the state.

Conclusion

From these critical contributions, it is clear that there exists, among secondary commentators, extensive support for Carl Boggs' claim that the strategy of the Southern European communist parties, and the PCI in particular, represents 'not an optimistic third path but a return to the original path of Bernsteinian social democracy'.[37] There is also evident a widespread, if not universal, belief that orthodox Leninism does not offer a satisfactory alternative. But while the standing of the PCI's '*terza via*' as an alternative to either social democracy or Leninism is thus repeatedly questioned, counterposed 'authentically' distinctive and radical accounts of 'the third way' are, at best, rudimentary. Though not wholly unsupported, the advocacy of 'anti-passive' revolution or 'sweeping transformation of the state' gives very little indication of what an alternative 'third way' would entail in practice in, for example, the Italian context. This is clearly one source of the PCI's impatience with its 'overly-theoretical' critics.

If the suggestions of Buci-Glucksmann, Poulantzas and others are too general and programmatic, it is possible that a practical alternative to the established party interpretation of the '*terza via*' might be sought among differing positions *within* the PCI.[38] If we take the PCI's most recent strategy – the pursuit of the Democratic Alternative – it is indeed possible to identify significant divergences between right and left. As presented by Berlinguer, the strategy of Democratic Alternative was seen to consummate a breach with the Historic Compromise – a move away from Christian Democracy in favour of a left alternative, a move away from an exclusive reliance upon parliamentary alliance in favour of 'a mobilization of social forces and movements'. But he continued to emphasize that the party's 'electoral strength . . . is still the decisive factor in changing the balance of forces in favour of the alternative', while Napolitano, speaking for the right of the Party, has tended to view the Democratic Alternative as a strategy for Party and parliamentary alliance with the PSI, as the basis of a government able to pursue 'a policy for the relaunching of (economic) development in such a way as to avoid fuelling inflation'.[39] By contrast, Pietro Ingrao, spokesperson of the left of the Party, has insisted that 'the alternative is not simply a proposal for central government' and he has given much more weight to the promotion of a more general radical social movement organized around the pursuit of radical social alliances, built upon greater local autonomy and in-party democracy.

But it is not clear that (even) this left variant of the Democratic Alternative has defined the grounds upon which a more radical '*terza via*' could be constructed. Indeed, the experience of the PCI strategists themselves lends considerable support to the belief that there are chronic difficulties in overcoming the social democracy-Leninism divide from within even a broadly-conceived Marxist framework. For example, the experience of the 'new social movements' – to which all sides of the PCI express themselves to be open – illustrates the considerable difficulties of comprehending the diversity of contemporary 'emancipatory struggles' with the tools of conventional Marxist class analysis. Similarly, the ambivalence of state action – neatly captured in Offe's claim that 'socialism in industrially advanced societies cannot be built *without* state power and it cannot be built *upon* state power' – is ill-comprehended by classical Marxist accounts of 'the capitalist state' and its 'withering away'.[40]

In short, the evidence of the Italian experience suggests both that an emancipatory politics is perhaps not best understood as the pursuit of 'a third road to socialism' and that, in fact, such a politics cannot now, if ever it could, be exclusively based upon Marxist premisses. Contemporary circumstances suggest the need for a new evaluation of the nature of state and civil society and a view of democracy and pluralism quite at variance with the rudimentary positions of both social democracy and Leninism.

If the capacity of the left wing of the PCI to respond to this challenge is doubtful, the prospects of the mainstream PCI meeting it are minimal. For it is resolutely committed to a reformist interpretation of the '*terza via*' in which a deeply-entrenched commitment to Marxism 'as an objectivistic theory of social development' seems to legitimate, as it did for the Second International, a largely reformist practice.[41] But, at the same time, it should be clear that this is a commitment which arises less from doctrinal preferences than from the institutional and practical dilemmas experienced by any socialist party seeking mass electoral support. It is a difficulty starkly posed by Przeworski: 'Participation in electoral politics is necessary if the movement for socialism is to find mass support among workers, yet this participation seems to obstruct the attainment of final goals.'[42]

Under the peculiar 'exclusionary' circumstances of Italian politics, this problem is especially pronounced. In the election of 1983, under the new strategy, the Communist vote held up quite well, (down 0.5 per cent at 29.9 per cent), while the DC tumbled from 38.3 per cent to 32.9 per cent. In the European elections of 1984, the PCI even crept ahead of the DC. But despite these historical reversals for Christian Democracy, Italy continued to be governed by a DC-PSI coalition, under the premiership of the PSI leader Bettino Craxi. Committed to an electoral strategy, the Italian Communists – powerful in the unions, strongly embedded in civil society, experienced and widespread in local government, consistently able to secure around a third of the popular vote – still found themselves excluded from governmental power.

The irony of the PCI's position is neatly caught by Middlemas:

> The PCI has come closer than any other CP to bridging the ancient gap between the Second and Third Internationals, yet the only fruit appears to be that it has inherited what in the halcyon mid-70s it used to call 'the crisis of social democracy'.[43]

While elements of a radical 'third way' may indeed be found in the experience of Italian Marxism, the PCI repeatedly finds its options foreclosed, on the one hand, by the limitations of social democracy and, on the other, by the unacceptability of Leninism. Indeed, its continuing difficulties, in the face of its very considerable strengths, lends further support to the claim that even a quite radically reconstructed Marxism is inadequate to the task of defining a satisfactory basis for a democratic socialist politics. This is evident in the circumlocutions in which the PCI has found itself involved in reconciling its day to day political practice to the broadest parameters of Marxist analysis. I defer to the concluding chapters a fuller consideration of the ways in which an alternative democratic socialist politics might seek to confront this problem.

5
Sweden
Beyond Welfare Capitalism?

In the last chapter, I considered the evolution within the Italian Communist Party of '*la terza via*' – a strategy for pursuing 'a third road to socialism', that was to avoid the pitfalls and excesses of both traditional Leninism and the social democratic management of advanced capitalism. But the practice of the Swedish labour movement has itself been long and widely presented as constituting a distinctive 'third way' – distinguished from the adversarial inequalities of advanced capitalism to the west and the excesses of bureaucratic socialization to the east – and, in recent years, it has been increasingly widely cited as a practice potentially capable of moving beyond the traditional dichotomy between Leninism and social democracy. Indeed, at least from the publication in the 1930s of Maurice Childs' *Sweden: The Middle Way*, the model of Sweden as 'the prototype of modern society' which, through pragmatism and 'cautious gradualism' practised by temperate social democrats, has succeeded in 'subjugating' or controlling capitalism and harnessing its massive productive potential to the building of an affluent and egalitarian welfare state, has been widely canvassed by modernizing 'right wing' social democrats in Western Europe. Organizing their critique of capitalism not around private ownership of the means of production, (attenuated, anyway, by the managerial revolution), nor around exploitation at the point of production, but rather around the *inequalities* of wealth and consumption that it generates and its *inefficiency* in employing the nation's human and material resources, these social democrats – best represented in Britain by Tony Crosland – were able to present Sweden as 'a socialist's ideal of the "good" society'. They felt able to commend to the traditional class-based parties of labour in 'old' Europe, the successes of the modernizing and pragmatic Swedish Social Democrats.[1]

Of course, this attribution of pragmatism has never been unequivocally welcomed by the Swedish Social Democratic Party, (SAP). Certainly, it dropped its official affiliation to Marxism during the 1950s and among those who have sought to present Swedish social democracy as a model 'for all of the Western European Social Democratic parties', much of the Party's success is attributed to its 'dissolution of socialist ideology'. But it is worth noting that leaders such as Ernst Wigforss, a principal architect of the 'Middle Way' in the 1930s, always maintained a commitment to the transformation of capitalist society and to the establishment of social control over the means of production.[2] His belief that gradualism is not straightforwardly conterminous with pragmatism was reinforced by the publication, in the 1960s, of Adler-Karllson's *Functional Socialism*, which envisaged socialist transformation through a gradual appropriation of those many proprietorial rights which together constitute the ownership of capital, and we shall see below that a similar commitment to a radical gradualism is a major element in contemporary assessments of the state of Swedish social democracy.

Sweden's 'Historic Compromise'

In the last ten to fifteen years, the compromise upon which the prototypically modern Sweden was seen to have been built has itself been seen to be increasingly imperilled, partly by the circumstances of international economic recession but also through the accumulation of contradictions which have arisen from within the compromise itself. In this period, as Jonas Pontusson notes, the Swedish labour movement, which was 'once a model for the right wing of European social democracy . . . has become a model for its left wing'.[3] Indeed, since the late 1970s, a number of works have appeared which argue from an explicitly (and, at times, surprisingly orthodox) Marxist position, that the period of 'historic compromise' between Swedish labour and capital, forged in the 1930s, is past and that the contemporary strategy of the labour movement, in a newly polarized Swedish society, is both an effective strategy for the democratic transition from welfare capitalism to socialism in Sweden and, by extension, a model for similar democratic socialist transition in other advanced Western capitalist societies.

These anticipations of the favourable prospects for democratic socialist transition are built upon a very particular understanding of the history of Sweden since the emergence of the organized labour movement. A small, sparsely populated, export-oriented, late and rapid industrializer, with substantial indigenous sources of wood and iron ore, and comparatively free from religious, linguistic or ethnic cleavages, Sweden was, from very early in its development as an industrial nation, distinguished by the highly formalized and centralized representation of both labour and capital, in the Swedish

Confederation of Labour, (LO), and the Swedish Employers' Confederation, (SAF). Dating from 1898 and 1902 respectively, their 'December Compromise' of 1906 established the long-standing basis of contested union-management relations in Sweden. Under the agreement of 1906, the right of workers to organize unions and bargain collectively was recognized in exchange for the trades unions' acceptance of management's right to hire and fire workers and to organize the process of production itself, (the celebrated Article 32). Reversals following the defeat of the General Strike of 1909 notwithstanding, the following twenty-five years were a period of growing unionization and also of historically high levels of industrial conflict, the result of both lock-outs and strikes. A law of 1928, which made collective agreements legally binding while, as interpreted by the newly established Labour Courts, doing nothing to undermine management's prerogatives under Article 32, had little impact upon these high levels of conflict.

However, levels of industrial action did drop drastically following the accession of a (minority) Social Democratic government in 1932. Although progressive legislation, (guaranteeing rights to unionize, to maternity benefit and to statutory holidays), and a Keynesian fiscal policy followed, the newly negotiated LO-SAF Basic Agreement of 1938, while securing to the trades unions new rights to joint consultation, left managerial prerogatives materially unaffected. In his influential work on *The Working Class in Welfare Capitalism*, Walter Korpi deduces that this decisive change in levels of industrial conflict in the mid-1930s was not, as has been so widely maintained, associated with the growing institutionalization of class conflict. Rather, it reflected that change in political power which the accession of the Social Democrats, intimately associated with the LO from the turn of the century, had effected. For Korpi, the accession to power of the Social Democrats represented a signal change in the balance of power between labour and capital, heralding 'a stable division of economic power and governmental power between opposing classes'.[4] These changed circumstances persuaded both the leaders of the labour movement and the representatives of capital 'to re-evaluate their earlier strategies of conflict' and to move towards what Korpi calls the 'historic compromise' of the 'Swedish model'.

In Korpi's account, this is presented as a compromise based on the mutual acknowledgement by both organized capital and organized labour, that neither would be able to exercise unmediated power over the other. Recognizing this stalemate, it formalized a division of economic and political control and a division of the spoils of continued and agreed capitalist development. Korpi cites the most prominent leaders of the labour movement of the 1930s – including Minister of

Finance, Wigforss, and Prime Minister, Hansson – to the effect that this 'Swedish model' was not a *resolution* of the differences between capital and labour but a temporary, (albeit long-term), *compromise* dictated by the existing equilibrium of class forces. However, Korpi is insistent that the Social Democrats' position also embraced the further expectation that continued capitalist development, which the 'historic compromise' would allow and indeed encourage, would, in accordance with Marxist economic anticipations, deliver the Swedish labour movement onto ever more favourable terrain.

The essence of the compromise was that capital would maintain intact its managerial prerogatives within the workplace, subject only to guarantees on rights to unionization, and capitalist economic growth would be encouraged. At the same time, the Social Democratic government would pursue Keynesian economic policies to sustain full employment and use progressive taxation to reduce economic inequality and promote provision for collective needs, such as education, health, and housing. When in the post-Second World War period the defence of welfare institutions and full employment threatened inflation and the loss of international competitiveness, the compromise was complemented by the adoption of the 'Rehn' model, which entailed first, an 'active manpower policy' – facilitating the redistribution and reallocation of labour and capital from less to more efficient enterprises – and secondly, a 'solidaristic' wage policy, which would allow for the centralized negotiation of wages and the reduction of wage differentials, through a principle of equal pay for equal work, irrespective of a given company's capacity to pay. In this way, it was hoped that welfare provision and a rising standard of living for the working population could be reconciled with continuing non-inflationary economic growth.

'Breaking the Mould'

Indeed, the 'historic compromise' brought with it many advantages for both labour, (full employment, improved wages and welfare), and capital, (high mobility of capital, large profits, low levels of social ownership and the curtailment of industrial conflict). It was this 'positive-sum period' of the 'historic compromise', when both Swedish labour and Swedish capital seemed to gain unproblematically from growing affluence, that was to inform those accounts which saw in Swedish industrial and social progress the fruits of an 'end of ideology' and unproblematic economic growth. But, Korpi insisted, those who depicted Swedish welfare capitalism as 'the "happy ending" to the conflicts which have beset Western countries ever since the Industrial

Revolution', had mistaken for 'the final chapter' what was 'only a long episode in the development of a capitalist democracy', itself determined by a long-standing equilibrium of class forces.[5] Increasingly, in the late 1960s and the early 1970s, the compromise was seen to be endangered not only by its failures but also increasingly by the disutilities that arose from its 'successes'.[6]

We have seen that one of the principal terms of the 'Swedish model' accommodation was the retention of managerial prerogative at plant level, within a strategy designed to give continued economic growth. Over time, this need to achieve continuing economic growth, under circumstances in which the managerial prerogative within the plant and the process of production was non-negotiable, led to an intensification of pressure upon workers at the point of production and an accompanying growth of unrectified workplace grievances, job dissatisfaction, physical and nervous diseases, absenteeism, and so on. These problems were intensified by the concentration of union resources and efforts at the national level – at which the solidaristic wage policy was pursued – and the continuing incapacity of the union to deal effectively with local, plant-based dissatisfactions.

A second set of difficulties surrounded growing hostility to the disorientations and disutilities involved in the 'active manpower policy'. While this policy had long been comparatively successful in promoting full employment without fuelling inflation, under conditions of intensifying economic recession, the policy became more disruptive in shifting labour geographically and occupationally at the same time as it became increasingly difficult for displaced labour – especially among groups marginalized by age or disability – to re-enter the active work-force. At the same time, the labour movement's commitment to securing economic growth through untramelled capitalist development, while funding what was, by international standards, a high level of general social welfare, tended to intensify economic inequalities and generate large and concentrated accumulations of private capital. In fostering this continuing economic growth, both the Social Democratic Party and the unions lost conviction as forces for radical social change.

These pressures – which led both the LO and the TCO (the principal white-collar trades union organization) to set up working parties on industrial democracy in the late 1960s – were most clearly evident in the disruption that followed upon the major iron-workers' unofficial strike of 1969–70, which served to highlight what was already widely recognized among some sections of the labour movement's leadership – that it was no longer possible to secure the support of its membership while devolving to management exclusive control over the process of production.

Legislative Intervention and the Wage-Earners' Funds Proposal

During the first half of the 1970s, the response this elicited from both government and unions gave rise to a quite impressive – if sometimes uneven – array of industrial legislation designed to displace the established system of industrial joint consultation by one of joint regulation. Between 1972 and 1976, laws were introduced to put employee representatives on company boards, to expand health and safety regulations and to give new powers to union safety stewards, to control the powers of management to hire and fire and to give priority to union interpretations in cases of dispute. Most substantial of all was the legislation of 1976 which annulled the traditional Article 32, (leading, in its turn, to the dissolution of the 1938 Basic Agreement), formalized joint determination in the workplace and obliged management to negotiate with and furnish information to the trades unions. The legislative innovation of these four years, upon Andrew Martin's account, 'adds up to a major transformation of the structure of authority in Swedish enterprise'.[7]

But the single most radical initiative of this period was the LO's advocacy of '*Lantagarfonder*' or wage-earners' funds. The first outline of the wage-earners' funds – prepared in response to an LO Congress proposal of 1971 – was presented by an LO working party, under their principal economist Rudolf Meidner, in 1975. They too were seen as a progressive reponse to anomalies which had been generated by the period of 'historic compromise'.

The initial problem to which wage-earners' funds were to be a response was that the trades unions' solidaristic wage policy – in which nationally negotiated pay rates were, as we have seen, to be related to the work undertaken rather than to a given company's capacity to pay – generated a problem of 'excess profits' in highly efficient firms. While some of this excess was undoubtedly offset against local wage drift, the unions did not want to resolve this problem in a way that would prejudice their commitment to equalize incomes. At the same time, they wished to confront and overcome others of the problems generated by the long period of 'historic compromise'. Among the most important of these, Meidner listed the need 'for the community and the trades unions to acquire a greater say in the allocation of profits for investment purposes', 'to check the concentration of wealth among traditional groups of owners' and 'to increase employee influence'. But in meeting these ambitions, any proposal had also to maintain a high level of capital formation, to promote economic growth and to be 'neutral with respect to costs, wages and prices'.[8] The principle of the Meidner proposal, which was to reconcile these several constraints and ambitions, was quite straightforward:

> The ownership of a part of the profits which are ploughed into an
> enterprise is simply transferred from the previous owners to the
> employees as a collective. A proportion . . . [Meidner proposed
> 20%] . . . of the profit is set aside for the employees. This money does
> not however leave the business. Instead, a company issues shares to that
> amount, and these are transmitted to the employee fund.[9]

Meidner supplemented this stark proposal with a consideration of some
of the most important questions that it necessarily brought in its wake.
These included deciding between plant-based, regional or national
funds, considering the electoral position of consumers, the position of
multinational corporations and the possibility of capital flight.

In fact, the Meidner proposals have met with a very uncertain
response – not only, as one would expect, from the representatives of
capital and the parties of the right but notably from the leaders of the
SAP. Their reaction has been to temporize and dilute the original
radical posture of the Meidner plan. When wage-earners' funds were
finally introduced in January, 1984, though resistance was fierce and
the leader of the Swedish Conservatives denounced the government for
'declaring open war on a majority of the Swedish people', they were
much attenuated compared with the original proposals of 1975.
Furthermore, in the 1985 elections, the Social Democrats stated that
the wage-earners' funds would be making no further investments after
1990, by which time they would own just 8 per cent of all equities on the
Swedish stock exchange.[10]

However, I do not want to discuss in any detail here the rather
chequered history of Meidner's proposals. For our purposes, it will
suffice to have in mind the broadest principles of the wage-earners'
funds proposals. For in the remainder of this chapter I intend to
concentrate upon the way in which the wage-earners' fund proposals,
allied to the reforming legislation of the early 1970s and read in the
light of the interpretation of the historical evolution of the labour
movement in Sweden which I have already discussed, yields an
anticipated strategy for democratic socialist transformation in Sweden
and, by extension, in other, comparably placed, advanced capitalist
societies.

The Contradictions of Welfare Capitalism as the Basis for Socialist Transition

I have already drawn attention to Walter Korpi's account of an 'historic compromise' between capital and labour in Sweden during the 1930s and of its breakdown from the late 1960s onwards. It would be mistaken, however, to suggest that Korpi understands this breakdown as arising exclusively, or even principally, from the unintended and dysfunctional consequences of an increasingly unworkable historical settlement. For Korpi is insistent that the historic compromise of the 1930s was entered into by Social Democratic leaders such as Hannson, the Myrdals and, above all, Wigforss, not simply in recognition of the parity – or, at least, stalemate – of the powers of capital and labour, but in the confident expectation that the terms of this class compromise would themselves foster a pattern of continued capitalist economic growth which would, in time, strengthen the strategic position of the labour movement.

Korpi, and those, such as John Stephens, Ulf Himmelstrand et al. who sympathize with his interpretation, go on to argue that the 'historic compromise', at first entered upon because of the comparative *weakness* of the labour movement, is exhausted because of this same labour movement's comparative *strengths* over against capital.[11] This account – which is explicitly grounded in a Marxist model of capitalist development – has a strong whiff of Kautskyan or Bernsteinian evolutionary optimism about it. But it is buttressed by considerable empirical evidence. The period since the 1930s, it is argued, has brought changes in the Swedish class structure which strongly favour social democratic interests. First, the continuing process of industrialization has increasingly marginalized the once substantial agrarian interest, (forcing the Agrarian Party to reconstitute itself as the Centre Party). At the same time, while the proportion of blue-collar workers has first stabilized and then, since the early 1960s, declined, the proportion of the economically active citizenry who are wage-earners has risen – by the 1970s, to over 90 per cent.[12] Though the capacities of this 'extended working class' as an effective political actor may have been curtailed by internal divisions, these are seen to have been limited by the LO strategy of wage solidarity and the general process of de-skilling. Above all, it is stressed that both blue-collar and white-collar workers have achieved an extraordinarily high degree of unionization, a level which Korpi claims is approaching 'a point of saturation'.[13] While Korpi correspondingly argues that 'the organizational basis for the working class to act as a "class for itself" has matured only in the postwar period', this did mean that the working class became an effective force in a period of sustained social democratic governmental hegemony, a period in which full employment and growing welfare provision were effectively secured under what Castles calls 'the social democratic image of society'.[14]

At the same time as the powers of the labour movement have, in these various ways, been expanded, those of capital have contracted. Some weight is given by Himmelstrand et al. to those powers of capital which were expanded by the period of (untramelled) capitalist development under the 'historic compromise' – continuing managerial prerogatives, minimal public ownership and the acute concentration of private wealth. But these strengths were increasingly to be offset by high unionization, low unemployment, the growth of work in the non-manufacturing public sector and, increasingly, by the enactment of legally guaranteed trades unions' rights at the point of production. Himmelstrand's conclusion in 1980 – in what was probably the most sustained analysis of the countervailing powers of capital – was that 'the systemic power of Swedish capital has been falling during the last ten to fifteen years, and particularly after 1976.'[15]

Thus, the dissolution of 'the Swedish model' is not the result of the general, international economic recession which swept the advanced capitalist world in the early 1970s nor of the historically high levels of unemployment that followed in its wake – both of which, Korpi insists, *post-date* the earliest signs of the break-up of the 'historic compromise'. Rather, does it arise from the changing balance of forces between capital and labour in favour of the latter, a change which is itself a product of the processes of capitalist development, carried out under the hegemony of a progressive Social Democratic government. In this way it falls more or less unproblematically into a tradition, running from Branting to Palme, of the development of Sweden as a process of the gradual affirmation and expansion of democracy. Indeed, in *The Democratic Class Struggle*, Korpi traces a unilinear, though of course contested, development from universal suffrage (political democracy) through the welfare state (social democracy) towards the canvassing of wage-earners' funds (economic democracy).

'Lontagarfonder' as Means of Transition to Socialism

This evolutionary model of the development of Swedish democracy is taken up with particular enthusiasm in John Stephens' *The Transition from Capitalism to Socialism*. Here, the advocacy of Swedish social democratic practice as a model, under broadly Marxist assumptions, for gradualist democratic transition to socialism within advanced capitalism, is made quite explicit. This begins from Stephens' rather remarkable claim that 'the transition to socialism actually begins . . . when the workers stage the first successful strike', at which point 'the social order in question can no longer be said to be . . . purely capitalist.'[16] However improbable, this expectation that capitalism, from its very inception, is already in a process of transition to socialism is an underlying premiss of Stephens' account. Arguing that 'there are no purely *theoretical* reasons why the transition from a capitalist social order to a socialist social order cannot be evolutionary', he seemingly follows Kautsky in suggesting that:

> Socialism can only be created through the abolition and transcendence of advanced capitalism, not because history is predetermined but because socialism is nothing more than the negation of capitalism, the reclamation of the potentialities created by capitalism but suppressed by its contradictory structure.[17]

Mobilizing empirical evidence against those who argue that the power and redistributive efficacy of the welfare state is unrelated to the incumbency of social democratic governments, he argues that 'the welfare state is a product of labour organisation and political rule by labour parties and *thus* represents a first step towards socialism'[18] (my emphasis). Stephens does not argue that the emergence of a welfare state *necessarily* presages a transition to socialism. He cites France under the Fifth Republic as an example of the conservative administration of a welfare state yielding a non-socialist 'corporate collectivism'. The British welfare state is seen to lie somewhere between the Swedish and the French experiences. But, Stephens argues, under the particular circumstances of Sweden – the strength of the labour movement in the unions and the government – the welfare state is 'characterised by high levels of expenditure and progressive financing and *thus* represents a transformation of capitalism towards socialism' (my emphasis). 'This claim', he acknowledges, 'is the key to our contention that a parliamentary road to socialism is a possibility and, indeed, is under way'.[19]

This claim rests, in turn, upon Stephens' borrowing from Adler-Karllson of the concept of capitalist ownership as 'a bundle of rights', rights which can be gradually appropriated by labour and its representatives, leaving capital with an increasingly beleaguered and minimalized economic control.[20] In this strategy of gradual transition to socialism through the incremental appropriation of the property control rights of capital, very special status is given to the proposals for wage-earners' funds. Building upon the limited, though widely contested, programme of pension funds first introduced, in the face of bitter opposition, in the late 1950s, the wage-earners' funds proposal is greeted by Stephens as 'a brilliant solution to the political and tactical problems of social democracy in its attempt to go beyond the welfare state towards socialism'. Although Stephens is not uniformly optimistic in his anticipations of the SAP's making effective the LO's proposals for wage-earners' funds, he seems to share with the employers' federation, (SAF), the belief that the implementation of wage-earners' funds 'would change the economic system of society'.[21]

Although Korpi and Himmelstrand et al., like Stephens, do give some consideration to the forms of resistance that capital will adopt in the face of attempts to introduce wage-earners' funds, they too are essentially optimistic about the transitional possibilities these afford. Korpi, while criticizing the limitation of control over the funds exclusively to producers – favouring the introduction of citizens' funds controlled by parties to wage-earners' funds controlled by the unions – praises the principle of the LO proposal inasmuch as it 'allows for a gradual transferring of economic power from private capital to democratically governed collectivities in ways which will minimize disturbances in the economy'. His confidence that the wage-earners' funds will be able to mobilize sufficient popular support to make them effective he grounds in those 'changes in the distribution of power resources in society which tend to accompany the maturation of capitalism'.[22] Himmelstrand is still more confident. For him, the reforming legislation of the early 1970s has already vindicated the capacity of *legislative* intervention to alter the balance of forces between capital and labour. He concludes that 'there are *no significant structural constraints preventing a new era of labour party majorities in Parliament, and a stepwise change of Swedish society to resolve the contradictions of welfare capitalism.*'[23] In contrast to all those revolutions for which the Bolshevik 'Revolution against *Capital*' is the model, Korpi, and, still more explicitly, Stephens and Himmelstrand see in the adoption of the wage-earners' funds the means of realizing the classically Marxist expectation of transition to socialism through the 'ripening' of the contradictions of capitalism. For Himmelstrand, the gradual take-over of society's productive forces, envisaged in the wage-earners' funds proposals, embodies 'the classical Marxian hypothesis about the transition to socialism in the terminal phase of capitalism'.[24]

'Lontagarfonder': Beyond Social Democracy?

Although the arguments of Korpi, Stephens, Himmelstrand *et al.* are carefully organized and buttressed with considerable empirical evidence, it would indeed be remarkable if their account of Swedish social democratic practice as a process of transition to socialism *already underway* had met with universal approval even among socialist commentators. Here, as in the last chapter, I want to concentrate upon those criticisms which depict this strategic advocacy of contemporary social democratic practice not as a radical 'third way' to socialism but rather as a rehearsal of the 'errors' of the Second International.

Some of these criticisms almost certainly reach their target. In the account of a gradual transition from political, to social, to economic democracy, it is possible to identify echoes of Kautsky and Bernstein, particularly of the latter's expectation of an 'evolutionary socialism' based upon the expansion of workers' citizenship. This analogy is perhaps clearest in Stephens' characterization of capitalist ownership as 'a bundle of rights' and his depiction of the gradual transition to socialism as the process of incremental transfer of these ownership rights from the possessors of capital to the sellers of labour power. Upon this account, the transfer of economic rights is to be seen as completing the apparatus of democratic rights, (principally rights to parliamentary representation), and social rights, (the institutions of the welfare state), which the working class has wrested from the historically dominant bourgeoisie. Stephens goes to some lengths to show, contrary to the determinations of Wilensky, Parkin and others, that the re-distributive capacity of Western welfare states is not simply a 'by-product' of industrial development but is rather directly related to social democratic incumbency (and, one might add, following Castles, the weakness of parties of the right).[25]

This is a powerful corrective against those who deny any significance to the struggle of organized labour in securing the introduction of welfare measures and against that alternative and Marxist orthodoxy which argues that the working class can make no worthwhile gains under the aegis of 'bourgeois democracy'. But it must be repeated here that such an evolutionary account of the development of the welfare state, parliaments and democracy, however appealing, is untenable. Certainly, it is true that universal suffrage and the provision of welfare services were bitterly contested and represent real gains for organized labour, but at the same time it is equally true that suffrage and welfare were often conceded in forms or under circumstances which did not of necessity weaken the dominant position of the ruling class, that, as the literature on incorporation suggests, these concessions may indeed have very considerable benefits for ruling interests and/or that they may themselves generate *new* contradictions, presenting the organized labour movement itself with radically new and intractable problems. Perhaps most importantly, these gains cannot be seen as having been secured 'once and for all'.

All these insights are suppressed in the evolutionary model and most explicitly in Stephens' analysis. In the face of that literature which identifies in corporatism a withdrawal from the popular arena of parliamentary government and a disorganization of working-class interests, Stephens depicts 'corporatism' as a compromise imposed by the *strengths* of organized labour and tending towards a resolution in favour of the latter. Despite the evidence that the welfare state redistributes wealth for the most part *within* the wage-earning classes and, at the same time defrays some of the attritional and social costs of labour for capital, Stephens insists that, at least under Swedish conditions, the welfare state is necessarily an active step in the transition to socialism. The point, of course, is not to suggest that corporatism and the welfare state are unrelated to the strengths of the organized labour movement nor that they are unproblematically *'functional for capital'*. Rather is it to argue that the development of corporatism and the welfare state is itself *contradictory* and that these forms may have a crisis logic of their own, a logic that is not readily reducible to the traditional contradiction between capital and labour. I shall consider this extended contradictory logic in a later chapter. Here, I want only to stress that the abiding weakness of evolutionist accounts of social transformation is that they tend ironically to 'bracket out', as already in some sense 'determined', those very grounds upon which the struggle for social transformation must take place.

However, even within its own terms of reference, a number of very serious reservations have to be entered against this evolutionist model of social transformation. Once again, Himmelstrand, Korpi and Stephens mobilize considerable empirical support for their account of a preponderant extended working class. They trace the historical development of the growing proportion of wage-earners in the entire work-force – tying this to the processes of capitalist concentration and centralization – discuss the ambiguities surrounding productive and unproductive labour, the feminization of mental labour, the general 'de-skilling' of work tasks and so on. But it is not clear that this development lends unequivocal support to Korpi's contention that since the Second World War the extended working class has developed into a 'class-for-itself' that is a class aware of its shared interests and capable of intervention as a more or less unified political actor. Certainly, Sweden is characterized by extremely high levels of unionization – though the nature of the memberships' commitment to the union is here, as elsewhere under advanced capitalism, increasingly open to doubt – and the LO strategy of 'wage solidarity' and the absence of a craft-union tradition may tend to lessen internal divisions of interest within this greatly extended working class. However, it is far from clear that the correlate of this is that the extended working class can be postulated as an effective political actor, united in its mobilization against the interests of capital. As Przeworski makes clear, rather than the working class being a preconstituted political actor which then engages in (class) struggle with the representatives of capital, the continually problematic constitution and reconstitution of those united by their interests as wage-earners as a class is a very large part of what political struggle is. This problem – constantly re-posed and never definitively settled – of the constitution of wage-earners as a class and the corresponding political struggle over the formation and reformation of classes is, as Przeworski further points out, more or less neglected in evolutionary Marxist accounts from Kautsky onwards.

Indeed, these recent accounts of anticipated socialist transition in Sweden generally convey very little sense of active and contested political struggle. In so far as it is recognized at all, political class struggle is seen to be mediated either through parties or through the formal organizations of labour, (the trades unions), and capital, (the SAF). Correspondingly, the model of transition – built around wage-earners' funds – itself tends to be technocratic, premised upon the resolution of a set of technical problems of accumulation through changes in formal ownership rather than upon the overcoming of the political contradictions established by capitalist development. Indeed, for its advocates, one of the great strengths of the wage-earners' funds policy is that it promotes a process of more or less painless and costless expropriation of capital. Thus, it is argued that it is possible to continue to enjoy, uninterrupted, the benefits of capitalist economic growth while gradually stripping capital of its effectiveness as a form of ownership. In this way, the problem of declining productivity occasioned by economic disruption and capital flight/resistance, which is one of the most widely cited problems of mobilizing mass support for the transition to socialism, can be avoided. Seen from a rather different angle, as Offe suggests, what seems to be offered is a technical (and *dirigiste*) strategy for changes in formal ownership without any indication of how this is to articulate with a mass movement for socialism.[26]

This overly sanguine view of the prospects for the extended working class as a political actor and the smooth transfer of economic power through the extension of wage-earners' funds has its counterpart in a systematic underestimation of the powers of capital and of the problems associated with its expropriation. Again, some of this 'optimism' is 'built into' the model of contemporary Swedish welfare capitalism. For Korpi, for example, the premiss of capital's strength is seen to reside in division among the wage-earners. He concludes *The Working Class in Welfare Capitalism* by insisting that 'where the competition among the wage-earners ceases, the foundation of capitalism has eroded.'[27] But while competition among wage-earners is clearly a major strength for capital – especially pronounced in a period of recession and high unemployment – to allow to it the sort of categorical status that Korpi does is surely mistaken. Even where competition among the wage-earners is severely attenuated, as Korpi clearly feels he has shown to be the case in contemporary Sweden, this cannot be said to have removed *all* of capital's sanctions, particularly in a society where manufacturing industry is so heavily concentrated in private hands and which is so strategically placed *vis-à-vis* the international capitalist market. By concentrating so heavily upon capital's reliance upon divisions within an increasingly preponderant wage-earning class, which Korpi's figures on union density shows to be increasingly homogenized, (though only in this limited sense), Korpi is able to depict Swedish capital as chronically weakened over against the collective force of the united labour movement. In this way, he is able to canvass the gradual expropriation of capital as a political power without any serious interruption in the process of capital formation and accumulation, as a process to which resistance will be severely limited.

Wage-fund Socialism?

It would be a mistake to underestimate the ingenuity and importance of Meidner's wage-earners' funds proposal. The implementation of even an attenuated version of the 1975 proposal would still place Sweden indisputably in the van of European social democracy. But it is clear that it is a model which is particularly vulnerable to the kind of reading that Korpi and Stephens offer, in large part because it abstracts from the very circumstances of economic crisis out of which it arose. Certainly it is perceived as a remedy for certain (rather formally conceived) contradictions of capitalism, problems associated with the long-term skewing of wealth, difficulties of long-term accumulation and control over the process of production. But under those circumstances in which wage-earners' funds might be used as a means of transition to socialism, it is not simply a question of redirecting the fruits of unproblematic economic growth, but rather a question of intervening within a crisis of the circumstances of continued accumulation. While such crises are indeed the circumstances under which capital is reorganized, the process of its reorganization is bound to be open-ended and contested. Furthermore, while wage-earners' funds certainly promise the possibility of intervention in the direction of the processes of production, they still constitute a strategy tied to continued economic growth. But the problematic of continued economic growth and its attendant disutilities is itself politically contentious ground. Korpi himself concluded that the SAP's historic electoral defeat of 1976 was in large part attributable to its continuing commitment to economic growth, (as manifested in its commitment to a civil nuclear fuel policy). In addition, wage-earners' funds continue to do little to address the political issues of point of production and labour process politics which were themselves clearly a major source of the wage-earners' funds' initiative. Indeed, in concentrating more or less exclusively upon a politics of producers, the wage-earners' funds not only neglect what are widely conceived to be major contemporary political problems – such as civil and military nuclear policy, enviromental and sexual politics – they also neglect that growing number of citizens who lie outside the active working population. For, while the trend *within* the working population may be towards growing 'proletarianization', the more general social trend is for growing numbers – among them those in higher education and particularly old-age pensioners – to be located *outside* the categories of wage labour and capital, and correspondingly to be open to 'politicization' around quite differing issues. In the face of this, it would appear that any effective socialist or – more properly – 'emancipatory' politics is bound to be defined around an alliance that goes beyond the preponderance of wage-earners.

Limitations of the Marxist Account of Democratic Socialism

In the last section of this chapter, I want to consider the extent to which these particular criticisms can be seen to be symptomatic of the more general weaknesses I have sought to isolate in the Marxist appraisal of socialism and democracy. Of course, it can be argued that the experience of the Swedish Social Democrats is a quite inappropriate source for drawing such general conclusions. After all, the SAP abandoned its official affiliation to Marxism during the 1950s. However, we have seen that the leading advocates of a radical social democratic strategy in Sweden ground their advocacy upon formally Marxist premises and that the radical strategy that they advocate, while innovative, is perceived as following logically and consciously from the social democratic practice of the past forty years. Still more importantly, Korpi, for example, is quite explicit that, in fact, Swedish social democracy is farther down the road to socialist transformation than its seemingly more radical sister movements in France and particularly in Italy. The 'historic compromise' which, for Sweden, is drawing to a close is only beginning for the Italian Communist Party. Despite their many differences, it is, in this sense, Swedish social democracy that is showing to the Italian labour movement its own future. Similarly, Himmelstrand makes it clear that he perceives Sweden to be the one advanced capitalist society in which capitalism has matured to the point at which, in accordance with Marx's model in *Capital*, it is ready to be transcended by socialism.

This expectation that Sweden constitutes the most mature form of capitalism both justifies our considering it in terms of the Marxism-democracy-socialism nexus and alerts us to the particular kinds of weaknesses we should anticipate. For it shares many of those faults which I have identified in that Marxist model which anticipates socialism arising (necessarily) out of the circumstances of advanced or mature capitalism. Thus, preponderant weight is given to establishing that the balance of forces is such as to favour transition to socialism. The continuing process of the concentration and centralization of capital, the decline of transitional modes of production (and with them of intermediary classes) and the homogenization of wage-earners through unionization and de-skilling are seen, in classical Marxist manner, to deliver a preponderant majority in favour of systemic change. Upon this reading, the wage-earners' funds are a solution to the problem of the fetters which capitalism eventually places upon its own further development and which must, correspondingly, be 'burst asunder'. Furthermore, picking up, as does Stephens, upon Avineri's account of Marx's seeming advocacy of universal suffrage as a transformative principle, it is suggested that, given the enormous institutional and numerical weight of the social democratic movement, it may prove possible through legal enactment to effect a radical though gradual transition to socialism.[28] I have already indicated that it is quite inappropriate to extrapolate unproblematically from the economic category of wage labour to the actively political proletarian class and this divergence is only affirmed rather than overcome by circumlocutions over the passage from 'class-in-itself' to 'class-for-itself', (which usages reappear, of course, in Korpi's account of the development of the Swedish working class). While the category of wage labour clearly remains an important dimension of cleavage and unification, it cannot do the work that Marxist evolutionary accounts require of it.

We have also seen in earlier accounts – those that have been derived from the model of *Capital*, rather than those which Marx himself offered – how this supposition of class-based politics rendered the particular nature of the state in some sense unproblematic. Evidence of just such a view is repeatedly apparent in contemporary advocacy of Swedish social democracy. For it is argued that, created under social democratic governmental hegemony, the welfare state is more or less uniformly an imposition of the wage earners upon capital *and* a first step in the transition to socialism. What this fails to acknowledge, as I shall argue in the following chapter, is that the welfare state is a contradictory and contested development, emerging from the respective strengths and weaknesses of both capital and labour and subject to its own forms of cumulative contradiction, summarized, by Offe, as the 'crises of crisis management'. Failure to recognize this draws attention away from actual state strategies and practices, from internal struggle and contradictions *within* the state and points towards a crudely instrumental view of the state as a unified political actor expressing, through the elected government, the interests of the broad mass of the population.

Such a misrepresentation of the nature of the state seems to be the almost universal fate of those accounts which seek to 'derive' political practice from an 'external' economic logic. Indeed, as we have seen, the strategy of wage-earners' funds is marked by a curiously non-political account of social transformation. Wage-earners' funds – as the technical solution to problems of capital formation generated by capitalist development itself – are presented as if the mobilization of mass popular support would be superfluous. It is hard to be as sanguine as are many of Meidner's supporters as to the quiescence of Swedish capital in the face of its (gradual) expropriation.

Furthermore, the absence of any very satisfactory explanation of the relation between political and economic struggles is further evidenced by the comparative silence of the advocates of a radical social democracy on the question of political issues defined *outside* the sphere of production. These commentators should surely have been sensitized to such issues by the SAP's 1976 electoral defeat which we have seen that Korpi himself attributes not so much to the unpopularity of the wage-earners' funds proposals as to the government's commitment to nuclear power. The attitude to civil and military nuclear power is widely perceived to be among the most pressing, contentious and class-crossing of contemporary political issues. It would seem that it was the Social Democrats' insistence upon understanding this nuclear issue exclusively in terms of its commitment to continued economic growth – itself a politically contentious issue in Sweden, as Korpi and others concede – that helped to occasion the government's downfall.

On the evidence of this and the previous chapter, it would appear that a democratic socialist practice based upon a Marxist model of capitalist development may be extremely effective in mobilizing particular and often very broadly based political interests. However, it has been repeatedly embarrassed by the emergence of political interests and aspirations that lie outside this framework and can hardly be said to have generated a compelling and effective democratic socialist *practice* that transcends the theoretical impasse of Leninism and social democracy. Grounded in an historicist account of capitalist development, these Marxist accounts have been increasingly driven to deny the autonomy of the political sphere, to neglect issues defined outside the realms of class and/or production, to view democracy not as a process of discursive will-formation but as the means of articulating given majority interests, and, through identifying emancipation with socialization, greatly to contract the possibilities for an alliance of emancipatory struggles under advanced capitalism.

In the final chapters, I turn to some of the recent innovations that have arisen from dissatisfactions with the more orthodox Marxist political tradition and consider the extent to which these new departures have themselves generated a more compelling basis for a democratic socialist practice.

Part Three
Departures?

6
Exercising Power
'The Achilles Heel of Marxism'

Writing in 1970, Ralph Miliband insisted 'that the exercise of power remains the Achilles Heel of Marxism.'[1] More recently, John Dunn has made much the same point in his essay on *The Politics of Socialism.* Here, he argues that socialist writers have generally sought to avoid the problems surrounding the exercise of power by concentrating their attention upon 'the [critical] analysis of existing societies' and 'the theory of social and political goods' to the exclusion of a consideration of 'how what exists can be sustained or improved and how social and political goods can in practice be realized'.[2] Despite the supposed interdependence of theory and practice in Marxist analyses, it has proved possible, in this way, to secure an ever more effective division of mental labour between, on the one hand, the social and political critique of advanced capitalism and, on the other, the promotion of effective socialist strategies and practices.

Recasting Democratic Socialist Theory

In the foregoing chapters, I have argued that it is not simply this hiatus between theory and practice but, in fact, the very political and social analyses of advanced capitalism and the counterposed socialist strategies and practices advocated, that have proven to be the debilitating weaknesses of the Marxist political tradition. I have sought to show that these weaknesses, with their origins in Marx and quite explicitly seen in the disputes of the Second International, continue to misinform the strategy of contemporary Marxist political theorists. In these closing chapters, I want to consider the ways in which a number of recent critics have sought to overcome these several weaknesses, building their differing accounts of state, society and democracy upon a critique of the more familiar premisses of conventional Marxist analysis.

Of course, criticisms of the categorical weaknesses of Marxism – its commitment to historicism, derivationism, essentialism, and so on –

have long been voiced, perhaps most prominently by Karl Popper and J. L. Talmon, in defence of established liberal democracies and in support of H. B. Mayo's claim that 'Marxist theory . . . is at odds with the democratic use of political action to build the free and just society.'[3] However, in more recent years, many of the same criticisms have been taken up by a range of political theorists who are united less by a shared antipathy to the established Marxist political tradition than by a desire critically to appropriate what are seen to be the authentic insights of Marxist analysis within an eclectic project, drawing upon several theoretical traditions and directed towards synthesizing a viable, libertarian theory of democratic socialist change. The central organizing principle of this theoretical reorientation has been an encounter with existing (and unsatisfactory) Marxist accounts of the state and of democracy, and the attempt to recast the relations of state and (civil) society, to take account both of these insufficiencies and of changes in the nature of the state-society relation in contemporary advanced capitalist societies. In this and the following chapter, I consider this reformulation and critically examine the claim that it can be said both to have overcome the weaknesses of existing Marxist interpretations and to have provided the bases for the development of a coherent and democratic socialist strategy.

From Gramsci to Poulantzas

In some sense, these recent theoretical innovations may be read as a contribution to the political project initiated by Gramsci, to establish the premisses for socialist advance under the circumstances of advanced capitalism. Though I have discussed Gramsci principally, (and rather briefly), in the context of his contested contribution to the Italian Communist Party's '*terza via*', it would, of course, be quite inappropriate to consider him as a 'parochial' Italian figure. Indeed, in many accounts, he now enjoys the uncertain distinction of ranking alongside Lenin as an authoritative interpreter of Marx's work and, particularly in the last fifteen years, he has been a major influence upon neo-Marxist political theory in Western Europe, encouraging Paul Piccone, for example, to anticipate that the 1980s would prove to be 'the decade of Gramscism'.[4] Accordingly, while often sceptical of the claim that Gramsci's work can, in any very straightforward sense, be interpreted as the development of a 'Leninism in the West', many contemporary democratic socialist writers continue to be profoundly influenced by characteristically Gramscian themes – the uniqueness of given nation state formations, the necessity of alliances and the importance of non-class social forces and non-state institutions, the importance of securing hegemony and, perhaps above all, the particular nature of the relationship between state and civil society in advanced capitalism.

We have already seen that these characteristically Gramscian concerns are quite clearly to the fore in the influential and agenda-setting work of the later Poulantzas. In *State, Power, Socialism*, Poulantzas – hailed by Bob Jessop as 'the single most influential Marxist political theorist of the postwar period' – sought to break decisively with the 'Leninist vanguardism' of his own earlier *Political Power and Social Classes*.[5] Rejecting the account of the state as necessarily representing the unified power of a single class, Poulantzas argued that 'popular struggles are inscribed in the state not because they are exhaustively included in a totalizing Moloch-state, but because the state itself bathes in struggles that constantly submerge it.'[6]

But this did not lead him to endorse the parliamentary and reformist practices of present-day social democracy. Rather, for him, as we have seen, since both social democracy and Leninism favoured strategies which finally collapsed into varying forms of 'authoritarian statism', the decisive challenge was to generate a strategy which was able:

> Radically to alter the state in such a manner that the extension and deepening of political freedoms and the institutions of representative democracy (which were also a conquest of the popular masses) are combined with the unfurling of forms of direct democracy and the mushrooming of self-management bodies.[7]

Indeed, it is this seemingly intractable problem of how to defend existing and cherished liberties and democratic institutions and massively to extend the democratic control of society and personal autonomy, without lapsing into the 'statist' traps set by both traditional Leninism and traditional social democracy that could be said to summarize the agenda of recent democratic socialist theory.

Offe: Towards 'A Non-statist Socialist Strategy'

Because of his untimely death, Poulantzas' own contribution to this project remained largely programmatic. However, a still earlier, substantial and continuing source of new theoretical perspectives on state and civil society has been the increasingly influential work of Claus Offe. A brief consideration of his work – spanning the period from the early 1970s to the early 1980s and concentrating on the welfare state as the generic form of the contemporary advanced capitalist state

– will deliver us firmly onto the most advanced ground of contemporary heterodox democratic theory.

The occasion for Offe's consideration of the prospects for democratic socialist strategy is the pressingly topical breakdown of the post-war welfare state consensus. Offe follows classical Marxism in arguing that the '"privately regulated" capitalist economy' is innately crisis-prone and this is the basis of his understanding of the emergence of the welfare state – seeking to 'harmonize the "privately regulated" capitalist economy with the processes of socialization this economy triggers' – as both the generic form of the advanced capitalist state and as a form of systemic 'crisis management'.[8] But this process of reconciliation under the aegis of the welfare state proves impossible as the welfare state is subject to a particular crisis logic of its own and is repeatedly confronted by its own forms of cumulative self-obstruction. It is this that leads Offe to make the focus of his analysis of the welfare state 'the crises of crisis management.'

For Offe, it is characteristic that, under late capitalism, *economic* contradictions of capital accumulation express themselves in a *political* crisis of the welfare state. As the basis of fiscal viability (through taxation and borrowing) and thus of mass loyalty (through administrative and welfare provision) the successful functioning of the (capitalist) economy, built upon profitable commodity exchange, is indispensable to the long-term viability of the welfare state. 'The key problem' for this capital-dependent welfare state is that capitalist development, in fact, shows 'a constant tendency to paralyse the commodity form of value',[9] and thus to imperil the state's principal source of revenue. For fear of antagonizing capital, the state cannot generally intervene directly in the accumulation process to overcome this paralysis. Instead it has to proceed indirectly to try to re-establish the conditions under which capital and labour will be drawn into (profitable) commodity exchange, through regulations and financial incentives, public infrastructural investment and the sponsoring of neo-corporatist institutions. This strategy Offe styles 'administrative recommodification'. Its vitiating weakness is that, in practice, it promotes *de*-commodification, that is, in intervening to secure the general conditions for effective commodity exchange it places ever greater areas of social life *outside* of the commodity form and *outside* the ambit of market exchange.

Offe identifies three manifestations of this principal contradiction of the welfare state as being of particular importance:

1 *The fiscal crisis of the welfare state*. The state budget required to fund strategies of recommodification tends to grow uncontrollably and to become increasingly self-defeating, occasioning (through high taxation

and welfare provision) both a 'disincentive to invest' and a 'disincentive to work'.[10]

2 *Administrative shortfall*. The welfare state repeatedly fails to live up to its own inflated programmatic-administrative claims, a failure variously attributed to the ineffectiveness of the indirect instruments of public policy, to struggles *within* the state and to the external imperatives of public accountability, democratic representation and short-term political expediency.

3 *Legitimation shortfall*. Under these circumstances of fiscal crisis and administrative shortfall, state intervention is seen to be increasingly particularistic and *ad hoc* and this undermines the political norms of 'equality under the rule of law', leading to a short-fall of mass loyalty/legitimacy. (This is perhaps the least secure point of Offe's argument, though the undermining of the achievement principle, the emergence of 'post-material' values and, above all, a loss of faith in the capacity of the welfare state to resolve its own problems, is real enough.)

Offe suggests three ways in which these contradictions of the welfare state might be resolved. The first possibility – a strategy of 'reprivatization' – Offe rejects as 'unworkable' because of the reliance of capital upon the state's provision of public goods (and public contracts) and because of the 'irreversible' gains of the labour movement within organized capitalism. (Such a sanguine view reminds us that Offe's primary referent is West Germany rather than Britain.) A second possible strategy – the (re)emergence of corporatist arrangements – is also rejected as unworkable, since corporatism is seen by Offe to be the characteristic form in which the crisis of the welfare state arises. As such, it is seen to be a persistent symptom rather than a possible cure.

A third and favoured strategy – the transition towards 'a democratic and socialist welfare society' – inheres, Offe argues, in the possibilities opened up by the very crisis-ridden corporatist structure of the existing welfare state. The practices of corporatist politics, he argues, have destroyed the bourgeois conventions of a division between politics and economics and of politics defined as the struggle for institutionalized state power. At the same time, they have precipitated a crisis of legitimacy for existing trades unions, parties and the party system generally, while promoting the organization and mobilization of political interests outside the conventional political system. The complex institutional structure of the welfare state itself – particularly as the 'local' state – provides the (often new) terrain on which 'political' struggles may be fought out and the emergence of new social movements – feminism, enviromentalism, the peace movement – means that there are new media, 'outside the system', through which an interest in welfare as the promoter of 'authentic needs' may be pursued. For Offe, it is the very contradictions which the welfare state solution embodies and which have rendered 'statist strategies of societal transformation "clearly unrealistic"' that have promoted the circumstances under which a non-statist socialist strategy may be possible.[11]

Towards an Alternative Account of the State

Both Poulantzas and Offe clearly represent, in their differing ways, a decisive break with traditional Marxist teaching on the state, civil society and democracy. At the same time, they both retain a commitment to certain characteristic Marxist claims – in Poulantzas' case, to the centrality of class struggle, in that of Offe, to the cumulative self-obstruction of organized capitalism's 'sub-systems'. In recent years, this 'post-Marxist' initiative – seeking critically to appropriate Marxism, and to reconcile it with quite distinct theoretical traditions, without ever wholly rejecting it – has been extended in a way which has carried its proponents still further away from Marxist orthodoxy. It is upon these developments and the extent to which they have or have not confronted the specific weaknesses of more traditional Marxist political analysis that I turn in the rest of this chapter.

In fact, these recent theoretical innovations are not exclusively oriented around the inadequacies of classical Marxist accounts of the state. As well as the weaknesses of Marxism's radical anti-statism and the contrast of this with the overbearing statism of 'actually-existing socialism', these commentators are much concerned with the bureaucratic statism which they identify with social democracy. Correspondingly, they seek to develop an account of the proper role of the state which can meet objections not only to Marx's radical anti-statism and the statism of 'actually-existing socialism' but also to the statism of 'actually-existing social democracy'.

However, at the centre of their attention is the comparatively recent revival of Marxist interest in the state and the point of departure of their analyses may quite properly be retraced to those issues that arose in the Miliband-Poulantzas and subsequent state derivation debates of the early- and mid-1970s. The dispute between Miliband and Poulantzas should be too familiar to require extended rehearsal here. Both authors, it will be recalled, were anxious to define the particular nature of the capitalist state. Miliband sought to give the lie to the bourgeois political orthodoxy of a neutral state, obedient to its freely elected masters, arguing that the capitalist state was controlled, either directly or through sets of interwoven elites, by the economically ascendant capitalist class. Poulantzas, while acknowledging the importance of

Miliband's 'demystification' of the bourgeois account of a neutral state, insisted that an empirical rebuttal of bourgeois orthodoxy was quite inadequate. For Poulantzas, it was not the occupation of state positions by bourgeois personnel nor the capacity of the state to act as the instrument of this ascendant class which marked out the state as capitalist. Rather, this state was defined by its position *within the capitalist mode of production*, (CMP), as 'the factor of cohesion or unity in a class-divided social formation', the state not of the capitalists but of capitalist society. Indeed, the 'relative autonomy' of the state from the immediate interests of mutually competing capitals within a market economy was a decisive feature of its capacity to act in the general and long-term interests of capital.[12]

Staatsableitung

A second major source of Marxist state theory in the 1970s – arising in part from dissatisfaction with the analyses of both Miliband and Poulantzas but equally from local political circumstances – was the German *Staatsableitungdebatte*, (state derivation debate).[13] Broadly conceived, the state derivationists' intention was to 'derive' the form of the state from the imperatives of the capitalist mode of production. In contrast to what was seen as the 'class-theoretical' accounts of both Miliband and Poulantzas, the state derivationists insisted that both protagonists had mistakenly sought to isolate from one another the political and economic levels. This they attributed to a misreading of Marx's *Capital* which, they insisted, is not an economic critique of capitalism, to be complemented by a distinct though related political critique, but is rather a *materialist critique* of political economy – a critique not only of the economic but also of the political form of the capital relation. For them, the necessity of the political form of the state could be derived either from the requirements of the processes of continued capital accumulation, (Müller and Neusüss, Altvater), or from the shared interests of all commodity owners (capital and labour) at the 'surface' of society where they meet and exchange as equals, (Flatow and Huisken, 'Project Klassenanalyse').

That such positions are strongly functionalist in character – capitalism gets such state forms as are consonant with continued accumulation – and that they correspondingly underplay struggles within and about the capitalist state is clear. Later contributors to the debate were much more sensitive to such criticisms. Hirsch, for example, while maintaining the possibility of 'deriving' the form of the capitalist state, recognized that the contradictions of capitalist society are reproduced *within* the state and that the particularistic interventions that the state is increasingly called upon to make in the interests of the dominant monopoly fraction of capital leads to 'serious difficulties and conflicts' in its wider brief of both securing the general conditions for the reproduction of capital as a whole and keeping the class struggle latent. He also sought to give his analysis of the state relation a dynamic and historical component, by connecting it with the perceived *contradictions* of continued capital accumulation, (the tendency of the rate of profit to fall and its counteracting tendencies), calling for the development of 'a conceptually informed understanding of an historical process'.[14] Heide Gerstenberger's breach with state-derivation was still more explicit. She insisted that:

> The logical analysis of the conditions of capitalist development certainly provides no basis for understanding how state activity, which on closer inspection is amazingly unsystematic, always establishes, as if by a trick of reason, exactly that which can be regarded as functional at the time for the concrete conditions of capital accumulation.[15]

It was possible, she argued, that 'actual state activity is not always the adequate expression of the interests of capital as a whole.' This led her to call for a focus upon 'the concrete course of social strategies', (not always unproblematically 'functional for capital'), and to insist that a more adequate analysis could not be based upon an ever closer consideration of *the* form of *the* capitalist state but rather required the study of a diversity of forms of actually existing capitalist states. Such a redefinition of the problem, she concluded, rather despairingly, 'poses problems for the materialist analysis of the state which we have not yet begun even to think about'.[16]

The Under-determined State

It is precisely these kinds of doubts and reservations, expressed by Hirsch and Gerstenberger, that have been taken up and expanded upon in recent 'post-Marxist' analyses. First, there has been a decisive break with what has been widely regarded as the *sine qua non* of historical materialist accounts of the state – a rejection of the claim that the state can be 'explained' by its derivation (as class- or capital-determined) from the capitalist mode of production and of the supposition that the state (either instrumentally or relatively autonomously) functions unambiguously in the interests of a single class. Such criticisms clearly represent part of a much more general breach with the broadest explanatory bases of Marxism. Correspondingly, they are pressed with particular conviction in Giddens' recent work – centrally, though not exclusively, in *A Contemporary Critique of Historical Materialism* – on the latently functionalist and evolutionist elements within Marxism which disenable it as a mode of social explanation. In suggesting that the state could be read off from other, principally economic, areas of his social theory, seeing it as necessarily mobilizing the interests of the economically ascendant class, and anticipating that its disappearance would be conterminous with the dissolution of classes defined around ownership of the means of production, Marx systematically under-explained the particular nature of the state. Under the influence of Saint-Simon and in a manner characteristic of nineteenth century social theory, he is seen to have misappraised 'the role of the state as the agent of surveillance and the purveyor of military violence'.[17] Lenin's cataclysmic treatment in 'The State and Revolution' notwithstanding, it is argued that 'the state is a much more formidable phenomenon than Marxism has traditionally allowed for.'[18] Thus, denying that there is any useful sense in which the state can be explained in terms of its 'functioning' in the interests of a ruling class, and tracing the history of the varyingly independent *loci* of allocative and authoritative powers, Giddens argues that the (flawed) explanatory framework of Marxism has systematically failed to give an adequate account not only of 'the capitalist state' but still more importantly of the state under socialism and/or of its transcendence.

Materially similar reservations are expressed by John Urry. Considering Marx and Engels' varying approaches to the state, Urry concludes that within them, even upon the most generous reading, 'there is still nothing resembling a theory of the state in capitalist societies.'[19] In counterposing the criteria for a more adequate theory of the capitalist state, Urry argues that this must be 'based on the specific characteristics of capitalist societies', yielding an account in which 'the state is not reduced to the economic, or seen as the instrument of the dominant economic class.' From this it follows that the state must not be viewed 'functionally'. Urry is insistent that 'it must not be assumed that each state always has the most functional consequences for the overarching structure', for, he argues, 'the state does not develop automatically but . . . in the context of individuals, groups, and classes, struggling to sustain their material conditions of life.'[20]

The State as 'An Arena of Struggle'

The latter claim could be read in a 'minimalist' sense to mean that the actions of the capitalist state meet with varying forms of class and popular resistance. But in any more 'active' reading, this claim sanctions a second, quite radical divergence from the Marxist account of the state – that is the claim that the state is not a centralized-unified political actor but 'an arena of struggle', constituted-divided by quite opposing interests. The point is well made by Esping-Andersen et al. who, in their discussion of 'Modes of Class Struggle and the Capitalist State', insist that 'the internal structure of the state is simultaneously a product, an object and a determinant of class struggle.'[21] Urry goes still further, arguing that 'the development of the state [is] significantly the outcome not directly of the capitalist interest but of that of wage-labourers,'[22] while Giddens maintains that the characteristic mistrust of the state among the capitalist class is largely attributable to 'the power that the organized working class [has been] able to mobilize vis-à-vis the state.'[23] The point is made with particular vehemence by Boris Frankel who insists that 'state institutions in capitalist countries have not just reproduced capitalist relations . . . they have also undermined the reproduction of dominant values and practices.'[24]

Significantly, none of these commentators is correspondingly committed to a reformist view of the gradual securing of working-class interests within unproblematically growing and benign welfare states. Urry, for example, is insistent that 'working-class and popular struggles do not effectively transform such states into a popular or workers' state able to eradicate capitalist relations.'[25] They all recognize, with Offe, that the characteristic condition of the contemporary Western welfare state is one of being divided by its own forms of contradiction. In Esping-Andersen's account, 'the political question for the working class is never whether or not contradictions exist within the state, but rather how intense those contradictions are and how they can be exploited by the working class.'[26] This question of the possibilities afforded to the working class by contradictions within the state is taken up by Giddens. For if we take seriously the characteristic of the state as 'an arena of struggles', so Giddens argues, 'the state can in some part be seen as an emancipatory force', as 'neither a class-neutral agency of social reforms (the theory of industrial society, social-democratic political theory), nor a mere functional vehicle of the "needs" of the capitalist mode of production (functionalist Marxism)'.[27]

Of course, the contemporary state cannot be understood exclusively by reference to this potentially emancipatory moment. Indeed, Giddens insists that one of the greatest weaknesses of traditional Marxist analysis is that it has 'no tradition of theorising violence', and the consequences of this absence are acute in relation to its analysis of the state both internally, (repression and surveillance), and externally, ('the "world violence" of the contemporary system of power-blocs and nation-states').[28]

Disaggregating 'The Capitalist State'

These contradictions point us towards a further weakness of traditional Marxist accounts – that is their tendency to treat generically of 'the capitalist state', as if there were a single characteristic model to which the state in any and all capitalist societies approximated. This perspective can now be seen to be flawed in at least two respects. First, the intervention of the labour movement within the state makes problematic the extent to which the state in capitalist societies can be usefully described as a 'capitalist' state. As Peter Hall suggests, 'theories of the state have posited a powerful set of explanations for why the state tends to function on behalf of capital; but when confronted with the need to account for systematic variation among the policies of different nations, these theories explain too much.'[29]

This directs attention towards a second and perhaps still more important weakness of traditional Marxist analyses – that is their willingness to treat of 'the capitalist state', independent of the history and particular circumstances of individual nation states, (including 'actually-existing' socialist states), and with no regard for the international dimensions of trade, alliance or domination. As John Urry notes, 'there is no capitalist state, merely a multiplicity of conflicting nation states' and these are, of course, both economically and militarily vastly unequal and their relations are organized, often on the basis of threats and sanctions, in ways which are often more or less explicitly coercive. This requires analytically that we should displace analysis of 'the capitalist state' with a consideration of the *histories* of particular societies in an *international* complex of unequal nation states and with a concern for intra- as well as inter-state relations.

With the abandonment of the conception of unitary state power and the recognition of the state as an arena of struggles penetrated by working-class and popular interests there goes, as in Poulantzas' *State, Power, Socialism*, a rejection of the traditional strategic perspectives of dual power and 'smashing the state'. As the debates surrounding the emergence of Eurocommunism in the mid-1970s made clear, these are amongst the most fiercely contested and defended claims of traditional Marxist analysis. Not only do the 'post-Marxist' theorists side more or less uniformly against the Leninists' frontal assault on the state, some go still further towards a fundamental breach with the ubiqiutous socialist ambition of exercising state power. André Gorz, for example, argues that it is not at all clear 'that power should be *seized*, rather than dismantled, controlled if not abolished altogether'. Indeed his quite unconventional account leads him to argue that 'the essential purpose of politics is not the exercise of power . . . [but] to delimit, orient and codify the actions of government, to designate the ends and means they should use, and to ensure that they do not stray from their mission.'[30]

This is a rather unusual position for a socialist writer to adopt but it is characteristic of the 'post-Marxist' view inasmuch as it recognizes, following Poulantzas, that the state is not an institution that can be 'occupied' and that state power is not an essence that can be seized or smashed. Similarly characteristic of the 'post-Marxist' view is the endorsement of Boris Frankel's impatience with 'the abstract utopianism of stateless socialism'.[31] Here again, Poulantzas is the model and criticism is mobilized against both 'Stalinism' *and* traditional social democracy which, despite everything that distinguishes them, are seen to show 'a fundamental complicity . . . marked by *statism* and profound distrust of mass initiatives'. Both are seen to give rise to *'the techno-bureaucratic statism of the experts'*.[32]

In fact, these critics tend to identify statism not with the existence of the state as such but with those strategies that attempted either to deny the continuing importance of the state under socialism, (Leninism, Stalinism), or to envisage socialism developing exclusively within the parameters of existing (bureaucratic and repressive) state institutions. Much more typical of the 'post-Marxist' position is the attempt to redefine the relation of state and society, (rather more in line with Poulantzas' own problematic), stressing the necessity of both as autonomous regions and recognizing the necessity of the former as the guarantor of the independence and institutions that must flourish within the latter. On this, Gorz is characteristically clear and heretical: 'The only hope of abolishing relations of domination is to start by recognizing that functional power is inevitable. This recognition will enable us to look for ways of effectively restricting it to areas where it cannot be dispensed with.'[33]

Very similar concerns are expressed by Held and Keane, who argue that:

> Without a secure and independent civil society of autonomous public bodies, goals such as freedom and equality, participatory planning and community decision-making will be nothing but empty slogans. But without the protective, redistributive and conflict-mediating functions of the state, struggles to transform civil society will become ghettoised and divided, or will spawn their own, new forms of inequality.[34]

This means recognizing that the state cannot be 'overcome' and that it will not 'wither away'. While not a necessary evil, being in some circumstances an enabling institution, it must however always be subject to strict delimitation and control. This may be summarized as a call for the effective restriction of a necessary state power.

On Civil Society and 'Social Pluralism'

Even more than a reconsideration of the state, these positions imply a quite radical re-evaluation of the category of civil society. Indeed, they are more or less diametrically opposed to the classical Marxist account of the state-civil society relation. This classical view we saw in Marx's own earliest (philosophical) writings in which the division between civil society (as the realm of needs, of the private *'bellum omnia contra omnes'* of a market society) and political society (the modern representative state) is seen to be the characteristic institutional form of liberal capitalism. For Marx, no amount of reform could alter the nature of this polity. 'True Democracy', he had insisted, was premised upon the overcoming of the division between civil and political society, the supersession of the state and 'the end of politics', in the replacement of 'the government of men' by 'the administration of things'.

This anticipation of a 'seamless' democracy was among the most prominent targets of Marx's liberal detractors, but in the most recent 'post-Marxist' theory it has become a target of writers otherwise quite out of sympathy with this liberalism.[35] Thus, the claim that it is the *division* of state and civil society that is, in some sense, at the root of political alienation is vigorously rejected and the expectation that such political alienation might be overcome through the coalescence of civil and political society is seen to be Utopian and extremely dangerous.

This radical conclusion is drawn with particular clarity by André Gorz. Having recognized the indispensability of the state, as the retort of 'functional power', Gorz insists that it is essential 'to dissociate power from domination, keeping the first where necessary, doing away with the latter everywhere and upholding the specific autonomies of civil society, the political society and the state'.[36] 'The existence of a state separate from civil society, able both to codify objective necessities in the form of law and to assure its implementation' is, he argues, 'the essential prerequisite to the autonomy of civil society and the emergence of an area outside the sphere of heteronomy in which a variety of modes of production, modes of life and forms of cooperation can be experimented with according to individual desires'.[37] In practice, Gorz maintains, it is only through the existence of laws and the state, and the possibility they afford for the 'trivialisation of relations regulating the sphere of necessity' that it becomes possible 'to establish a sphere of the fullest autonomy, in which individuals are free to associate according to their desires in order to create what is beyond necessity'.[38] The problem then, according to Gorz, is not the abolition of the state but the abolition of domination with which law and the state have been historically, but not necessarily, connected. The initiative to unyoke state and domination will not, however, issue, unprompted, from within the state itself:

> The state can only cease to be an apparatus of domination over society and become an instrument enabling society to exercise power over itself with a view to its own restructuring, if society is already permeated by social struggles that open up areas of autonomy keeping both the dominant class and the power of the state apparatus in check.[39]

It is the aspiration of new social movements within civil society – often dissociated from political parties which are themselves disenabled by representational crises and by what is, in the Gorzian account, an inappropriate concern with competition for state power – that prompts and promotes this transformation within the sphere of the state. At the same time, civil society, as the sphere of autonomy, should be characterized by a heterodox plurality of movements and aspirations. Such a plurality, conceived as 'the coexistence of various ways of working, producing and living, various and distinct cultural areas and levels of social existence', has ever presented a serious difficulty for a monolithic and moralistic 'classical socialist doctrine'.[40] But it is precisely the claim of liberal democracies to have preserved, albeit in a deformed and distorted way, popular aspirations for plurality that has secured them continuing support and it is, Gorz insists, 'precisely because the socialist movement has failed to embrace and enrich this pluralist perspective that it has condemned itself to a minority position even among the working class'.[41]

Significantly similar conclusions arise from Jean Cohen's critique of conventional Marxist political analysis. Arguing that, in envisaging 'a collectively planned, fully socialized society', Marx lapsed into 'a rationalistic myth combined with a technocratic utopia', Cohen takes up the necessity of providing a new theory of civil society.[42] In reducing the realm of civil society to the '*bellum omnia contra omnes*' of a market economy, Marxism has tended to resolve all struggles for liberation into forms of class struggle. In this way it has failed both to comprehend the diversity of institutional forms within civil society and to understand the variety of 'emancipatory struggles' which traverse it. Marxist class theory is simply inadequate to the task of explaining and mobilizing the wide range of emancipatory struggles to be found within the contemporary state and civil society. To meet this weakness, Cohen advocates the development of 'a *post-Marxist* critical *stratification* theory' which will redeem the systematically neglected sphere of civil society as a realm in which divergent struggles for emancipation – on the basis of, for example, race, gender, and anti-militarism as much as upon class – can be pursued. The upshot is a call for a political strategy directed towards securing 'a socialist and pluralist civil society'.

A very similar concern is to be found in the already cited work of John Urry. Echoing Cohen's criticism of the *narrowness* of the Marxist analysis, Urry argues that the struggle of classes to reproduce the conditions of their existence are 'a part of, but not exhaustive of, civil society'. Civil society is also populated by a variety of other social groupings, particularly those based on gender, race, generation and nation.[43] Avoiding the reduction of civil society to 'the economic', Urry defines it as:

> That set of social practices outside the state and outside the relations and forces of production in which agents both are constituted as subjects and which presuppose the actions of such subjects – first, in the sphere of circulation directly; second, in those relations within which labour-power is reproduced economically, biologically and culturally; and third, in the resultant class and popular democratic forces.[44]

Towards an 'Autonomous Public Life'

Among the most important responses to Cohen's call for 'a pluralist and socialist civil society' is John Keane's advocacy of an 'autonomous public life'.[45] Keane's discussion is concentrated upon a critique of both bureaucratic domination, as the organizing principle of both private and public life under late capitalism, and of the ways in which this domination has been understood in German social theory from Weber to Offe and Habermas. In circumstances in which social democracy, associated with the expansion of bureaucracy and the curtailment of democracy, 'is rapidly ceasing to be a viable and legitimate political option', the central thrust of Keane's argument is that 'the radical reform of late capitalist societies depends crucially upon the weakening of the power of corporate and state bureaucracies through the establishment and strengthening of spheres of autonomous public life.'[46]

Keane is sharply critical of Weber's codification of 'the impossibility of defending autonomous public life against the "forward progress" of bureaucratic domination', and of the 'thesis of total administration' that emerged, under Weber's influence, from within the Frankfurt School.[47] He is somewhat less critical of Offe and Habermas, who, as the contemporary inheritors of the critical theoretical tradition, recognize this bureaucratic domination within late capitalist states to be subject to its own forms of systematic self-contradiction. However, he is insistent that Habermas, at least, continues to concede too much to the bureaucratic principle and that his political advocacy of 'universal pragmatics' is 'unable to offer many insights into the substantive aspects of contemporary struggles for autonomous public life'.[48]

For Keane, the pressing need is to elaborate forms of socialist public life which are genuinely accessible to ordinary actors in ways that the principles of 'universal pragmatics' are not. In practice, certain forms of public life have survived, often under plebeian pressure, in a period more generally characterized by techno-bureaucratic domination. Keane cites the survival of civic humanism and citizenship, to which might be added the retention of trial by jury. He concludes that 'a socialist theory of public life . . . can ignore these tradition-informed struggles only at the cost of excessively empty and abstract-general formulations.'[49] Given these premises, it is clear that, for Keane, 'the democratic "road to socialism" can be envisaged only as a difficult and extended process of decentralization of decision-making power to a plurality of public spheres', as a strategy directed 'toward a "socialist civil society" of non-patriarchal public spheres that relate to state institutions only at the levels of criticism, negotiation and compromise'.[50]

On Democracy

It should, by now, be clear that this recent critique of Marxist understandings of the relations of state and civil society also occasions a breach with traditional Marxist accounts of democracy. Although there is little homogeneity in those accounts of democracy with which Marxist orthodoxy is countermanded, there is near universal support for Keane's contention that 'the radical wish for a perfectly substantive democracy unhindered by problems of legitimacy, power, obedience, and conflict must be rejected for what it is: an exaggerated, anti-political, and never-to-be-realised utopia.'[51]

For some commentators, this yields something close to an uncritical endorsement of the existing institutions and practices of Western liberal democracies. A. J. Polan, for example, in his passion definitively to settle accounts with Lenin's 'police-socialism', contrasts political repression in Eastern European states with liberal democracy, in which politics is seen as 'the discourse of the necessary interplay between the interests and ideologies articulated in the decision-making processes that are allocated to the state'.[52] 'It cannot be repeated too often', he insists:

That without a genuine process of discursive will-formation, there is no politics that merits the name, and there is no democracy that is not a travesty of the meaning the concept holds. And such a process of will-formation can only take place in a polity that is composed of voluntary associations of individuals who are legally constituted as trans-situational citizens, entitled to a framework of legally safeguarded institutions wherein a public sphere may form reinforced and sustained by informal and myriad modes of communication and publicity.[53]

Existing bureaucracies and parliaments are seen to have their faults – which are platitudinously seen to be shared with all human institutions – but these are to be overcome by 'development' rather than dissolution.

The position that I have maintained throughout this book should make it clear that to criticize Polan is in no sense to defend Lenin's counterposed account of democracy and the state. However, even the brief résumé of Keane's work above should indicate that precisely those relations and practices which Polan assumes to be present within liberal democracies are themselves acutely problematic. In endorsing the 'so fruitful' tradition of bureaucratic analysis from Weber to Habermas, Polan has 'bracketed out' that problem of bureaucracy as a limitation upon democratic practices grounded in the division of state and civil society, which is the central concern of Keane's work.

In Hindess' *Parliamentary Democracy and Socialist Politics*, a similarly severe breach with orthodox Marxist politics yields a somewhat less sanguine view of existing liberal democratic practice. Hindess argues that both 'revolutionary' and 'reformist' variants of Marxism are vitiated by their reliance upon an (albeit mediated) economically determinant basis to politics and particularly by the expectation that capitalism necessarily generates an inherent working class majority for socialism. At the same time, he criticizes that contrasting (and largely social democratic) tradition which has sought to focus attention exclusively upon the indivisible 'sovereignty of parliament', to the neglect of all those governmental decisions that are made outside the parliamentary arena. Disconnecting the concept of democracy from any notion of sovereignty, he argues:

Opens up the possibility of assessing any putatively democratic mechanism in terms of its specific determinations and limitations by identifying first its scope and how that scope is determined and second, the way it is organized and other conditions under which it operates, and third, the identifiable constraints on discussion and voting, limitations of scope, and other effects which they impose.[54]

Such an approach, Hindess insists, affords the possibility of promoting democratic reforms both within and outside parliament, the promotion of the legitimacy of extra-parliamentary as well as parliamentary struggles and the organization and mobilization of broadly conceived social alliances around broadly progressive democratic programmes. Although Hindess is clear that extra-parliamentary action is a quite legitimate brand of democratic struggle, it is equally evident that he regards parliament as the principal focus of alliance-based democratic mobilization. Some commentators have gone still further. John Keane, for example, insists that 'the "parliamentary road" can no longer be seen as privileged, as occupying the centre stage of politics.'[55] Other writers, particularly those among the 'new social movements', and drawing inspiration from the 'representational crisis' of traditional party organizations, have similarly drawn attention to democratic struggles outside the parameters of party and parliamentary organization.[56]

While it is possible, then, to find considerable variation among contemporary assessments of democratic practices and institutions, a number of claims can be seen to be very widely endorsed across the spectrum of 'post-Marxist' thought. These include the recognition that representative parliamentary democracy, 'the public sphere' and many of the rights and liberties secured within it, are real though limited popular achievements and the insistence that any attempt to replace all forms of representative democracy by exclusively direct democracy will issue in statism. To this is added a trenchant defence of pluralism, not only as a claim to the formal plurality of political parties, but also as an advocacy of the broadest possible plurality of aspirations, ideologies and 'ways of life'.

At this point, it may prove useful to summarize the most important of these claims as a set of brief theses:

1 On the State

1 The state does not, (either instrumentally or relatively autonomously), function unambiguously in the interests of a single class.
2 The state is not a centralized-unified political actor. It is 'an arena of struggle', constituted-divided by quite opposing interests.
3 There can be no satisfactory, general analysis of the (capitalist) state. The proper subject of study is given nation states in their historical and international particularity.
4 The state is not an institution that can be 'occupied'; state power is not such that it can be 'seized'. Transformation of the state may be 'profound' but it will also be gradual and, at least in part, internal.

5 The state cannot be overcome and will not wither away; it is essential to any developed society. While not a necessary evil, it must however always be subject to strict delimitation and control. This may be summarized as a call for the effective restriction of a necessary state power.

2 On Civil Society and 'Social Pluralism'

6 Any form of socialism which is to realize aspirations for both liberty and equality must be based not upon the overcoming of the division between state and civil society but rather upon their increasingly clear and formalized differentiation.

7 Rather than fostering a socialist morality, civil society must be the site of a legally guaranteed plurality of aspirations, ways of life and ideologies.

8 Anticipations of 'the end of politics' and the end of conflict over the distribution of means and resources (even under circumstances of abundance) are Utopian, as is the corresponding expectation of the overcoming of the necessity of law. Under these circumstances, an (extended) set of civil and political rights, and the state as legal guarantor of these rights, is indispensable.

9 All forms of emancipatory struggle under late capitalism are *not* reducible to forms of class struggle. An emancipatory politics must therefore recognize the significance of new movements, (often single-issue campaigns), and recognize the necessity of alliances of liberating forces within a popular-democratic (rather than exclusively class-based) struggle.

3 On Democracy

10 Representative parliamentary democracy and many of the rights and liberties secured under it are real though limited popular achievements.

11 Any attempt to replace all forms of representative democracy by exclusively direct democracy will issue in statism.

In this chapter, I have dealt, in some detail, with a wide range of theorists who have attempted, in a critical though not wholly antipathetic way, to confront the severe limitations of Marxist accounts of politics evidenced in the opening chapters of this study. It has been possible to trace the way in which a concern with the sufficiency of existing Marxist accounts of the state has broadened into a quite decisive break with many of the essential claims of more traditional Marxist teaching. For the most part, these developments, which afford a far more compelling account of the enabling and oppressive nature of state institutions, of the necessary division between state and civil society, of the strengths and weaknesses of pluralism and existing democratic practices, are to be welcomed. Collectively, they represent a significant advance in the attempt to generate a compelling account of a democratic socialist politics. But substantial difficulties remain. It is, for example, quite unclear that these initiatives have recognized the extent to which their breach with certain claims of Marxism, however well justified, means a general loss of the explanatory comprehensiveness which has ever been one of Marxism's most theoretically appealing features. At the same time, even the most developed and considered of these accounts, for example, Jean Cohen's *Class and Civil Society* and John Keane's *Public Life and Late Capitalism*, remain largely programmatic, while others, such as Gorz's *Farewell to the Working Class*, are explicitly speculative. This simply underlines the extent to which these initiatives have, as yet, failed to carry us very far towards a more comprehensive account of what a democratic socialist political *practice* should look like.

It is these weaknesses that I take up in the following chapter, discussing two linked areas in which these theoretical innovations have been applied – in the attempt to elaborate a socialist theory of rights and a socialist account of the rule of law – and assessing the extent to which it is possible to extrapolate strategic conclusions from these programmatic critiques.

7
Socialist Rights and a Socialist Rule of Law?

It would be as well to begin this discussion of contemporary advocacy of socialist rights and a socialist rule of law by reminding ourselves of the classical Marxist position against which these recent accounts are so frequently set. Rather than rehearse the respective positions of Marx, Lenin, Bernstein, Kautsky and Luxemburg – already extensively discussed in earlier chapters – I want here to consider the contribution of Evgeny Pashukanis, whose *Law and Marxism* has sometimes been taken to be the definitive statement of the Marxist theory of law and which has itself enjoyed something of a renaissance within the more general flowering of an English-speaking 'Marxist jurisprudence' over the last ten years.

Pashukanis: 'Towards a Critique of the Fundamental Juridical Concepts'

A Bolshevik, writing and working in the earliest years of the Soviet Union, Pashukanis' intention was to establish a Marxist account of the law which would share the authority of, because it was derived from, Marx's much more fully considered critique of political economy. Disavowing the possibility of recreating a coherent Marxist position from Marx's own scattered and unsystematic writings on the law, and criticizing those accounts which either reduced all law to a purely *ideological* manifestation or else were exclusively concerned with criticism of the *content* of existing bourgeois law, Pashukanis insisted that it was essential to study the material *form* taken by bourgeois law.

There were, he insisted, the closest imaginable similarities between the commodity form, which was at the heart of Marx's detailed critique of political economy, and the legal form, which was to be the centre piece of Pashukanis' parallel critique of bourgeois jurisprudence. Both commodity and legal form had existed only 'embryonically' in pre-capitalist societies. Their twin dominance arose simultaneously with the displacement of feudal privileges by the bourgeois-capitalist system of equivalent exchange. Repeatedly, Pashukanis stressed the parallels between the categories of bourgeois jurisprudence and those of political economy. He pointed to the coeval emergence of commodity form and juridic individualism, insisting that 'man becomes a legal subject by virtue of the same necessity which transforms the product of nature into a commodity.'[1] Juridical individualism and 'the person', as a legal subject availed of a set of justiciable rights, were thus identified with the rise of capitalism and an economic order which was constituted by 'the conflict of private interests' of the individual owners of commodities in a system of formally equivalent exchange. This 'conflict of private interests', so Pashukanis argued, is 'both the logical premise of the legal form and the actual origin of the development of the legal superstructure'.[2] He concluded that 'it is readily evident that the logic of juridical concepts corresponds to the logic of the social relations of a commodity-producing society.'[3]

Of course, it will be readily recalled that one of the main burdens of Marx's analysis of the commodity form was to demonstrate its *historical* origins and to disclose the (mistaken and ideological) presumption of bourgeois political economy that this was a natural rather than an historically given category. Pashukanis drew a parallel and contermi-nous conclusion for the legal form and its historical 'bearer', the legal subject. For, just as the commodity form which arose with the capitalist mode of production based upon the conflicting interests of individual-ized commodity-producers is destined to 'wither away' with the supersession of capitalism by socialism, so too is legal regulation based upon the conflict of private interests – and, for Pashukanis, *all* law is finally reducible to this category – itself destined to 'wither away' under socialism.

This elimination of the law does not bring with it, Pashukanis insisted, the elimination of *all* forms of social regulation. In a number of spheres of social and industrial life – Pashukanis cited the example of running a railway network – technical rule-following is essential to ensure safety and efficiency. But abiding by technical and thus, for Pashukanis, neutral codes of practice, it would come to be increasingly detached from the adversarial, legal categories of 'liability . . . predicated on private choices, private, differentiated interests'.[4] Pashukanis drew similar conclusions about the changing nature of the criminal law. Though attenuated by the elimination of capitalism, Pashukanis did not anticipate that antisocial behaviour would 'wither away' under socialism. But he did suggest that the criminal law, with its categories of individual responsibility, punishment and retribution would increasingly give way to a 'curative' attitude to offenders, to a therapeutic intervention directed towards their rehabilitation and a full and early return to normal 'mental health'. In a transitional period, while the 'narrow horizon' of equivalent exchange is not yet crossed, the legal form would be retained. But Pashukanis' quite radical conclusion was that, under developed communism, 'the withering away of the categories of bourgeois law will . . . mean the withering away of law altogether, that is to say the disappearance of the juridical factor from social relations.'[5] Anticipating a shift 'from rights to utility', Pashukanis insisted that the legal regulation of a society of rights-exercising, justiciable private individuals would increasingly yield to 'a social system which enables people to build and conceive of their interrelations in terms of the clear and simple concepts of harm and advantage'.[6]

Contemporary Marxism and 'the Withering Away of the Law'

Pashukanis' radical conclusions on the withering away of the law were originally intended as a polemical intervention in the face of the contemporary advocacy of a transition to 'proletarian law' in the post-revolutionary Soviet Union. It is not perhaps surprising that Pashukanis' account did not long enjoy official favour. Criticized by Yujdin and Vyshiinsky, it was soon displaced by the latter's account of the *positive* role of the law under socialism, an account which was much more consonant with the immediate interests of the Soviet state under Stalin.[7] Though recent Marxist commentators have tended to be more sympathetic – Pashukanis was, after all, eventually to be 'liquidated' under the jurisdiction of 'proletarian law' – they have not, for the most part, identified with Pashukanis' most radical expectations for the withering away of the law. Much more widespread has been a (sometimes conditional) commitment to the continuing necessity of law under socialism, but to a law exorcized of the appeal to rights and the ideology of the rule of law.

Hugh Collins' own much more recent discussion of *Marxism and Law* furnishes a particularly outspoken statement of this position. Having flirted with the endorsement of Pashukanis' expectation of the withering away of the law under socialism, (through the overcoming of alienation), Collins is eventually compelled to conclude that, since 'Marxism only provides a few foggy notions about the organization of a Communist society' (and given 'the probable opportunities for conflict and misuse of power'), 'the contention that the law will wither away must appear unrealistic.'[8] He is much less reserved, however, in his judgement upon rights and the rule of law. Rights are to be valued only as 'a stepping-stone towards true democracy based on a Communist mode of production' and, while rights that promote the class struggle are to be vigorously prosecuted, Collins perceives 'a danger that continued discussion of petty incursions of civil liberties found in the criminal process will raise the rights infringed to the status of ends rather than means'. In this way, he argues, it is possible that 'the class struggle would degenerate into a defence of the Rule of Law.' In a Marxist ranking of political principles, he concludes, 'a concern for legality and liberty is unlikely to score very high.'[9]

Similar conclusions – if less fundamentalist premises – underpin Sol Picciotto's position on 'the theory of the state, class struggle and the rule of law'.[10] Dissatisfied with existing accounts of the rule of law organized around the 'ambiguous dichotomy of coercion/legitimacy', (he cites E. P. Thompson and Stuart Hall), or around instrumentalist or derivationist principles, Picciotto maintains the necessity of concentrating upon legal forms 'as *part* of social relations as a totality'. Arguing that 'the most basic aspect of the fetishization of social relations under capitalism is the separation of the economic and the political and the autonomization of the state', Picciotto insists that 'the first moment of the capitalist state is to *establish and guarantee exchange* as the mediation of production and consumption.' This, in turn, requires 'the creation and maintenance of individuals as *economic and legal subjects*, the bearers of reified property rights'. Pashukanis was right then, Picciotto avers, in arguing that the basic legal category is the subject as the bearer of a bundle of rights and duties and that it is 'his individual legal subjectivity [which] is enshrined and maintained by legal procedures'.[11]

The pursuit of class interests under the rubric of rights, Picciotto argues, places systematic limitations upon the kinds of gains that can be secured. For example, gains formalized as rights tend, through their individualist bourgeois legal form, to have an 'isolation effect', fragmenting the collective experience of class solidarity. Thus:

> Substantive gains are achieved through collective struggles building up class solidarity: the channelling of such struggles into the form of claims of bourgeois legal right breaks up that movement towards solidarity through the operation of legal procedures which recognize only the individual subject of rights and duties.[12]

This does not mean that 'the legal form of "rights" should be ignored as totally illusory' – the struggle for rights has generally been historically progressive and 'a right encapsulated in bourgeois form is certainly better than no right at all' – but since 'the individual legal subject is essentially the bearer of commodities, the owner of economic assets producing a revenue', this subject's exercise of his or her rights, however expansive, can never overcome the limitations of what is seen to be an essentially bourgeois form.[13]

In fact, Picciotto argues, the 'rule of law', which was long seen to be the necessary institutional framework under which rights could be exercised, has, under the conditions of twentieth century monopoly capitalism, become increasingly problematic. Repeatedly, the capitalist state has been forced to make particularistic interventions in the interests of sustaining profitable capital accumulation and has thus broken with the principles of generality, impartiality and equivalence which are seen to underpin the ideology of 'equal rights' and the 'rule of law'. However, in the face of these developments, Picciotto insists:

> The strategy for a working-class movement must be, not to uphold the impossible ideals of the liberal form of state and the 'rule of law', but to insist on the necessity that it be transcended, in forms which challenge the dominance of capitalist social relations.[14]

Hirst: 'Law, Socialism and Rights'

A view still more sharply critical of Pashukanis' presumption in favour of the withering away of the law is taken up by Paul Hirst.[15] Rejecting Pashukanis' central claim that all law is, in essence, private law, a mediation of the conflicting interests of private commodity-owners, Hirst is insistent that 'all states, as complexes of agencies of decision, *must* take a public law form.'[16] Indeed, 'socialist states, by increasing the scope and variety of state agencies and functions, accentuate rather than reduce the need for an effective framework of public law to regulate the "public" domain and its relations with other agents.'[17] Pashukanis' assumption that under socialism what had previously been political decisions, subject to some (albeit deformed) means of legal constraint, would be rendered purely technical-administrative and politically neutral, is vigorously resisted. Hirst argues that, especially in the light of the unhappy record of 'actually existing' socialist societies, 'the idea that a framework of legal regulation and review be replaced by apparatuses of "social defence", subject only to considerations of administrative objectives and effectiveness is disastrous.' By contrast, he insists upon the indispensable 'necessity for a framework of legal definition and regulation in socialist states'.[18]

However, taking issue with Ronald Dworkin, as 'the most sophisticated representative of modern Anglo-Saxon analytic philosophy', Hirst denies that this necessity can be met by 'taking rights seriously'.[19] For, he insists, claims to rights, as of sovereignty, are seen to be 'derivative of ontological doctrines in which institutions and laws are conceived as the expression or recognition of certain prior or privileged attributes of subjects'. Such doctrines 'lead to a conception of social organization as expressive of a principle, a singular and homogeneous derivative of the will of subjects or individuals [and] are incapable of sustaining the complexity and heterogeneity of state institutions and social relations'.[20]

Where he breaks decisively with Pashukanis is in arguing that the supervention of rights is not equivalent to the overcoming of the law in general nor of certain forms of legal guarantee or protection in particular. The appeal to rights, he acknowledges, will always call forth 'the claims of rival ontologies, to parallel the rights of one agent with the conflicting claims of those of another', and as Macintyre makes clear in *After Virtue*, there is no further principle through which such competing rights' claims can be adjudicated. But while the 'categories of "right" cannot assist in the resolution of complex questions of social policy', he insists that 'laws can serve objectives of social policy, regulating the conduct of individuals, without interpellating subjects as bearers of possessive right.'[21]

Through a discussion of abortion legislation in England, the competing rights' claims that have surrounded it and the irreducible legal, social and public policy components it entails, Hirst seeks to show that 'categories of "right" cannot assist in the resolution of complex questions of social policy.'[22] If, as Hirst maintains, law is indispensable under socialism, this requires that we should recast the consideration of 'civil liberties' not in terms of rights, as the prized possessions of alienated subjects, but rather as the maintenance of 'the conditions for securing forms of regulation, inspection and interdiction of the actions of state agencies'.[23]

Hirst's account certainly avoids many of the criticisms that might be raised against a position much closer to Pashukanis. While critical of 'the rule of law' as an ideology associated with a polity securing freedom of contract under generally applicable laws, Hirst is not an opponent of legal provision in itself and while critical of rights' disourse, he is not hostile to the legal protection of citizens' interests. But even this more circumscribed position has been subject to substantial criticism. Alan Hunt, for example, raises the telling, if somewhat 'common-sense' objection, that whatever the philosophical merits of Hirst's objections to rights' discourse, 'no amount of critical commentary removes the appeal to "rights" from the language of politics and therefore from the terms within which politics are fought out.'[24] He further insists that there is no staging post between Hirst's rejection of rights as ontological and irredeemable and a fully positivist account of the law, in which only those rights which are entrenched in statute law can be said to exist. In its turn, this positivist position, inasmuch as it can acknowledge only such rights as have been sanctioned by the state, is subject, Hunt argues, to an 'inherent statism'.[25]

Defending 'Socialist Rights'

Of course, the most effective rejoinder to Hirst, as indeed to all those who are more closely associated with Pashukanis' account of rights, would be a demonstration that an account of socialist rights could be effectively defended. Just such a claim is made by Tom Campbell, who, seeking to redeem rights' discourse from its familiar association with the 'possessive individualism' of a competitive market society, sets out to demonstrate – against 'the revolutionary left', paradigmatically represented by Pashukanis – the 'reformist' case that rights are essential, not only within non-socialist societies, but also as an integral element of any envisageable form of socialism.[26]

The nub of this reformist position, Campbell claims, is that, under socialism, 'the whole approach to rights will change from a situation in which rights mark the boundaries of legitimate, self-regarding behaviour to one in which they are part of the rule-governed framework within which the individual can fulfil his potential as a social being.'[27] To substantiate this position, Campbell deals systematically with four facets of rights against which the Marxist critique has generally been directed: first, their (inappropriate) appeal to moral values, secondly, their association with the law, thirdly, their corresponding reliance upon coercion and fourth, their irredeemable commitment to competitive individualism.

He accepts the inappropriateness of an appeal to *moral* rights, insisting that such a usage strips the appeal to rights of its distinctive quality and 'submerges it in the mass of undifferentiated general terms of moral approval, such as "right", "good" and "desirable"'. In fact, he insists, rights' discourse has 'an important function of its own to fulfil in moral and political discourse', namely 'to identify those ingredients of human life which are protected and furthered in a particular way, that is by *the acceptance within a community that certain actions are or are not permitted or required*'[28] (my emphasis).

Having accepted the inadmissability of moral rights, Campbell seeks, through a critique of the three remaining points of the revolutionary Marxist position, to establish the coherence and indispensability of a body of socialist rights that is consistent with just these distinctive qualities of rights' discourse. Thus, he decisively rejects the association of rights with law and coercion, arguing that rights are not conterminous with (coercive) law but rather with the existence of 'societal rules'. Indeed, Campbell seemingly goes beyond Hirst in conceding that law may (putatively) be overcome under socialism but he is insistent that even 'altruists in a conflict-free society require societal rules' and the intervention of 'monitoring, rectifying and preventative agencies'.[29] He argues that:

> Inevitable limitations in human knowledge, the requirements for educating the young into the way of life of socialist societies and the need to establish normative standards of what counts as harm and benefit, plus the high standard set by socialists for mutual assistance, would generate in a socialist society rules which might differ from – but whose function would be the same as – those rules which are at present used to control human behaviour in order to minimise harm and maximise benefit.[30]

Since even perfect altruists are fallible, these rules will from time to time be broken and this, in turn, dictates, for Campbell, the continuing necessity of rights, (albeit that their exercise will tend to be non-controversial and administrative rather than legalistic and adversarial).

The Marxist criticism that rights are irreducibly 'individualist' and thus associated with the characteristic vices – selfishness, competitiveness, acquisitiveness – of the individual under capitalism, Campbell meets half-way. Conceding that rights are indeed associated with some species of individualism, this is recognized only contingently to be the 'possessive individualism' of a competitive capitalism, while a 'fully human' individualism is seen to be among socialism's highest aspirations. While possessive individualism is premised upon contract or power theories of rights, Campbell argues that the most appropriate basis for fully human individualism is to be found in the appeal to an *interest* theory of rights, under which social rules are held to protect the interests or concerns of individual right-holders. It is possible, Campbell insists:

> To detach 'interest' from 'selfishness' and 'obligation' from 'burden' and so open the way for a socialist concept of rights which retains the individualism inseparable from the idea of obligations being owed to others, but interprets the relevant interests in such a way that they do not amount to self-regarding behaviour and the correlative obligations in such a way that they are not typically viewed as burdensome.[31]

In this way, Campbell argues, the seemingly indissoluble tie between rights and self-interest can be broken.

Further support for many of Campbell's criticisms can be found in the work of A. E. Buchanan. Buchanan argues that while Marx's strictures upon rights may be cogent in respect of the right to private property, his claim that 'the *other* rights of man' – Buchanan cites the right to equality before the law and the right to free speech – 'are valuable only or even chiefly for the isolated, egoistic individual of civil society is much less plausible'.[32] He goes on to elaborate five ways in which rights might prove valuable under socialism, but 'which do not presuppose either egoism or class conflict'. These are:

1 as constraints on democratic procedures (securing the protection of minorities) or as guarantees of access to such democratic procedures;
2 as constraints upon paternalism;
3 as constraints upon what may be done to maximize social welfare;
4 as safeguards defining the ways in which coercion or penalties may be used to secure the provision of public goods;
5 as a way of specifying the scope and limits of the obligation to provide for future generations. [33]

If Campbell, complemented by Buchanan, has had some success in criticizing the premises for the Marxist hostility to rights, it is much less certain, as one would expect, that the *positive* side of his account of rights is just as compelling. To a very considerable degree, the conviction that such an account can hope to carry relies upon its ability to give a compelling explanation of what is, in fact, to count as a right-generating interest. Campbell, himself, stipulates what is to count as such an interest by a further appeal to the concept of 'human needs'. Conceding that such a category is necessarily 'elusive and open-ended', he insists that it is possible to clarify it further in terms of first, basic course-of-life needs, a minimal 'welfare principle' and secondly, 'a higher conception of need . . . that which is required if those "in need" are to reach a level of equal benefit'.[34]

Here an analogy may usefully be drawn with the similar two-tier classification offered by Albert Weale. Weale insists that there is a normative basis for the mandatory provision of a welfare minimum, premised upon the 'overriding imperative' of the principle of autonomy which requires 'that all persons are entitled to respect as deliberate and purposive agents capable of formulating their own projects, and that as part of this respect there is a governmental obligation to bring into being or preserve the conditions in which this autonomy can be realised'.[35] For Weale, the provision of this minimum, corresponding to Campbell's minimal 'welfare principle', is a binding obligation upon government. Further provision, to meet 'relative deprivation', in line with Campbell's 'higher conception of need', is seen to be guided largely by contractarian principles and falls legitimately within the contested terrain of democratic liberal politics. Campbell argues that the first (minimum) principle is already partially operative within existing welfare states; both principles would form the legitimate basis of right-generating interests under socialism. He goes on to insist that such an account of rights premised upon needs and interests can be seen to yield a compelling defence of 'traditional' civil and political rights, the 'new' economic and social rights and even of the notoriously problematic 'human' rights.

In fact, it is far from clear that Campbell's account, even when buttressed by Weale's parallel treatment, is actually able to deliver a *compelling* account of what socialist rights should be. Campbell himself recognizes that rights, interests and needs, which all play such a central role in his justificatory apparatus, are extremely elusive conceptions. His seeming acceptance that a right is conditional upon community support and endorsement – rights, as we saw, being premised upon 'the acceptance within a community that certain actions are or are not permitted or required' – may be well-founded but it is not categorically distinguishable from the much-circumscribed claims of positive rights. Yet, for its everyday users, rights' discourse is perceived to be so powerful precisely because a rights' claim is seen to be a claim that requires no prior or further justification. As such, Campbell's account may well be open to Hirst's (possibly unanswerable) criticism that eventually all opposing rights' claims are reducible to rival ontological presumptions, which cannot be discursively redeemed.

However, it may well be that the real strength of Campbell's position does not lie in his claim to *ground* an account of socialist rights, a claim which we have already seen to be subject to very serious reservations. Rather, its strength may lie in its outline of a suggested programme of rights appropriate under socialism and perhaps, above all, in the support that it lends to the claim that, whatever the perceived basis of rights, a *practice* of rights is indispensable given that it is impossible to conceive of a society, in other than almost wholly Utopian conditions, that is 'beyond the circumstances of rights'.

Defending a Practice of Rights

The breach that this concern with rights *as a practice* effects with a more orthodoxly Marxist position is still more pronounced in the work of E. P. Thompson. The parameters of his position, briefly alluded to in chapter 3, are quite clearly shaped by those historical studies in which he traces the development of the English working class as substantially a process of struggle for, and the gradual implementation of, a growing body of civil, political and social rights. Thompson's historical work is dotted with evidence of working-class or plebeian struggles taking the form of mobilization behind a variety of rights' claims, but the clearest general statement of this principle is to be found in his essay on 'The Secret State':

> In area after area, the 'common people' insisted that the civil rights of the 'freeborn Englishman' were not the privileges of an elite but were the common inheritance of all: freedom of press, speech and conscience, rights of assembly, inhibitions upon the actions of military or police against crowds, freedom from arbitrary imprisonment or unwarranted arrest and entry upon private premises. The insurgent British working class movement took over for its own the old Whiggish bloody-mindedness of the citizen in the face of the pretensions of power.[36]

The aspiration to an equality of citizenship, Thompson insists, represented 'a new way of reaching out by the working people for *social control* over their conditions of life and labour', and the civil liberties that underpinned this citizenship 'were wrested *from* authority and not granted by it, were greatly disliked by government and created intense difficulties'.[37] Under these circumstances, Thompson is profoundly critical of that Marxist orthodoxy which sees in civil liberties only the rights' basis of capitalism, that is the constitution of persons able to enter into free and equivalent exchange as commodity-owners. He attacks that highly schematic (and, as he sees it, 'structuralist') Marxism, for which 'the rule of law is only another mask for the rule of class' and for which the law is ('in the last instance') a superstructural expression of an essentially economic relation. He cites as a particularly telling (and imperilled) counter-example the maintenance of the jury system which, he argues, 'is not a product of "bourgeois democracy" (to which it owes nothing) but a stubbornly maintained democratic *practice*'. Indeed, he concludes that 'one way of reading our history is as an immensely protracted contest to subject the nation's rulers to the rule of law'.[38]

This approach reaches its apogee in the conclusion to *Whigs and Hunters*. Here, Thompson appears, at first, only to be endorsing 'the obvious point, which some modern Marxists have overlooked, that there is a difference between arbitrary power and the rule of law' and that 'law has not only been imposed *upon* man from above: it has also been a medium within which other social conflicts have been fought out.' Drawing upon the evidence of practices surrounding the introduction of the Black Act, (1723), Thompson argues that while the law was undoubtedly a highly effective instrument for the imposition of the interests of the ruling class, at the same time, 'the law mediated these class relations through legal forms, which imposed again and again, inhibitions upon the actions of the rulers.' The law itself became 'a genuine forum within which certain kinds of class conflict were fought out'. For Thompson, it is apparently a short distance from this claim that 'there is a very large difference . . .between arbitrary extra-legal power and the rule of law' to the claim that 'the notion of the rule of law is itself an unqualified good.' He concludes that 'to deny this good', as, he claims, does a broad spectrum of Marxist orthodoxy, 'is, in this dangerous century when the resources and pretensions of power continue to enlarge, a desperate error of intellectual abstraction'.[39]

There is undoubtedly much to commend Thompson's position. He is right to draw attention to 'the ambivalence within "the Left" towards civil liberties' and to isolate in this 'the most alarming evidence that the libertarian nerve has become dulled'. At a time when the radical right is claiming to itself a monopoly in the defence of freedom and autonomy and yet the coercive and surveillance arms of the state are being strengthened and traditional civil liberties, (for example, of free movement, of trial by jury, of membership of trades unions), are seemingly under increasing threat, the importance of Thompson's call is reinforced. Yet it is not clear, as Thompson supposes, that such a short distance separates the distinction 'between arbitrary extra-legal power and the rule of law' and the far more sweeping claim that the rule of law is itself 'an unqualified good'.[40] As Bob Fine very properly observes, 'the rule of law does not have to be an unqualified human good for its superiority over authoritarianism to be recognized and acted upon.'[41] Much depends both upon the way in which the rule of law is understood and, particularly, how extensive a principle it is held to be. Many socialists would resist the suggestion that the rule of law should constitute nothing more than the freedom of individuals to enter into legally binding contracts, and the government's role as overseeing and adjudicating these, especially where this is seen to be exhaustive of the proper premises of political association. Even Hunt, who is generally very supportive of Thompson's position, is critical of his 'surprisingly narrow view of the rule of law which equates it with adherence to procedural justice'.[42] Nor is it clear that the hostility to rights' discourse can be properly attributed to an Althusserian or structuralist Marxism – a criticism which Hirst dismisses as 'an illiterate jibe'[43] – for, in fact, the anticipation of a consociational society in which individuals mutually support and assist each other without the mediation of laws and injunctions, is a recurring socialist aspiration which long pre-dates Marx.

Furthermore, it is possible to perceive in Thompson's historical work a rather Whiggish account of a faltering and contested 'forward march of labour', subsumed under the banner of an extension of citizenship rights and the rule of law. Yet, Stuart Hall, for example, is insistent that the consequences of the extension of the rule of law have been much more ambivalent for the labour movement. He follows Thompson in arguing that 'the working-class movement must count the extension of the rule of law, the freedoms of speech and assembly, the right to strike and to organise in the work-place, as its own victories . . . won only as a consequence of more or less continuous struggle at key points and moments.'[44] Yet, 'while the substantial gains which working people have made from the enforcement of the "rule of law" and other legally sanctioned rights must not be overlooked', he argues that 'on the other side, we should not neglect what it performs – not necessarily in a concealed, but often in a perfectly open and "legitimate" way – in the long-term service of capital.'[45] He cites the ambivalent consequences of the legal protection of private property and contract, the securing of 'public order' and the interpellation of individuals and corporations as legal subjects. If the law is authentically 'an arena of (class) struggle' it is clearly one in which both victories and defeats are possible.

Marxism and the Rule of Law: Squaring the Circle

In his contribution to *Capitalism and the Rule of Law* and, much more substantively, in the later *Democracy and the Rule of Law*, Bob Fine attempts to reconcile the authentic insights of these several, often quite opposed, accounts into a comprehensive view of Marxism, rights and the rule of law. He criticizes Pashukanis *and* Thompson, (as well as Foucault, whose somewhat tangential contribution is not considered here), by comparing both unfavourably with a position derived from Marx. Fine bases his critique of Pashukanis upon the claim that while Marx derived the legal form from the relations of commodity production, Pashukanis derived the law from the form of commodity exchange. This, upon Fine's account, is 'the essence of their difference'.[46] It was to lead Pashukanis to give an overly abstract, generic and uniformly negative account of 'the legal form in general'. Abstracting exchange from production, he was unable to recognize, as Marx had done, that under differing social conditions the law might embrace a quite varying content. Thus, for example:

> While he learnt from Marx that equality before the law necessarily entails inequality in fact, he did not appear to learn either that equality

before the law provides a measure – albeit limited and formal, but not illusory – of equality, or that the inequalities which it entails are of an entirely different order depending on whether they derive from commodity, capitalist or socialist relations of production.[47]

It is a part of Fine's case that Marx did indeed see legal forms under these differing modes of production as being significantly different.

At the same time, Pashukanis' undifferentiated hostility to the law was matched by an unproblematic commitment to the possibility of enacting 'technical' social norms and regulations which could be purely administrative and which would not express relations of social control. This supposition – criticized so extensively since the publication of Braverman's *Labour and Monopoly Capital* – Fine attributes to Pashukanis' 'misunderstanding of Marx's category of the "technical division of labour"'. It was a mistake which was to sanction an unfettered state and bureaucracy, of which Pashukanis himself was eventually to fall the fatal victim.

In turning to Thompson's account of the rule of law, Fine, like Stuart Hall, is not unremittingly critical. Despite some reservations, he maintains that 'the general thrust of Thompson's critique of statist and nihilistic currents within Marxist theory of law and the state is . . . pertinent, correct and in accord with Marx's own writings.'[48] But he insists that in reducing the law 'to one essential function: that of inhibiting power', Thompson is himself guilty of that same essentialism which he had earlier exposed as a recurrent vice of an overly formal Marxism. He resists Thompson's claim that 'the determination of law by its economic base reflects not the essence of law but its distortion.'[49] Against this, Fine insists both that the rule of law mediates many relations other than the inhibition of centralized power – clearly it is, in part, itself a medium of the exercise of such centralized power – and that there are many popular forms of restraint upon state power other than the rule of law, among them parliamentary and industrial mobilization. Fine argues that in seeking to abstract the 'essence' of the law and in defining it as the means of exercising constraint over centralized power, Thompson has neglected the intrinsically contradictory aspects of the rule of law – both restrictive *and* enabling – and has failed to recognize the very considerable differences in the forms of law which, Fine suggests, can be seen to characterize differing modes of production. The most pronounced expression of this short-sightedness is seen to lie in Thompson's inability to recognize the possibility of moving beyond the rule of law by moving beyond the state.

Fine seeks to overcome the weaknesses of both Pashukanis and Thompson by arguing that both represent a regression from Marx's analysis of rights and the rule of law. In Marx's development of this analysis, through a critique of liberal jurisprudence, Fine identifies four stages. In the first stage, Marx adopted 'the liberal concept of the rational state as a synthesis of individual liberty and the universal will of the whole,' but he scrutinized critically the further liberal claim that this ideal was realized in the form of the existing state.[50] In the second stage, he went beyond this contrast between the ideal and the actual state, 'to reveal the limitations of mere political emancipation', arguing, as we saw in chapter 1, that purely political emancipation could never fulfil the aspiration for fully human emancipation. In the third stage, Marx again moved beyond the contrast of the rationality of the state and the irrationality of civil society to posit 'the alienated social character of the rational state itself'. At this juncture, Marx perceived that 'human emancipation required the withering away of the state and of law alongside that of private property.'[51]

The 'final stages' of Marx's position on the law were rather more diffuse. From these later writings, it is certainly possible to construe Marx as having believed that juridic forms are essentially an epiphenomenal expression of a determinant economic base. However, at the same time, Marx may also be seen to have held 'that capitalist relations of production express themselves at one and the same time through the juridic forms of private property, law and the state *and* the economic forms of value, price, money, capital, profit, and so on'. In this way, both juridic and economic forms were the expressions of certain material relations and, correspondingly, legal forms 'should not be conceived as mere masks concealing class relations but rather as real mediations'.[52] This recasting of the account of legal form enabled Marx to offer 'a more dialectical critique of the contradictions between juridic forms of freedom and equality and their class content in capitalist society than he had previously been able to do'. This was principally effected though his reconsideration of the category of private property, no longer viewed as an economic form determining particular juridic forms, but as, itself, the simplest juridic form. Correspondingly, 'the relation between private property and the law is not one between the economic and the juridic but a relation within the juridic sphere alone.'[53]

Crucially, for Fine's argument, this recasting of legal forms allows for the historical development of quite differing relations between private property, law and the state:

> Within the general context of capitalist productive relations, changing relations between labour and capital give rise to quite distinct forms of the state and distinct relationships between private property, the law, the

state executive and parliament. Further, in the socialist transition, new and more democratic forms of private property, law and state should emerge, leading eventually to their dissolution under communist relations of production.[54]

The advance effected by the later Marx was then to be able to reveal 'the inherently contradictory character of these [legal] forms'. In this way, he was able to combine 'a critique of the alien social content of private property with an appreciation of the real significance of its formal attributes'. He was able to show 'that while the freedom, equality and universality associated with wage labour are compatible with class subordination they are nonetheless material factors which give capitalism its emancipatory potential'.[55]

This allows Fine, in turn, to establish as Marx-derived his central contention that the form of state, law and private property differ decisively (and develop progressively) under differing modes of production. He insists that

> When Marx referred to the withering away of private property, law and the state, he had in mind not merely their abolition but also their replacement by *more* democracy and *more* individual liberty than is possible within their confines . . . For Marx, the withering away of juridic forms signified a process of democratization and extension of individual rights to the point of the dissolution of the juridic sphere in its entirety.[56]

In this, Fine has certainly outlined an interesting view of the possibility of changing relations of juridic forms under socialism. But it would seem to be clear that his is, in fact, a far more innovative position than he himself recognizes. While Fine's is a possible, and 'sympathetic' reading of Marx, it is very uncertain that Marx's own commitment to the expansion of autonomy can be properly comprehended under the forms of more formal and representative democracy, and particularly unclear that the extension of freedom could, for him, mean an expansion of rights.

Some weight is given to these doubts by the conclusions of the painstaking re-evaluation of Marx's view of rights and justice undertaken by Buchanan. Conceding that a less thoroughgoing reading of Marx's position than his own is possible, Buchanan argues that Marx is best seen as being committed to 'a very radical position on rights and justice'.[57] Upon this radical interpretation, Buchanan insists that:

> Marx thought of rights exclusively as boundary markers which separate

competing egoists in circumstances of avoidably severe scarcity, which absolve them of responsibility for each others' good, and which, through the coercive guarantees of the state, keep class conflict from erupting into outright war, while at the same time helping to preserve the dominant class's control over the means of production.[58]

He concludes that Marx apparently took these to be 'the defining functions of rights and hence that a conception of rights is needed only to cope with such egoistic conflict in class-divided societies'.[59]

This does not mean, Buchanan stresses, that Marx was not committed to an expansion of liberty and (what had under capitalism been only formal) freedoms. Rather does it suggest that Marx's understanding was that 'under communism the sources of conflict will be so diminished that there will be no need for a system of rights to *guarantee* the individual's freedom to enjoy his share of the social product or to *guarantee* him a share of control over the means of production.' It is, seemingly, in the expectation of abundance that 'Marx's materialism precludes any major explanatory role for juridical concepts.'[60]

Such an account is not easily reconciled with Fine's expectation of a changing and expanding body of legally guaranteed forms and practices. In fact, it appears to be much closer to the account arrived at in the opening chapter of this study, both analyses tending to suggest that Marx's account can only be made coherent by confining communism to 'circumstances beyond rights'. Upon such an account, Pashukanis may be read as an acutely one-sided and unilinear advocate of the Marxist position on rights but not as breaking with an essentially libertarian and rights-expansive Marxist tradition. By the same token, Fine's account of changing juridic forms should be seen as a sympathetic, but innovative contribution to the body of 'Marxist jurisprudence'.

Conclusion

Having outlined in Parts One and Two what I take to be the most significant generic weaknesses of the Marxist political tradition – in both its classical and contemporary forms – it has been the purpose of this and the previous chapter to offer an indication of some of the most important recent attempts to overcome these weaknesses through an eclectic confrontation of the most valued elements of the Marxist tradition with the most cherished claims of libertarian or liberal democratic theory.

The results must be said to be uneven. Certainly, much has been gained by opening up Marxist analyses to the insights of libertarian thought and by systematically criticizing the formulaic and essentialist rigidities of traditional Marxist analysis. Conversely, Marxist analysis continues to expose as pretty threadbare much of that ideological clothing with which liberal democracy shrouds many of its most unattractive features. But the marriage of Marxist and libertarian insights has proven to be much more difficult than many of its advocates may have anticipated. This became particularly clear in the discussion of recent attempts to promote socialist rights and a socialist rule of law. The experience of many of those theorists who have undertaken this synthesis has been that these duplex terms are extremely difficult to substantiate.

It is to a further consideration of these difficulties and attempts to overcome them, in the broadest context of the strengths and limitations of Marxist political analysis, that I turn in the concluding chapter.

8
In Defence of Socialist Politics

At the outset of this study, I suggested that the closest contemporary political analysis is likely to come to an axiomatic claim is in the widespread recognition that we face a more or less general crisis in the explanatory powers of conventional Western political theory. I argued that Marxist political theory, though once promoted as a means of escape, has increasingly been seen to be deeply implicated in this general impasse and that this 'crisis of Marxism' has, if anything, become still more acute in the wake of recent developments in advanced capitalism. Although the evidence of this study supports the claim that both Marxism, and perhaps Western political theory more generally, do indeed face some sort of crisis, its early chapters indicate that, so far as Marxist political thought is concerned, this is neither new, nor should it be unexpected. Rather than this crisis being brought on, as is sometimes suggested, by changes in late capitalist societies – political dealignment, the 'marginalization' of the traditional working class, changing patterns of state intervention or whatever – I have suggested that the roots of the Marxist incapacity adequately to comprehend political processes must, in fact, be sought in the theoretical writings of 'classical' Marxism. Rather than retrace the historical evolution of these theoretical weaknesses, often tempered in practice by an acute awareness of political actualities, I want here to abstract from this historical account an 'ideal typical' model of what may be seen to be the most important generic weaknesses of this 'classical' Marxist political analysis.

1 Historicism

Historicism – as confidence in immanent if tendential laws of historical development – is extraordinarily deep-seated in Marxist theory. From the neo-Hegelian anticipation of 'True Democracy' as 'the first true unity of the particular and the universal' to the overcoming of the cumulative self-obstruction of productive forces under developed capitalism through the socialization of ownership, the expectation that continued development favours progressive social forces with an interest in socialism is a ubiquitous Marxist claim. Marx's own sensitivity to the interdependence of theory and practice and Luxemburg's seemingly open-ended anticipation of either 'socialism or barbarism' notwithstanding, the Marxist tradition has been preponderantly committed to the evolutionist expectation that historical development favours progress towards socialism. In certain forms, it has also carried the much more radical claim that historical development, albeit in passing through a period of greatly intensified social struggle, can carry society into circumstances where formal political institutions – the state, political parties, representation, rights' claims and so on – will become obsolete. With hindsight, such evolutionary optimism – best seen in Marx's anticipation of 'True Democracy' as the realization of 'fully human emancipation' – can be seen to be misplaced and even pernicious.

To challenge this evolutionary historicism is not, of course, to deny – as Marx, among many others, was correct in observing – that the historical changes associated with the rise of capitalism and the industrial revolution favour the emergence of an organized labour movement, mobilizing a newly emergent working class in pursuit of a socialist ideology. Nor should 'the poverty of historicism' be seen to lie principally in the supposed 'irrefutablity' of Marx's social theory or its faith in 'predicting the future'. The point is rather that posed most starkly and simply by Gorz, namely that there is 'no point in . . . seeking to identify with laws immanent in historical development'.[1]

A second and ironic weakness of Marxist historicism lies in its tendency to suppress history. For the Marxist conception of history, conceived as the realization of an immanent purpose, is very difficult to reconcile with the history we recognize as 'happenstance', as an accumulation of non-determined, often unintended and frequently contested institutions, practices and events. Any more compelling account is correspondingly obliged to abandon the belief that socialism and/or communism constitute the innate and already given purpose of historical development, and to recognize them as, at best, an historical project or, more properly, projects carried out under circumstances which historical development makes more or less propitious. Above all, socialism cannot be seen as the end-point of humanity's pre-history.

2 The 'derivation' of the political

A second pervasive characteristic of Marxist analysis has been its tendency to seek to 'derive' political institutions and practices from other aspects of a materialist analysis. This was particularly clear in Marxist accounts of the state. Here the point is not to deny the interdependence of state and economy or, more broadly conceived, of state and society but rather to challenge the claim that the nature of this state can be derived from, for example, the 'irreconcilability of class contradictions' or 'the capital form'. For such a claim necessarily entails the subordination of political (and ideological) struggle to economic forms and a sublimation of struggles around differing political axes to struggles based upon class. The consequence of this Marxist position seems to be that (all) politics is, in some sense, class politics. Other forms of struggle – over such issues as gender, race and the environment – are allowed some autonomy, but all are seen, in a more or less explicit 'last instance', to be subordinated to the principal lines of political cleavage defined around social class. The consequences of this attempt to derive all political struggle from class become still more acute where class is itself characterized in an acutely derivative form, as in its definition around formal ownership or non-ownership of the means of production. Some of the most damaging consequences of this highly formalized conception of class politics are posited, in rather bold colours, in A. J. Polan's *Lenin and the End of Politics*, but, in fact, its consequences are quite as debilitating for the Kautskyan tradition of Marxism, whose politics is so heavily reliant upon socialist transformation through the development of a preponderant working class.

In her critical work on *Class and Civil Society*, Jean Cohen traces these weaknesses back to Marx, particularly to 'the base/superstructure model' in which 'state, law and ideology are conceived as *determined* ("in the last instance") by the mode of production.' Such a model, she argues, mistakenly implies 'that political power and domination represent something else: the economic power of the bourgeoisie'.[2] Nor is she alone in arguing that later Marxist accounts of the state have obscured rather than overcome this mechanistic determination. Hindess, for example, insists that the recently popular advocacy of the 'relative autonomy' of the political and 'determination in the last instance' of the economic 'are gestural evasions of a problem that cannot be resolved'. There is, he argues, 'no coherent way in which political life can be conceived as different from and irreducible to the economy and the distribution of the population into classes on the one hand and in which the economy is conceived as playing the ultimately determining role on the other'.[3]

The principal charge against this Marxist determinism, as we have seen, is that it denies the very space in which an authentically non-determined and discursive politics could arise.

3 Essentialism

A third generic weakness of Marxist appraisals of the political may be seen to lie in the tendency to treat political institutions and practices as essences rather than as capacities. Here, Leninism has perhaps been the chief offender. In its formulaic insistence that, for example, every state represents the unmediated rule of a single class or that democracy necessarily mobilizes the dictatorship of a particular class, state and democracy are seen to have essential and categorical qualities. This both draws attention away from the contingent, historical and contestable elements *within* given states and democratic practices and promotes strategies for socialist transformation which are themselves essentialist – 'smashing the state', displacement of 'bourgeois democracy' by 'proletarian democracy' – the severe consequences of which were extensively considered in the opening chapters. Also damaging is the widespread Marxist conception that the (capitalist) state necessarily acts in the interests of the ascendant (capitalist) class, whether in a crudely instrumental sense, (as 'the tool of the ruling class'), or in that more elaborate form which recognizes internal divisions of the state, but only as the expression of the divided interests of particular fractions of capital. More damaging still is the expectation that the state, as an expression of the irreconcilable contradictions inscribed in the existence of classes, can be overcome or 'wither away' where these contradictions founded upon *class* cease to operate.

But such essentialism cannot properly be seen to be confined to the Leninist reading of Marx. For that same essentialism which leads Leninists to underestimate the possibilities inherent in the parliamentary institutions of 'bourgeois democracy', leads the heirs of Kautsky to overestimate the plausibility of a straightforward parliamentary transition to socialism. For the latter tend to depict parliament as both an expression of, and means of articulating, the 'real' balance of social forces within a given society and as a means of exercising effective control over the entire apparatus of the state.

4 Holism

A fourth critical weakness of Marxist political analysis resides in its thoroughgoing commitment to holistic modes of social explanation. Here again, my intention is not to deny the very considerable value of such forms of explanation, nor to deny that the application of Marxist methods has often effected a very considerable advance upon traditional institutional, constitutional and liberal pluralist accounts of the political. But though the reasons for Marxism's seeking society-wide or even world-wide explanations is clear, it is no less evident that not all forms of significant political struggle can best be understood in this context. This is true not only of inter-state struggles, which are massively evident but rather poorly explained within conventional Marxist analyses, but also of (conceptually) localized disputes within societies – which may not have a national or class-based significance – but which are nonetheless important sites of the struggle to secure autonomy. The possibility this raises of socialist pluralism – as anything other than the rather fanciful 'disappearance' of significant political disputes under communism – is very poorly conceptualized by a Marxism overwhelmingly committed to holistic patterns of social explanation.

Revolution With and Against *Capital?*

Such a summary account of the weaknesses of Marxist political analysis may itself be too categorical. Yet the contrasting experiences of 'the left' in Sweden and Italy, which I discussed in Part Two, afford ample evidence of the several difficulties faced by those seeking to develop an effective transformative political strategy for advanced capitalist societies from within the parameters of the 'classical' Marxist framework.

The intellectual origins of the Italian project are very properly seen to lie in the writings of Antonio Gramsci. Although, by force of notorious circumstance, Gramsci's own contribution was substantially theoretical, his was a practico-critical theory oriented around an immediate intervention in the particular and peculiar circumstances of contemporary Italian society. In the period after 1920, it is clear that his thinking differed in several decisive respects from the mainstream of the 'classical' Marxist tradition. Thus, he broke not only with the formalism and immobilism of the Second International but also, (the contentious issue of his attitude to the Leninist party notwithstanding), with the Bolshevik insurrectionary strategy of 1917. At the heart of Gramsci's critique was the insistence that the Marxism of neither the Second nor the Third International was able to comprehend, and thereby effectively to confront, the particular nature of bourgeois rule in Western Europe. Such a comprehension, upon the Gramscian account, was impossible without a reconsideration of many of the axiomatic claims of previous Marxist political theory and, in particular, a reformulation of the nature of, and the relation between, the state and civil society. The mechanistic reduction of the state to the organized means of exercising violence and of civil society to the *bellum omnia contra omnes* of a market society was rejected in favour of an account which, for all its considerable internal variation, sought consistently to show that, in Western Europe at least, bourgeois rule was not simply sustained through the coercive and repressive apparatuses of the state but, in fact, through a variety of institutions and practices inscribed in both the enlarged/integral state and civil society. Any oppositional strategy for the West had correspondingly to take full account of these distinctive structural features and it was indeed this relationship between state and civil society which underpinned Gramsci's own advocacy of class alliances, differing roads to socialism and revolution in the West as an attritional struggle for (civil) hegemony. To continue, under these changed circumstances, to pursue unamended the political project of either the Second or the Third International, would be to court either total immobilism or abject defeat.

Much of the rest of that chapter was devoted to a consideration of the way in which these Gramscian initiatives were subsequently subject to a very particular (and partial) reading in the PCI's evolution of its *'terza via'*. Throughout this period, we saw that the practice of the PCI was ever more firmly defined as lying within the pale of the existing constitution and that increasingly socialist revolution was de-emphasized in favour of 'structural reforms' carried out under a 'progressive democracy'. Many commentators argued that while there were indeed very good grounds for breaking with the Marxism of the Second and Third Internationals as sources for political practice in contemporary Western Europe, there were similarly good grounds for suggesting that the PCI, in its advocacy of Eurocommunism, far from offering a radical and distinctive 'third way' had settled back into something very close to the Bernsteinian (and statist) social democracy of the Second International. Some argued that this 'lapse' could be overcome through a strategic return to 'the authentic Gramsci'. My own conclusion was that the recent PCI strategies of the Historic Compromise and the Democratic Alternative were to be understood less as 'a betrayal of Marxism' than as an (albeit unsatisfactory) response to the position of the PCI as a mass-based communist party in an advanced capitalist society. Whatever the inadequacies of the post-Gramscian leadership of the PCI – and it is far from clear that the party has been particularly poorly served in this respect – the failures of Eurocommunist strategy seem to be as much attributable to the weaknesses of Marxist theory as to the lack of revolutionary fervour among the party's leaders.

In the chapter that followed, I went on to consider the contrasting and complementary transitional strategy advocated by some on the left of Swedish social democracy. It was of particular interest that such an initiative should have been generated by Swedish experience. For long, Sweden has been regarded as being in the van of European social democracy while, at the same time, serving as a model for its right wing. Yet recent years have seen, for whatever reasons, a seeming breakdown of the consensus upon which Sweden's 'historic comprom- ise' has been based and it is in this context that the new strategic initiatives of the left have flourished.

It was clear that the Swedish social democratic left's model for transition to socialism could be summarily characterized as 'a revolu- tion *with "Capital"*'. If not quite, as Stephens supposes, 'a brilliant solution to the political and tactical problems of social democracy', Meidner's wage-earners' funds proposals were certainly innovative and proffered an ingenious solution to some of the perennial difficulties presented by an insurrectionary politics, (for example, problems of capital flight, international financial destabilization and unacceptable disruption to the national economy). But they were still proposals which were to form part of an overall strategy which was premised upon the expectations for capitalist development which had been classically developed in *Capital*.

As such, this strategy showed many of those weaknesses which I had sought to isolate in a political practice based upon the 'classical' Marxism of *Capital*. It was noted that the Swedish social democratic strategy was largely silent on the issue of *political* struggle as an active and non-determined sphere of contested claims rather than as an immanent expression of already posited economic interests. Despite its own account of the circumstances under which Sweden's 'historic compromise' began to break up, under the pressure of shop-floor grievances and the disutilities of nationally negotiated trades union- employer bargains, this recent strategy was also noticeably weak in its perception of struggle *at the point of production*. This neglect was in the face of the plethora of studies of the politics of the labour process that have followed upon Braverman's *Labour and Monopoly Capital*.

It was further suggested that the left social democratic strategy was overly reliant upon a 'classical' Marxist account of class which was increasingly inadequate to the changing circumstances of advanced capitalism. Thus, accounts of advancing proletarianization, upon which the expectation of a wage-earners' preponderance were premised, were seen to neglect both divisions among the category of wage-earners and the growing numbers who fall outside the productive categories of wage labour and capital within all the major advanced capitalist societies. This increasingly sectional emphasis upon the economically productive classes, tended to underpin a further difficulty in the Social Democrats' perception of contemporary political prospects, that is a failure satisfactorily to embrace those political interests that are wholly or partially defined outside the sphere of class politics. Of course, it would be wrong to accuse them of a total neglect of the politics of the new social movements, but it remains the case that theirs is a strategy for transition which is rooted in the circumstances of continued (productive) capitalist development. Yet it is clear that among several of the new social movements, and commanding considerable (electoral and other) support, is political mobilization around just these contested issues of continued economic development. The same productivist logic can be seen to underlie the evidently overly sanguine view of the way in which capital would react (passively) to the process of gradual expropriation which the wage-earners' funds would set in motion.

It is, of course, difficult to judge how successful this transformative strategy advocated on the left of Swedish social democracy will or, more properly, would prove to be. It seems unlikely that, in the near future, we shall see an implementation of a 'full-blooded' version of Meidner's wage-earners' funds proposals and we should expect resistance to any such initiative to be severe. But if the summary account of this position in chapter 5 does not wholly distort its content and intent, it is possible to identify within it a number of the very same difficulties that have earlier been seen to vitiate the Kautskyan strategy for socialist transformation. As we have seen, the Kautskyan heritage, once widely vilified and now rehabilitated, is far from unambiguous. However, it could clearly be seen, precisely through its adherence to a deterministic variant of Marx's expectation of capitalist development, to offer a mechanistic anticipation of socialist transformation that very largely sublimated the extraordinarily fierce political struggles without which it is difficult to imagine that such a revolutionary transformation could possibly be undertaken.

Both the SAP and the PCI are the firmly entrenched representatives of well-established labour movements. Yet, on the evidence of chapters 4 and 5, neither party's theorists can properly be said to have generated a compelling radical and transformative politics for the circumstances of advanced capitalism. This weakness is hardly to be uniquely attributed to their (anyway much disputed) unwillingness to break with the parameters of 'classical' Marxism. The experience of the massed ranks of more traditional social democracy is sufficient evidence, were such needed, that breaking with 'classical' Marxism is anything but a guarantee of political radicalism. However, I would argue, in the face of those Marxist accounts which attribute 'de-radicalization' to an abandonment of the 'essentials' of Marxist explanation, that it is as much what these theorists have retained of 'classical' Marxism, as that which they have abandoned, that vitiates their strategies for the transformation of advanced capitalism. Indeed, in the light of the three opening chapters of this study, I would conclude that the difficulties of contemporary Marxist political advocacy are but an expression of the more general incapacity of Marxism, in anything like its 'classical' form, to proffer a compelling account of the political. This is not, of course, to argue that the force of Marxism as a critique of existing political institutions and practices is exhausted, nor to suggest that political arrangements under a Marxist rubric must necessarily prove to be oppressive. It is however to insist that as the source for a radical and transformative political practice under advanced capitalism, even under what may seem to be, politically and intellectually, the most propitious circumstances, (in Sweden and Italy), Marxism has failed to deliver.

If it is clear that these strategic weaknesses can only be exacerbated by a return to a more orthodox Marxist position, it is just as evident that they cannot be overcome by a more enthusiastic embracing of the prevailing practices of social democracy. Indeed, both the PCI's *'terza via'* and the wage-earners' funds initiative of the Swedish Social Democratic left are already vulnerable to the claim that, for all their innovation, theirs are strategies which are little more than variants of (an historically discredited) social democracy. Thus, it might well be said of the left wing of Swedish social democracy, as does Middlemas of the PCI in its advocacy of the *'terza via'*, that the only fruit of its attempt 'to bridge the ancient gap between the Second and Third Internationals' has been its inheritance of '"the crisis of social democracy"'.[4] The Swedish and Italian experience offers telling evidence both of the acute difficulties of overcoming the social democracy-Leninism divide from within even a very broadly conceived Marxist framework and of the extent to which, under contemporary circumstances, the 'crisis of Marxism' can be seen to elide with 'the crisis of social democracy'.

I concluded the opening two thirds of the book by insisting that this crisis in the analytic and strategic powers of the Marxist political tradition, allied to the simultaneous crisis of social democracy and difficulties within the liberal democratic tradition, required a substantial recasting of democratic socialist theory. Correspondingly, in chapter 6, I turned to a critical consideration of some of the most important recent initiatives in this direction. Of course, these more recent accounts have not been conjured out of the air and they show a varying proximity to the major existing strains of socialist (political) discourse. Repeatedly and unsurprisingly, given his sensitivity to the particular difficulties of effecting a socialist strategy within advanced capitalist societies, Gramscian themes are to the fore. This was particularly clear in the work of the later Poulantzas, whose hostility to 'Leninist formalism' was complemented by an emphasis upon the centrality of struggles *within* the state. Hostility to formulaic rubric on the state, recognition of its enabling and emancipatory, as well as its repressive, moments, insistence upon the ubiquity of struggles within and about the state, the necessity of state institutions under socialism and a call for the careful study of particular state formations rather than the generic derivation of *the* form of *the* capitalist state, are perhaps the most prominent claims of this 'post-Marxist' initiative. What was also clear, particularly from Claus Offe's contribution, was that this is not only a crisis of the ways in which the state is understood (principally by neo-Marxist theorists) but also a crisis of the state form itself, a crisis of the welfare state as the characteristic form of the state under social democracy.

This reassessment of the state dictated, in its turn, a differing evaluation of the other term of the state-civil society relation. If the state was not the undivided and indivisible representative of the interests of a single class, if it had an emancipatory as well as a repressive potential and if, above all, it would not and could not 'wither away' under socialism, it was clear that the traditional Marxist understanding of civil society, exhaustively defined by the *bellum omnia contra omnes* of a market society, would have to be substantially amended. First and foremost, the belief that political alienation originates in the division of state and civil society had to be abandoned, and the aspiration to 'overcome' political differences through establishing the identity of state and civil society vigorously resisted as both Utopian and extremely dangerous. Although the state is regarded as irreversible, and this not simply as a necessary but wholly undesirable evil, it is also seen to embody chronic pretensions to exercise ever greater power, and the surest means of holding its powers in check is seen to lie in a vigorous, independent and legally guaranteed civil society.

This independent civil society cannot however be seen to be conterminous with the civil society of 'classical' Marxist theory. For it is not a sphere exclusively occupied by classes nor could the forms of struggle that of necessity traverse it be exclusively defined by differences of class interest. It is constantly stressed by 'post-Marxist' writers that the basis of a radical and socialist civil society should be a diversity of struggles prosecuted by a variety of overlapping but distinct popular groupings and alliances. At the heart of this advocacy of a reconstituted civil society lies the substantively unorthodox aspiration for a socialist pluralism.

In John Keane's work, this pursuit of 'a socialist and pluralist civil society' was seen to require the weakening of both public and private bureaucracies in favour of 'the establishment and strengthening of spheres of autonomous public life'. This entailed, in its turn, a reassessment of the 'classical' Marxist understanding of democracy. While this re-evaluation was subject to a good deal of internal variation, there was a more or less universal recognition that the Marxist aspiration to a 'True' or substantive democracy was impossible *and* undesirable and that existing (and inadequate) democratic practices were something to be retained and expanded upon wherever possible, rather than to be razed and replaced. Pluralism, not only of parties but also of ideologies and 'ways of life', was seen to be an indispensable feature of any satisfactory democratic polity.

Interesting as they were, the innovations that were discussed in chapter 6 were self-admittedly programmatic, if not openly speculative. In chapter 7, I addressed some of the difficulties that were faced in trying to give substance to these largely theoretical innovations. From this, it was clear that the process of 'fleshing out' these theoretical initiatives – here in respect of socialist accounts of rights and the rule of law – presented very considerable difficulties. Summarily, these could be seen to be of two kinds. First, there were the problems entailed in grafting traditionally liberal or libertarian principles onto (even a quite radically reconstituted) Marxist account of politics. 'Classical' Marxism, inasmuch as Pashukanis could be said to be its authentic interpreter, we saw to be violently hostile to any advocacy of rights and the rule of law, while those recent commentators who were more supportive of socialist rights and a socialist rule of law, such as Campbell and Thompson, had considerable difficulty in making their accounts theoretically and discursively compelling. Fine's own interesting and carefully argued position was seen to rely upon a distinctive and 'creative' reading of Marx. It became increasingly clear that to effect the kinds of radical changes that the advocates of chapter 6 had recommended might require a much more wholesale break with Marxism than many of their interventions had at first suggested. At the same time, this 'settling of accounts' with Marxism must be seen to have its 'debits' as well as its 'credits'. Breaking with Marxism clearly means losing much of its theoretical and practical vigour, and this cannot be straightforwardly appropriated by simply taking up what is found to be 'good' in Marxism, while exorcizing that which is 'bad'.

A second set of difficulties, less developed in this study but quite as problematic as the first, surround those very libertarian and liberal-democratic principles that contemporary socialist theorists have sought to appropriate. This is quite plainly the case with traditional liberal notions of rights which, no less than Campbell's advocacy of socialist rights, are vulnerable to Hirst's and Macintyre's insistence that competing rights' claims are, in essence, but the expression of irreducible and opposing ontological beliefs. But it is also a difficulty with, for example, the (indispensably) coercive elements of what is held to be an essentially libertarian conception of the rule of law, a problem which makes it difficult unreservedly to endorse Thompson's advocacy of the rule of law as 'an unqualified good'. Overall, the unsettling evidence of chapter 7 suggested that if a defendable democratic socialist theory must of necessity be eclectic, it cannot simply be reconstructed from a 'scissors and paste' amalgam of unreformed elements of the existing liberal and Marxist traditions.

'Public Spheres'

One interesting and innovative response to the multiple difficulties presented by the dual crisis of both Marxist and liberal political analysis is to be found in the attempt critically to appropriate and restructure the classical liberal principle of *the public sphere*. Here, the definitive source is Jürgen Habermas. Upon his account, the 'classical' public sphere, as the means of mediating relations between society and the state, was characterized by a set of institutions which guaranteed equal access of all citizens to a critical and discursive process in which public authority and political decision-making were to be subject to the rational scrutiny of a 'reasoning public'.[5] In practice, the ascendancy of such discursive public debate, 'both critical in intent and institutionally guaranteed', was seen to be historically confined to the period of the early development of a commercial society and 'the public' it embraced to a tiny elite. In practice, it was limited to the educated, male and property-owning readers and correspondents of what is presented as an essentially discursive, learned, practical and open-minded press. Indeed, the expansion of the public realm, through the emergence of forms of working class organization and the contemporaneous rise of commercial journalism, heralded the beginning of the end for the ascendancy of this classical model of the public sphere. Increasingly, through the nineteenth century, Habermas insists, politics can be seen to be based less upon this discursively formed, educated and rational public opinion, than upon 'the compromise of conflicting private interests' or the 'pressure of the street'.

Under contemporary 'social welfare state mass democracy', these tendencies become acute. With the growth of large-scale public and private bureaucracies, and the development of mass parties, the distinction between the public and the private becomes increasingly unclear. Under this 'interweaving of the public and private realm, not only do the political authorities assume certain functions in the sphere of commodity exchange and social labour, but conversely social powers now assume political functions'. Anticipating certain later analyses of corporatism, Habermas argues that this leads to 'a kind of "re-feudaliza- tion" of the public sphere' in which 'large organizations strive for compromises with the state and with each other, excluding the public sphere wherever possible'. Increasingly, the genuinely discursive will-formation of an authentic and critical public opinion is abandoned in favour of the manipulative strategies of 'publicity' and 'public relations'.[6] There are, Habermas insists, countervailing tendencies within the social welfare state, principally through 'the extension of fundamental rights', which affords the possibility that 'a public body of organized private individuals' could displace 'the now-defunct body of private individuals who relate individually to each other'. However, it remains the case, so Habermas argues in *Towards a Rational Society*, that:

> The depoliticization of the mass of the population and the decline of the public realm as a political institution are components of a system of domination that tends to exclude practical questions from public discussion. The bureaucratized exercise of power has its counterpart in *a public realm confined to spectacles and acclamation.*[7] (My emphasis)

Accordingly, he insists that the public sphere:

> Could only be realized today on an altered basis, as a rational reorganization of social and political power under the mutual control of rival organizations committed to the public sphere in their internal structure as well as in their relations with the state and each other.[8]

However uncertain we may be that the political processes of early commercial societies ever aspired in practice to the rational and discursive principles that Habermas outlines, this advocacy of the public sphere does have certain advantages over the often quite unclear call for 'a restitution of civil society'. Most immediately, it can be seen to give proper prominence to the 'epoch-making' importance of the securing of the public sphere, a development which, so Giddens argues, represents 'as fundamental a disjunction in history as the commodifica- tion of labour and property to which Marx showed it to be intimately related'.[9] At the same time, it makes it possible to recognize the lasting importance of the advances secured in the classic bourgeois political revolutions of the eighteenth century, without having to endorse either the claim that such gains can only be defended through the untramelled possession and exchange of private property, or the belief that they can only be fully realized through a recoalescence of public and private life. In this way, the public sphere may be seen to provide the basis for a critique of both Hayekian liberal democracy and Schumpterian social democracy, without endorsing the anti-modernism of Marx's 'seamless democracy'.

Again, in contrast to the more general advocacy of civil society, quite properly justified in terms of the need to counterbalance the overweening aspiration to power of the modern state, it is a strength of Habermas's analysis that it offers a specific, if somewhat formal, *historical* account of how and why the public sphere should have become imperilled under late capitalism. As importantly, Habermas's critique of organized capitalism, and its appeal to oppositional forces, is not definitively confined to, though it is extensively reliant upon, appeals to class and (organized and disorganized) labour. Articulation of the public sphere is seen also to be dependent upon the mobilization of a plurality of citizens and of citizens' initiatives in the face of the demobilization and de-politicization of their interests, and the idea of discursive political will-formation clearly precludes the identity of all oppositional interests and the assumption that there are pre-given (and majoritarian) coalitions that have only to shake off their false consciousness to disclose their 'true' unity of purpose. Indeed, the possibility of popular mobilization within the public sphere is itself to be discursively secured, raising the possibility of an indefinite number of particular public spheres and mobilizing a vast plurality of possibly quite keenly competing particular interests within the overall context of *the* public sphere. Such an account necessarily places an enormous weight upon the practices through which non-determined political strategies may be negotiated and redirects attention towards the kinds of institutional arrangements which the public sphere would prescribe, an area in which this kind of theorizing has traditionally been notoriously weak.

Yet, for all its considerable strengths, Habermas's account of the public sphere can hardly be said to have resolved the problem of an elision of 'authentic' liberal and Marxist insights. His justification of the principle of the public sphere and his expansive category of public opinion, for example, are heavily reliant upon his understanding of communicative competence and the ideal speech situation as providing the framework for the necessary background consensus upon which understanding rests, and these positions have themselves been extensively and effectively criticized.[10] Still more serious are those organizational and institutional questions which the advocacy of a socialist public sphere raises and yet which cannot be resolved in the manner ordained for the classically bourgeois public sphere. For of the essence of recent advocacy of a socialist public sphere is the insistence upon the citizen's legally guaranteed independence of the state and the call for some means of accommodating or reconciling those competing interests that are seen necessarily and legitimately to arise from within the public sphere. In classical bourgeois political theory these guarantees are afforded by the possession of private property and competing interests are mediated by the mechanisms of either the economic market-place (Adam Smith and classical political economy) or the political market-place, (Schumpeter, Downs).[11] These forms of guarantee and mediation are clearly unavailable to the advocates of a socialist public sphere, even those who will allow some circumscribed space to the market. Quite clearly this must raise the question of how the desired division between state and civil society is to be guaranteed and of how this is to be reconciled with the valued 'enabling' powers of the state. It also raises the issue of the sorts of sanctions that are to support the autonomy of citizens and of how their capacity to act independently is to be secured against the intervention of the host state or indeed of other states in the context of an international order of unequal nation states.

Similar difficulties surround the question of 'the organization of enlightenment' – parties, institutions and strategies – which is bound to present recurrent difficulties for any politics built upon the advocacy of the public sphere. Open to a variety of small-scale political pro-grammes, to a plurality of social and political aspirations, embracing a variety of large and small single-issue campaigns and massive cross-cutting political interests, it is quite unclear how systemic change could be promoted. If, as is widely supposed, there exists the potential for an 'alliance for enlightenment', how might that uniformity of interest be articulated? On the strategic issue of how the social and political goods that the socialist public sphere is to secure are to be delivered, Habermas's position looks extremely uninformative.

Despite these reservations, an abiding strength of Habermas's analysis is that it focuses attention upon processes of 'depoliticization', that is upon the ways in which politics as a process of discursive will-formation or, more prosaically, active decision-making is, both practically and theoretically, 'bracketed out' of contemporary political life. Perhaps the most pronounced variant of this 'depoliticization' is to be found, or so its opponents insist, in the characteristic practices of social democracy. Critics to both right and left tend to agree in characterizing social democracy as paternalistic and/or managerialist, reducing politics for the great mass of the population to the largely passive routine of 'spectacles and acclamation'. But whatever the justice of this claim against social democracy, I want here to consider 'depoliticization' as a context for examining the respective claims of liberal and Marxist political theory and for assessing the general prognosis for democratic socialist politics.

Liberalism and 'Depoliticization'

One of the great strengths of 'classical' Marxism lies in its critique of what, following Crenson, we may call the 'un-politics' of liberalism. This critique, definitively expressed in Marx's typification of the sphere of commodity production as the 'exclusive realm of Freedom, Equality, Property and Bentham', was focused upon liberal typifications of freedom, equality and dessert, and upon favoured liberal precepts, such as parliamentary sovereignty, the neutrality of the state and the rule of law. Above all, was it concentrated upon the liberal's anticipated division of political and economic life. Here, I concentrate upon traditional criticisms of two areas of liberal theory that have been extensively considered in this study – initiatives in favour of civil society and pluralism.

Generally among socialist commentators, the constitution of a separate civil society is seen to be associated with the *bellum omnia contra omnes* of an emergent market economy, with the reduction of human individuals to acquisitive and predatory egoists constrained only by the rule of law and the reduction of all forms of human interrelation to contractual relations backed by the sanctions of the law. Associative and affective relations are seen to be devalued in a system which gives very substantial means to the wealthy and strong to oppress the poor and the weak. Above all, it does violence to the principle of fraternity. The compelling strength of the specifically Marxist account, exhaustively developed in *Capital*, is that civil society defines that realm of authentic though purely formal freedom which is the necessary basis of substantive unfreedom and inequality. The process of free and equal exchange is seen to be the means by which the bourgeoisie expropriates the surplus value of the working class. The relations pertaining within civil society are seen to be systematically exploitative, if not unjust, and to be guaranteed by the untramelled claims of private property.[12] Thus capitalist society is condemned not simply because it does violence to the values of fraternity and solidarity, nor yet because it promotes vast inequalities of wealth and resources, but, above all, because it denies and conceals the exercise of power that apparently free and equal contractual exchanges necessarily enjoins.

Similar criticisms underpin traditional Marxist hostility to pluralism. At its most uncompromising, Marxism holds that the advent of socialism precludes pluralism as both unnecessary – given the actual and moral superiority of socialist principles over others – and impossible – given the incompatibility of socialism with the characteristic principles of liberalism and/or capitalism. This 'classical' Marxist position is not premised upon the suppression of a genuine plurality of interests, (other than, in the immediate revolutionary period, the interests of the tiny minority of the exploiting bourgeoisie), for it is argued that it is, in fact, possible to establish *objectively* the interests of the several social classes, and that those of the (massively predominant) proletariat accord with the transition to socialism. That sections of the working class should perceive themselves as having an interest in an other than socialist organization of production is attributable to a false and manipulated consciousness, lack of education and 'historical residues' and cannot be seen to be consonant with their *true* interests.

In this form, I should argue, the Marxist critique has a very limited purchase on the parameters of liberal pluralism. More telling is that second and less wholesale critique which is directed less against the principle of plurality than against the 'misleading' claims of liberal or liberal-capitalist pluralism. Here, the definitive 'classical' source is Marx's mature critique of political economy. We have seen how the formal plurality of free and equal individuals simultaneously provided the basis for, and a 'masking' of, those processes through which capitalism secures substantive inequality and unfreedom. It was the 'freeing' of individuals to pursue unfettered their several interests as the buyers and sellers of commodities (including labour power) that distinguished the inequities of capitalism from its feudal forerunner. In its turn, it is this formal plurality within the capitalist economy which effectively denies substantive pluralism to the great majority of its participants, who find themselves increasingly driven from a variety of modes of life towards a uniformly routinized and meaningless working life under the advanced division of labour.

Similar criticisms have been widely mobilized against much more recent advocates of pluralism. Those like Dahl, Truman and Lipset, who promoted the United States of the 1950s and 1960s as a model of pluralist democracy, have been subsequently, and deservedly, criticized for presenting an overly sanguine view of the representation of a plurality of interests in the United States, neglecting or excusing the way in which the American model of pluralism systematically favours big business and other organized corporate interests.[13] Such manifestations, it is argued, are the inevitable result of an advocacy of pluralism that fails to investigate those societal conditions that will always enable formal equality of access and representation to favour particular, and often numerically small, interests.

Recently, more critical pluralists, such as Charles Lindblom, have begun to take much fuller account of the distorting effect of the disproportionate powers of corporate interests upon pluralist political arrangements and this is one source of an apparent convergence of critical pluralist and critical Marxist positions. But even this more critical pluralism has found it difficult to resolve the *institutional* problems that such disproportionality poses and certainly the Marxist disclosure of the inequity of existing pluralist arrangements is a continuing challenge to any attempt to reconstitute a 'socialist and pluralist civil society'.[14]

Marxism and 'Depoliticization'

At the same time, it is imperative to acknowledge the considerable strengths of liberal accounts in seeking to expose the 'unpolitical' premises of Marxist analysis. At first sight, to criticize Marxism as 'unpolitical' must, even for its opponents, seem unreasonable, given the former's quite evident and passionate involvement in what can clearly be seen to be political struggles. Yet to politics in its (partial but indispensable) Habermasian sense, as the processes of practical, discursive will-formation, Marxist theory affords comparatively little attention. Again, we can assess this criticism through a brief consideration of Marxist positions on civil society and pluralism.

Certainly, Marxist writers have been right to question the substantive, as opposed to the purely formal, value of plurality and the 'bourgeois' rights and freedoms of civil society. Yet at least two serious reservations must be entered against this Marxist critique. First, it is clear that though limited, these liberties have been of enormous value to popular political movements and that they have exercised an (again limited) constraint upon more directly coercive elements of class rule. (Although, despite the occasional rhetorical flourish, it would be misleading to suggest that Marxism has displayed a generalized disregard for 'bourgeois freedoms'.)

A second and potentially more serious reservation focuses upon the conviction that some set of political institutions, albeit not those of liberal parliamentary democracy, are indispensable under *any* envisageable form of societal organization. I have argued that 'classical' Marxist expectations for passing beyond politics were, varying forms of transitional arrangement notwithstanding, wholly unrealistic. I have also argued against the historicist tendency to prescribe 'necessary' political conclusions from given historical developments. If post-revolutionary social arrangements cannot be post-political and if historical development does not determine given political consequences, it becomes clear that space must exist for politics as a sphere for the negotiation of legitimately competing programmes and practices – and this must mean, in its turn, formal political institutions and procedures. Here again some effort has been made, among critical Marxists, to reconcile these conclusions with more traditionally Marxist premisses. But as the contrasting yet complementary experience of Hindess et al. in their conclusions to *Marx's Capital and Capitalism Today* and the political strategists of the Swedish and Italian left suggests, the price of engaging political practice may be a breach with the parameters of 'classical' Marxism. For all that it is massively compromised by its identification with concealed structures of inequality and unfreedom, recognition of the necessity of political institutions is a real strength in the liberal critique of Marxism.

Similar arguments apply to the Marxian appraisal of pluralism. We have seen that this was telling against traditional forms of pluralism which mask systematic inequalities of access to power and decision-making under the formal rubric of equal access to a neutral and adjudicating state. At the same time, in the face of the evidence of forms of oppression not exclusively based upon class and of valued and legitimate differences within the working-class movement, more critical Marxists have made significant concessions to less unreservedly apologist defenders of plurality. The consequent diffusion of critical Marxist and critical pluralist perspectives has, as McLennan notes, made rigourous opposition of the two less compelling.[15]

Yet there are limitations upon what a Marxist perspective can yield to pluralism without thus losing claim to those very criteria that make it distinctively Marxist. Instructively, so far as 'classical' Marxism, rather than 'actually existing socialism', is concerned, the real difficulty does not lie, as its opponents so frequently insist, in opposition to pluralism, since we have seen that 'classical' Marxism is not, in fact, premised upon the suppression of a genuine plurality of interests. Rather does it rest upon the fact that such anticipations of plurality as one can find in 'classical' Marxism lack any *institutional* basis and seem to deny the possibility (under socialism) of a continuation of a *contested* plurality of interests, rather than simply of a 'diversity in abundance'.

Here again then, the radical weakness of 'classical' Marxism lies not in its embrace of a drab uniformity but rather in its unrealistic and unpolitical anticipation of diversity secured under circumstances which we have already seen to be almost unimaginably improbable. And again, for all that it is compromised by its association with the legitimation of an inequitable and oppressive social order, liberal recognition of the necessity of institutional plurality must be counted a strength against its 'non-political' Marxist opponents.

In Defence of Politics

If Habermas's counterfactual account of 'the public sphere' in itself yields few programmatic and procedural clues, it has at least directed attention towards important elements of the 'un-political' in both Marxist and liberal political traditions.

Though obviously important, liberal theory has only been addressed tangentially in this study and accordingly I confine myself in these closing pages to comments addressed to the Marxist tradition. Neither this, nor the generally critical tone throughout this study, should be taken to indicate either a belief that the liberal tradition is less prone to criticism or that my attitude to Marxism is unreservedly hostile.

In the course of the theoretical discussion above, I have stressed four key propositions – first, recognition of the indispensability of the state, secondly, recognition of the importance of independent institutions within civil society, thirdly, emphasis upon the procedural and institutional elements of democracy and fourth emphasis upon political plurality. In some sense, these constitute not a point of arrival but a (perhaps new) point of departure. Thus, for example, recognition of the state as potentially both enabling and repressive, calls for a consideration of the sorts of state institutions and practices that can facilitate effective mobilization while curtailing the abuse of power. This is an issue which, it seems to me, both Kautskyan and Leninist wings of Marxism have failed to address.

Again, socialist advocacy of civil society must be premised upon a radical overhaul of more traditional accounts of civil society. For, traditionally, Marxism and liberalism have been divided much more by their proscriptions for the future of civil society than by disagreements as to what civil society is. Yet, as Held and Keane make clear, settling accounts with the traditional understanding of civil society as 'a non-state sphere dominated by capitalist corporations and patriarchal families' – in favour of civil society as 'a non-state sphere comprising a variety of social institutions – production units, households, voluntary organizations and community-based services – which are legally guaranteed and democratically organized' – is, in large measure, just what socialist politics is.

This reconsideration of state and civil society dictates, in turn, the need to reassess the procedural and institutional elements of an anticipated democratic practice and the institutional bases of plurality. Traditionally, the presumed near-identity of socialism and democracy, the expectation of moving beyond 'formal' or 'procedural' models of democracy and the wish to resist 'Utopian' thinking has occasioned a very general neglect of detailed institutional questions of democratic organization. And nothing, of course, dates quicker than political 'tracts for our times'. Yet the reluctance to engage institutional and procedural issues must now be considered an unsustainable conceit. For given the conceptual space opened up by the division between state and civil society and the advocacy of a legally-guaranteed pluralism, it is extremely uncertain that democracy, as a particular set of *procedural* arrangements, can be seen necessarily to presage any specific substantive content, as, for example, socialist organization of production and exchange.

This does not necessitate a purely constitutionalist view of democracy nor an exclusive concern with procedure. It may, for example, be possible to invert the claims of the proponents of an (exclusively and necessarily) capitalist democracy, and to insist that those rights and freedoms which democracy is very generally said to exist to guarantee are ineffectual *without* socialist institutions. In this way, it may be quite proper to stipulate a socialist organization of production and exchange as a background condition, even as *the* background condition, for the effective enactment of democratic procedures. It is not however reasonable to argue that socialization can predetermine the outcome of these democratic procedures. Indeed, such an initiative requires that one address practical questions of what democratic practices should look like and, as importantly, how what we have now is supposed to yield to what we should have then. Here advocates of the promotion of a socialist democracy lack recourse to the brilliantly clear-cut and symmetrical lines of 'classical' Marxist theory which has been able, albeit in the face of much of the historical experience of the international labour movement, to cut through the tiresome rubric and messy practices of actual democratic institutions. For once the legitimacy of the division between state and civil society is welcomed, and pluralism embraced, it becomes impossible to proceed without asking how democratic politics is to be organized. The recent work of Gorz and of Carmen Sirianni indicates some of the ways in which such a project might be addressed – and suggests just how far there is still to go.

In its 'classical' form, we saw that the question of the 'tactics' for realizing socialism and the kind of fully formed socialism to which they were to give rise, turned upon the possibility of proceeding to a democratically expansive socialism through non-democratic methods. The sticking point, we saw in earlier chapters, was whether political 'dictatorship' could be the means of effecting transition to an emancipatory socialism. The effect of recent theoretical reformulations has been to render this particular dilemma redundant. For it is increasingly clear that democratic socialist politics is concerned above all with 'travelling in hope' and has precious little, despite the traditional language of 'forward marches' and 'privileged roads', to do with socialism as the terminus of humanity's prehistory. This does not mean that socialization or socialism is unimportant. It does however mean that socialism cannot be considered the end point of a democratic socialist politics. For it is increasingly clear that democratic socialist theory is not primarily about finding a democratic way of arriving at socialism – as it has been so frequently understood – but rather about a democratic socialist way of doing politics.

Notes

Introduction

[1] J. Dunn, *Western Political Theory in the Face of the Future*; A. Gorz, *Farewell to the Working Class*; A. Gamble, *An Introduction to Modern Social and Political Thought*.

[2] On the expectations and disappointments of recent Marxist political thought see, among others, R. Blackburn, (ed.), *Revolution and Class Struggle*; P. Anderson, *Considerations on Western Marxism*; A. Gouldner, *The Two Marxisms*; F. Parkin, *Marxism and Class Theory*; J. Dunn, *The Politics of Socialism*.

[3] Gorz, *Farewell to the Working Class*, p. 13.

Chapter 1

[1] L. Colletti, 'Introduction', in K. Marx, *Early Writings*, p. 45.

[2] B. Hindess, *Parliamentary Democracy and Socialist Politics*, p. 44; see also G. Della Volpe, *Rousseau and Marx and Other Writings*; A. M. Melzer, 'Rousseau and the Problem of Bourgeois Society'.

[3] This distinction between 'radical method' and 'conservative system' may more properly be associated with Engels – see 'Ludwig Feuerbach and the End of Classical German Philosophy', in K. Marx and F. Engels, *Selected Works*. On Hegel, see S. Avineri, *Hegel's Theory of the Modern State*; G. Lukács, *The Young Hegel*; H. Marcuse, *Reason and Revolution*; J. Ritter, *Hegel and the French Revolution*; C. Taylor, *Hegel and Modern Society*. On Marx and Hegel, see L. Colletti, *Marxism and Hegel*; S. Hook, *From Hegel to Marx*; S. Hippolyte, *Studies on Marx and Hegel*; A. Liebich, 'On the Origins of a Marxist Theory of Bureaucracy in *The Critique of Hegel's Philosophy of Right*'; D. McLellan, *The Young Hegelians and Marx*; H. Rubel, 'Notes on Marx's Conception of Democracy'.

[4] K. Marx, 'Critique of Hegel's Doctrine of the State', p. 137.

[5] K. Marx, 'On the Jewish Question', p. 233.

[6] Ibid., p. 233; 'Critique of Hegel', p. 146.

[7] Colletti, 'Introduction', p. 34.

[8] K. Marx, 'The Holy Family', in K. Marx and F. Engels, *Collected Works*, 4, p. 116.

[9] Ibid., p. 116.

[10] Marx, 'Critique of Hegel', p. 146.

[11] K. Marx, 'On the Jewish Question', p. 220.

[12] For an influential contemporary discussion, see C. B. Macpherson, *The Political Theory of Possessive Individualism*.

[13] Marx, 'On the Jewish Question', p. 219.

[14] Colletti, 'Introduction', p. 35.

[15] Marx, 'On the Jewish Question', pp. 226; 233; 'Critique of Hegel', p. 147.

[16] Marx, 'On the Jewish Question', p. 211.

[17] Ibid., p.217.

[18] Ibid., p. 221.

[19] Ibid., p. 222; for the early Engels' criticisms of 'the political', see F. Engels, 'The Condition of England', and 'Progress of Social Reform on the Continent'.

[20] K. Marx, 'Critical Notes on the Article "The King of Prussia and Social Reform. By a Prussian."', p. 419, 'On the Jewish Question', p. 234.

[21] Marx, 'Critique of Hegel', p. 87; 'On the Jewish Question', p. 234.

[22] Marx, 'Critique of Hegel', pp. 87–8.

[23] Ibid., p. 191.

[24] Ibid., p. 188.

[25] Ibid., p. 188.

[26] Ibid., p. 194.

[27] Ibid., p. 189–90; for an interesting recent discussion see R. Williams, 'Democracy and Parliament', *Marxism Today*, 26,6, 1982).

[28] Most influentially in L. Althusser, *For Marx*.

[29] N. Harding, 'Socialism, Society and the Organic Labour State', p. 8; see also R. Jessop, 'Marx and Engels on the State'; M. E. Spencer, 'Marx on the State'.

[30] K. Marx, 'Preface to *A Contribution to the Critique of Political Economy*', pp. 20–1.

[31] K. Marx, 'The Communist Manifesto', pp. 86–6.

[32] Ibid., pp. 86–6.

[33] Both Therborn and Moorhouse have provided evidence that might substantiate such a claim; see G. Therborn, 'The Rule of Capital and the Rise of Democracy'; and H. F. Moorhouse, 'The Political Incorporation of the British Working Class'; see also Rosenberg's claim that 'the social significance of general suffrage was greatly exaggerated before 1848 and just as greatly underrated afterwards' (A. Rosenberg, *Democracy and Socialism*).

[34] For two recent and contrasting assessments of the 'orthodox' reading of the Marx–Engels relationship, see T. Carver, *Marx and Engels: The Intellectual Relationship*; G. Welty, 'Marx, Engels and "Anti-Dühring"'.

[35] F. Engels, 'Introduction to Marx's *Class Struggles in France*', p. 290.

[36] K. Marx, 'The Chartists', p. 264; 'Speech on the Hague Congress', p. 324.

[37] K. Marx, 'Inaugural Address of the IWMA', p. 79; 'Instructions for Delegates', p. 89.

[38] K. Marx, 'The Class Struggles in France 1848 to 1850', p. 71; 'The Eighteenth Brumaire of Louis Bonaparte', p. 190.

[39] Marx, 'The Class Struggles in France', pp. 56; 134.

[40] Marx, 'The Eighteenth Brumaire of Louis Bonaparte', p. 210; for a distinctive view, see M. Johnstone, 'Marx, Blanqui and Majority Rule'.

[41] Marx, 'The Class Struggles in France', p. 125.

[42] Marx, 'The Eighteenth Brumaire of Louis Bonaparte', p. 238; see also the later influential accounts of F. Engels in 'Socialism: Utopian and Scientific'; 'The Origins of the Family, Private Property and the State'.

[43] K. Marx, 'First Draft of "The Civil War in France"', pp. 249–50; for a vivid account of the historical experience of the Paris Commune, see S. Edwards, *The Paris Commune*.

[44] K. Marx, 'The Civil War in France', p. 253; Marx, 'First Draft of "The Civil War in France"', p. 253.

[45] F. Engels, 'Introduction to Marx's *Civil War in France*', p. 259.

[46] K. Marx, 'Critique of the Gotha Programme', p. 355.

[47] See S. Avineri, *The Social and Political Thought of Karl Marx*, p. 204; H. Draper, 'Marx and the Dictatorship of the Proletariat'; H. B. Mayo, *An Introduction to Marxist Theory*, pp. 156 ff.; V. I. Lenin, 'The Proletarian Revolution and the Renegade Kautsky', pp. 256–7.

[48] K. Marx, 'Letter to Schweitzer', p. 146.

[49] This poses problems for those, such as R. N. Hunt and Michael Harrington, who argue that Marx attempted to 'utilize this space provided by bourgeois democracy for the achievement of socialist democracy'. See M. Harrington, 'Marxism and Democracy', p. 13; see also U. Cerroni, 'Democracy and Socialism'.

[50] A. Buchanan, *Marx and Justice*, p. 80; J. M. Maguire, *Marx's Theory of Politics*, p. 21.

[51] E. Kamenka, *Marxism and Ethics*, pp. 29–30.

[52] See, for example, C. Offe, *Contradictions of the Welfare State*, p. 246.

[53] H. Draper, *Karl Marx's Theory of Revolution: 1: State and Bureaucracy*, Vol. 1, p. 59; see also, L. Laurat, *Marxism and Democracy*.

[54] A. Gilbert, *Marx's Politics: Communists and Citizens*, p. 271.

Chapter 2

[1] A. Arato, 'The Second International: A Re-examination'; see also, T. Carver, *Marx and Engels: The Intellectual Relationship*.

[2] E. Bernstein, *Evolutionary Socialism*, p. x; on Bernstein, see P. Gay, *The Dilemma of Democratic Socialism*, P. Angel, *Eduard Bernstein et l' Evolution du Socialisme Allemande*; J. Hulse, *Revolutionists in London*.

[3] Bernstein, *Evolutionary Socialism*, pp. 1; 59.

[4] Ibid., p. 80.

[5] Ibid., p. 49.

[6] On Bernstein's contested relationship to Fabianism, see, in particular, Angel, *Eduard Bernstein et l'Evolution du Socialisme Allemande*, Hulse, *Revolutionists in London*.

[7] Bernstein, *Evolutionary Socialism*, pp. 142; 144.

8 Ibid., pp. 142–3.
9 Ibid., p. 146.
10 Ibid., pp. 218; 146–7.
11 Ibid., p. 167.
12 Ibid., pp. 217; 161; 167; 163–4.
13 Ibid., pp. 163–4; xvi; xxii; 197.
14 See E. Anderson, *Hammer or Anvil: The Story of the German Working Class Movement*; G. Roth, *The Social Democrats in Imperial Germany*; C. Schorske, *German Social Democracy, 1905-1917*.
15 R. Luxemburg, *Reform or Revolution*, pp. 13; 15.
16 Ibid., pp. 36–7; 'Social Reform or Revolution', in D. Howard, (ed.), *Selected Political Writings*, p. 93.
17 J. P. Nettl, *Rosa Luxemburg*, pp. 249–50.
18 K. Kautsky, 'Abschied Karl Kautsky über E. Bernstein', in *Vorwarts*, 22 Nov. 1932.
19 See F. Engels and K. Kautsky, 'Juridical Socialism'; K. Kautsky, 'Das Erfurter Programme', cited in M. Salvadori, *Karl Kautsky and the Socialist Revolution: 1880–1938*, p. 35.
20 K. Kautsky, *The Class Struggle*, p. 188.
21 Ibid., pp. 188–9.
22 K. Marx, 'The Communist Manifesto', p. 78; Kautsky, *The Class Struggle*, p. 191.
23 K. Kautsky, 'Das Erfurter Programme', cited in Salvadori, *Karl Kautsky and the Socialist Revolution: 1880–1938*, p. 36.
24 Salvadori, *Karl Kautsky*, p. 38.
25 Cited ibid., p. 37.
26 K. Kautsky, 'A Social Democratic Catechism', cited ibid., p. 41.
27 Bernstein, *Evolutionary Socialism*, p. 142.
28 K. Kautsky, 'Bernstein und das sozialdemokratisches Programme; Eine Antikritik', cited in Salvadori, *Karl Kautsky*, p. 66.
29 K. Kautsky, *The Dictatorship of the Proletariat*, p. 45.
30 Kautsky, *The Class Struggle*, pp. 197–8; 93.
31 Ibid., p. 93; K. Kautsky, 'The Erfurt Programme' in R. C. K. Ensor, (ed.), *Modern Socialism*, p. 318; K. Kautsky, *The Road to Power*, pp. 49–50; 29.
32 Cited in Salvadori, *Karl Kautsky*, pp. 41; 72; K. Kautsky, *Die Agrarfrage*, pp. 311–3, cited in Salvadori, *Karl Kautsky*, p. 59.
33 Cited in Salvadori, *Karl Kautsky*, p. 42; Kautsky, *The Class Struggle*, pp. 110–11.
34 Kautsky, *The Dictatorship of the Proletariat*, p. 26; for an interesting parallel, see T. Bottomore, P. Goode, (eds), *Austro-Marxism*.
35 Schorske, *German Social Democracy, 1905–1917*, pp. 180 ff.
36 See footnote 17, above.
37 Luxemburg, *Reform or Revolution*, p. 8; *The Mass Strike*, p. 70.
38 Luxemburg, *Reform or Revolution*, p. 22.
39 Ibid., p. 25.
40 Ibid., pp. 25–8.
41 Ibid., p. 28; K. Marx and F. Engels, *The German Ideology*, p. 39.

[42] Luxemburg, *The Mass Strike*, p. 75; *Reform or Revolution*, p. 28.

[43] Luxemburg, *Reform or Revolution*, p. 29.

[44] R. Luxemburg, 'Social Democracy and Parliamentarism', in R. Looker, (ed.), *Selected Political Writings*, p. 108; Luxemburg, *Reform or Revolution*, p. 47.

[45] Luxemburg, *Reform or Revolution*, p. 52–3.

[46] Ibid., p. 30.

[47] Ibid., p. 52.

[48] Ibid., p. 28; 'Social Democracy and Parliamentarism', pp. 107–9.

[49] Luxemburg, *Reform or Revolution*, pp. 49; 50; *The Mass Strike*, p. 61.

[50] R. Luxemburg, 'Speech to the Hanover Congress (1899)', in D. Howard, (ed.), *Selected Political Writings*.

[51] Luxemburg, 'Speech to the Hanover Congress (1899)', pp. 50–1.

[52] Luxemburg, *The Mass Strike*, pp. 73–4.

[53] Ibid., pp. 73–4; 'Democracy and Dictatorship', in Looker, (ed.), *Selected Political Writings*, p. 249.

[54] Cited in Salvadori, *Karl Kautsky*, p. 145.

[55] Ibid., p. 45; Kautsky, *The Road to Power*, pp. 49–50.

[56] Kautsky, *The Road to Power*, pp. 49–50; 51–2; 46.

[57] Ibid., pp. 49–50; 51–2.

[58] Ibid., pp. 51–3.

[59] Ibid., p. 64.

Chapter 3

[1] Kautsky, *The Dictatorship of the Proletariat*, pp. 1; 6–7; see also F. Claudin, 'Democracy and Dictatorship in Lenin and Kautsky'.

[2] Kautsky, *The Dictatorship of the Proletariat*, pp. 14–15.

[3] Ibid., p. 21.

[4] Ibid., pp. 23–4.

[5] Ibid., pp. 24; 38.

[6] Ibid., p. 26.

[7] K. Kautsky, *Terrorism and Communism*, p. 231.

[8] Ibid., p. 220; Kautsky, *The Dictatorship of the Proletariat*, pp. 98–9.

[9] K. Marx, 'Critique of the Gotha Programme', p. 355; Kautsky, *The Dictatorship of the Proletariat*, p. 45.

[10] Kautsky, *The Dictatorship of the Proletariat*, p. 58.

[11] Kautsky, *Terrorism and Communism*, pp. 217; 224.

[12] Ibid., pp. 227; 229; 232.

[13] Considerations of space preclude further consideration of Trotsky's own spirited defence of Bolshevik practice. However, his response to 'the renegade Kautsky' was materially very similar to that of Lenin. On this, see especially, L. Trotsky, *Terrorism and Communism*.

[14] A. J. Polan, *Lenin and the End of Politics*, p. 129.

[15] V. I. Lenin, 'Preface to the Russian Translation of K. Kautsky's Pamphlet *Social Democracy Wiped Out*', *Collected Works*, 10, p. 196; 'The Proletarian

Revolution and the Renegade Kautsky', *Collected Works*, 28, pp. 232; 235; 'Theses and Report on Bourgeois Democracy and the Dictatorship of the Proletariat', *Collected Works*, 28, p. 457; see also H. Carrere d'Encausse, *Lenin, Revolution and Power*.

[16] V. I. Lenin. 'The State and Revolution', *Collected Works*, 25, pp. 392; 477; 'The Tasks of the Proletariat in our Revolution', *Collected Works*, 24, p. 68; 'The Proletarian Revolution and the Renegade Kautsky', *Collected Works*, 28, p. 458.

[17] Lenin. 'The State and Revolution', *Collected Works*, 25, p. 428.

[18] Ibid., pp. 465–6; 'The Proletarian Revolution and the Renegade Kautsky', *Collected Works*, 28, p. 245; 'Theses and Report on Bourgeois Democracy and the Dictatorship of the Proletariat', *Collected Works*, 28, p. 465.

[19] Lenin. 'The State and Revolution', *Collected Works*, 25, pp. 427–8.

[20] See V. I. Lenin, 'Working Class and Bourgeois Democracy'; 'The Proletariat and the Bourgeois Democrats'; 'The Proletariat and the Peasantry'; 'The Revolutionary-Democratic Dictatorship of the Proletariat and the Peasantry'; 'The Democratic Tasks of the Revolutionary Proletariat', *Collected Works*, 8; 'Playing at Parliamentarism', *Collected Works*, 9; 'The Proletariat and the Peasantry', *Collected Works*, 10; 'Marxism and Revisionism', *Collected Works*, 15; '"Left-Wing" Communism – An Infantile Disorder', *Collected Works*, 31.

[21] Lenin, 'The State and Revolution', *Collected Works*, 25, pp. 398; 450; 459.

[22] Ibid., pp. 419; 405; *Marxism on the State*, p. 78.

[23] See N. Bukharin, L. Fabbri, R. Rocker, *The Poverty of Statism: Anarchism v. Marxism*; Lenin, 'The State and Revolution', *Collected Works*, 25, pp. 430–1.

[24] Lenin. 'The State and Revolution', *Collected Works*, 25, pp. 477; 407; 409; 467–8; 'The Proletarian Revolution and the Renegade Kautsky', *Collected Works*, 28, p. 256.

[25] Lenin, 'Theses and Report on Bourgeois Democracy', *Collected Works*, 28, pp. 466–7; 'The State and Revolution', *Collected Works*, 25, pp. 424–5.

[26] Lenin. 'The State and Revolution', *Collected Works*, 25, p. 437; see also, G. Ionescu, 'Lenin, the Commune and the State; V. I. Lenin, 'Plan of a Lecture on the Commune', *Collected Works*, 8; 'Lessons of the Commune', *Collected Works*, 13.

[27] Lenin, 'The Tasks of the Proletariat in Our Revolution', *Collected Works*, 24, p. 68, 'The Tasks of the Proletariat in the Present Revolution', *Collected Works*, 24, p. 23; 'Dual Power', *Collected Works*, 24, p. 39; 'The "Dictatorship of the Proletariat"', *Collected Works*, 30; see also 'The Constituent Assembly and the Dictatorship of the Proletariat', *Collected Works*, 30; '"Left-Wing" Communism - An Infantile Disorder'; 'The Essence of the Dictatorship of the Proletariat and of Soviet Power'; 'A Contribution to the History of the Question of the Dictatorship', *Collected Works*, 31.

[28] Lenin, 'The State and Revolution', *Collected Works*, 25, pp, 430–1.

[29] Ibid., pp. 468–9; for a recent discussion, see L. Holmes, (ed.), *The Withering Away of the State?*.

[30] Lenin. 'The State and Revolution', *Collected Works*, 25, p. 472.

[31] Ibid., p. 468.

[32] Lenin, *Marxism on the State*, p. 25; see also 'Letter to American Workers'; '"Democracy" and Dictatorship', *Collected Works*, 28; 'First All-Russia Congress of Adult Education'; 'Foreword to the Published Speech "The Deception of the People with Slogans of Freedom and Equality"', *Collected Works*, 29; 'The State and Revolution', *Collected Works*, 25, pp. 467; 479.

[33] N. Poulantzas, *State, Power, Socialism*; Luxemburg, *The Russian Revolution and Leninism or Marxism?*, pp. 37; 39; see also N. Geras, *The Legacy of Rosa Luxemburg*, J. P. Nettl, *Rosa Luxemburg*.

[34] Luxemburg, *The Russian Revolution*, pp. 29; 30; 56; 59–60.

[35] Ibid., p. 62.

[36] Ibid., pp. 63; 67.

[37] Ibid., pp. 77; 71.

[38] Ibid., p. 72.

[39] Ibid., p. 77.

[40] Ibid., p. 77.

[41] Ibid., p. 79; but see N. Geras, 'Classical Marxism and Proletarian Representation'.

[42] Cited in R. C. Tucker, *The Marxian Revolutionary Idea*; pp. 198–9; see also S. E. Bronner, 'Karl Kautsky and the Twilight of Orthodoxy'; L. Colletti, *From Rousseau to Lenin*; on the origins of Western Marxism's hostility to Kautsky's 'Automatic Marxism', see R. Jacoby, 'Towards a Critique of Automatic Marxism'; K. Korsch, *Marxism and Philosophy*.

[43] N. Harding, *Lenin's Political Thought: Vol. 2: Theory and Practice in the Socialist Revolution*, p. 314; P. Mattick, *Anti-Bolshevik Communism*, p. 10.

[44] See C. B. Macpherson, *The Real World of Democracy*, pp. 9–10.

[45] E. Laclau, *Politics and Ideology in Marxist Theory*; R. Jessop, 'The Political Indeterminacy of Democracy', in A. Hunt, (ed.), *Marxism and Democracy*; see also R. Jessop et al., 'Authoritarian Populism, Two Nations and Thatcherism'.

[46] E. P. Thompson, *The Making of the English Working Class*, p. 80.

[47] For contemporary non-liberal accounts of the consequences of Lenin's politics, see, for example, R. Bahro, *The Alternative in Eastern Europe*, P. Corrigan et al., 'Bolshevism and the USSR'; R. Medvedev, *Leninism and Western Socialism*.

Chapter 4

[1] See G. Amyot, *The Italian Communist Party: The Crisis of the Popular Front Strategy*.

[2] On Gramsci, see C. Buci-Glucksmann, *Gramsci and the State*; J. Cammett, *Antonio Gramsci and the Origins of Italian Communism*; J. A. Davis, (ed.), *Gramsci and Italy's Passive Revolution*, J. V. Femia, *Gramsci's Political Thought*; G. Fiori, *Antonio Gramsci: Life of a Revolutionary*; C. Mouffe, (ed.), *Gramsci and Marxist Theory*; C. Mouffe and A. S. Sassoon, 'Gramsci in France and Italy'; P. Piccone, *Italian Marxism*; 'Gramsci's Marxism: Beyond

Lenin and Togliatti'; A. Pozzolini, *Antonio Gramsci: An Introduction to his Thought*; A. S. Sassoon, *Gramsci's Politics*; P. Spriano, *Antonio Gramsci and the Party: The Prison Years*; G. A. Williams, *Proletarian Order: Antonio Gramsci, Factory Councils and the Origins of Italian Communism*.

3 P. Anderson, 'The Antinomies of Antonio Gramsci'.

4 A. Gramsci, *Selections from Political Writings 1921–1926*, p. 200.

5 A. Gramsci, *The Prison Notebooks*, pp. 243; 80 fn.

6 It is with this 'partial reading' of Gramsci that I am principally concerned here. It should, of course, be noted that others have sought in Gramsci a far more radical democratic theory. See R. Bellamy, *Modern Italian Social Thought*; N. Bobbio, *What is Socialism?*; Della Volpe, *Rousseau and Marx and Other Writings*.

7 Cited D. Sassoon, *The Strategy of the PCI*, pp. 4; 11.

8 P. Togliatti, *On Gramsci and Other Writings*, p. 72.

9 Ibid., p. 141.

10 Ibid., p. 258; 'Parliament and the Struggle for Socialism'.

11 D. Sassoon, *Strategy of the PCI*, pp. 99; 128–9.

12 Piccone, *Italian Marxism*, p. 154.

13 On Eurocommunism, see E. Balibar, *On The Dictatorship of the Proletariat*; S. Carillo, *'Eurocommunism' and the State*; D. Childs, *The Changing Face of Western Communism*; F. Claudin, *Eurocommunism and Socialism*; CPGB, *The British Road to Socialism*; L. Dunhamel, 'Lenin, Violence and Eurocommunism'; A.G. Frank, 'Eurocommunism: Left and Right Variants'; C. Gati, The '"Europeanization" of Communism'; R. Gordon and S. Haseler, *'Eurocommunism'*; J. Kautsky, 'Karl Kautsky and Eurocommunism'; R. Kindersley, (ed.), *In Search of Eurocommunism*; A. Kriegel, *Eurocommunism: A New Kind of Communism*; A.-M. Le Gloannec, 'Eurocommunism'; 'RDA and Eurocommunism'; H. Machin, (ed.), *National Communism in Western Europe: A Third Way to Socialism*; E. Mandel, *From Stalinism to Eurocommunism*; G. Marchais, *Le Défi Démocratique*; K. Marko, 'Real Communism or Eurocommunism'; P. Piccone, 'Labriola and the Roots of Eurocommunism'; G. Provost, 'Eurocommunism and the Spanish Communists'; G. Schwab, (ed.), *Eurocommunism: The Ideological and Political-Theoretical Foundations*; R .L. Tokes, *Eurocommunism and Detente*; P. F. de Torre et al., (eds), *Eurocommunism: Myth or Reality*; G. R. Urban, (ed.), *Euro-Communism*; H. Weber, 'Eurocommunism, Socialism and Democracy'; J. Woolacott, 'The Portuguese CP and the April 1983 Elections in Portugal'. On Eurocommunism in Italy, see M. Carrieri and L. L. Radice, 'Italy Today: A Crisis of a New Type of Democracy'; L. Gruppi, (ed.), *Il Compresso Storico*; P. Lange and S. Tarrow, (eds), *Italy in Transition: Conflict and Consensus*; A. Ranney and G.Sartori, (eds), *Eurocommunism: The Italian Case*; F. Rodano, *Sulla Politica dei Communista*; J. Ruscoe, *On the Threshold of Government: The Italian CP, 1976-81*; S. Serfaty and L. Gray, *The Italian Communist Party Yesterday, Today and Tomorrow*; E. Shaw, 'The Italian Historical Compromise'.

14 *Keesing's Archives*, 1982, p. 31456

[15] D. Sassoon, (ed.), *The Italian Communists Speak for Themselves*, p. 67.

[16] Sassoon, *The Italian Communists*, p. 64.

[17] G. Vacca, *Saggio su Togliatti e la tradizione communista*, p. 373.

[18] G. Napolitano, *The Italian Road to Socialism*, p. 83.

[19] E. Berlinguer 'Opening Address to the 16th Congress of the PCI (1983)', pp. 509–515.

[20] E. Berlinguer, 'Sixty Years of Democratic Struggles', pp. 76–8.

[21] Lenin, *Collected Works*, 28, p. 463.

[22] Cited J. Pontusson, 'Gramsci and Eurocommunism: A Comparative Analysis of Conceptions of Class Rule and Socialist Transition', p. 210.

[23] Ibid.

[24] Gramsci, *Selections 1910–920*, p. 133.

[25] C. Buci-Glucksmann, 'State, transition and passive revolution', in Mouffe, (ed.), *Gramsci and Marxist Theory*, p. 232–3.

[26] See Jessop, 'Nicos Poulantzas on Political Strategy, (*Politics*, 2, 1982).

[27] N. Poulantzas, *The Crisis of the Dictatorships*, p. 82.

[28] Poulantzas, *State, Power, Socialism*, p. 132.

[29] Poulantzas, *Political Power and Social Classes*, p. 271–2.

[30] Poulantzas, *State, Power, Socialism*, p. 251.

[31] Ibid., p. 252.

[32] Ibid., p. 253.

[33] Ibid.; for a quite different account, see E. Mandel, *Revolutionary Marxism Today*.

[34] Poulantzas, *State, Power, Socialism*, p. 256.

[35] Ibid., p. 256.

[36] Ibid., p. 258.

[37] C. Boggs, *The Impasse of European Communism*; p. 113.

[38] PCI, 'PCI: 1983 Manifesto'; 'For a Democratic Alternative'; 'The Democratic Alternative'.

[39] E. Berlinguer, G. Napolitano, 'Speeches to the 16th Congress of the PCI', *Communist Affairs*, 2, 1983, pp. 509–517; see also S. Gundle, 'The 16th Congress of the PCI'; 'In Search of the Arab Phoenix'.

[40] C. Offe, *Contradictions of the Welfare State*, p. 246.

[41] Piccone, *Italian Marxism*, p. 10.

[42] A. Przeworski, 'Social Democracy as an Historical Phenomenon', p. 38; see also 'Proletariat into a Class. . .'.

[43] K. Middlemas, *Power and the Party: Changing Faces of Communism in Western Communism*, p. 187.

Chapter 5

[1] For this 'classical' account, see A. Crosland, *The Future of Socialism*; H. Tingsten, *The Swedish Social Democrats*; R. F. Tomasson, *Sweden: Prototype of Modern Society*; 'The Extraordinary Success of the Swedish Social Democrats'; for the background to Swedish Social Democracy, see R. Scase,

Social Democracy in Capitalist Society; (ed.), *Readings in the Swedish Class Structure*.

[2] See T. A. Tilton, 'A Swedish Road to Socialism: Ernst Wigforss and the Ideological Foundations of Swedish Social Democracy'.

[3] J. Pontusson, 'Behind and Beyond Social Democracy in Sweden', p. 71.

[4] W. Korpi, *The Democratic Class Struggle*, p. 48.

[5] Ibid., p. 50.

[6] See R. Fulcher, 'Class Conflict in Sweden'.

[7] A. Martin, 'From Joint Consultation to Joint Decision-Making', in J. Fry, (ed.), *Industrial Democracy and Labour Market Policy in Sweden*, p. 14; 'Sweden: Industrial Democracy and Social Democratic Strategy', in G. D. Garson, (ed.), *Worker Self-Management in Industry*, (Praeger, 1977).

[8] R. Meidner, *Employee Investment Funds*, pp. 14; 17.

[9] Ibid., p. 47.

[10] I am grateful to Richard Scase for bringing this fact to my attention.

[11] See S. Bornstein, 'States and Unions', in S. Bornstein et al., (eds), *The State in Capitalist Europe*.

[12] U. Himmelstrand et al., *Beyond Welfare Capitalism*, p. 155.

[13] W. Korpi, *The Working Class in Welfare Capitalism*, p. 63.

[14] F. G. Castles, *The Social Democratic Image of Society*.

[15] Himmelstrand et al., *Beyond Welfare Capitalism*; 'Middle-Way Sweden at a Cross-Road', (*Acta Sociologica*, Supplement, 1978); see also G. Esping-Andersen, 'Re-casting Sweden's Middle Way'; 'Social Democracy', in M. Zeitlin, *Classes, Class Conflict and the State*; 'Social Class, Social Democracy and the State'; C. von Otter, 'Sweden: Labour Reformism Shapes the System', in S. Barkin, (ed.), *Worker Militancy and Its Consequences 1965-1975*; 'Swedish Welfare Capitalism: The Role of the State', in R. Scase, (ed.), *The State in Western Europe*.

[16] J. Stephens, *The Transition from Capitalism to Socialism*, p. 10.

[17] Ibid., pp. 6; 12.

[18] Ibid., p. 72.

[19] Ibid., pp. 129; 89.

[20] Ibid., p. 24; fig 2.1.

[21] Ibid., p. 190; cited Korpi, *The Working Class in Welfare Capitalism*, p. 329; see also S. Ersson and J.-E. Lane, 'Polarisation and Political Economy Crisis: The 1982 Swedish Elections'; for a contrasting view see M. Kesselman, 'Prospects for Democratic Socialism in Advanced Capitalism: Class Struggle and Compromise in Sweden and France'.

[22] Korpi, *The Working Class in Welfare Capitalism*, p. 351.

[23] Himmelstrand et al., *Beyond Welfare Capitalism*, p. 204.

[24] Ibid., p. 138.

[25] See Stephens, *The Transition from Capitalism to Socialism*, pp. 89 ff; F. Parkin, *Class Inequality and Political Order*; H. Wilensky, *The Welfare State and Equality*.

[26] See A. Emmanuel, 'The State in the Transitional Period', pp. 111–131; B. Gustaffson et al., 'Beyond Welfare Capitalism: Review Symposium'.

[27] Korpi, *The Working Class in Welfare Capitalism*, p. 335.

[28] Stephens, *The Transition From Capitalism to Socialism*, pp. 12–3.

Chapter 6

[1] R. Miliband, *Class Power and State Power*, p. 154; for the development of Miliband's position, see also *Parliamentary Socialism*; *The State in Capitalist Society*; *Marxism and Politics*; *Capitalist Democracy in Britain*.

[2] Dunn, *The Politics of Socialism*, p. 71.

[3] H. B. Mayo, *An Introduction to Marxist Theory*, p. 280; see also J. L. Talmon, *The Origins of Totalitarian Democracy*; *Political Messianism: The Romantic Phase*; K. Popper, *The Open Society and Its Enemies*; and J. Plamenatz, *Democracy and Illusion*; *German Marxism and Russian Communism*.

[4] P. Piccone, 'Gramsci's Marxism: Beyond Lenin and Togliatti', p. 485.

[5] Poulantzas, *Political Power and Social Classes*; R. Jessop, 'Nicos Poulantzas on Political Strategy', p. 3.

[6] Poulantzas, *State, Power, Socialism*, p. 141.

[7] Ibid., p. 256.

[8] Offe, *Contradictions of the Welfare State*, p. 51.

[9] Ibid., p. 122.

[10] Though I concentrate here upon Offe's contribution, this is not to deny the definitive contribution of J. O'Connor's *The Fiscal Crisis of the Welfare State*; see also I. Gough, *The Political Economy of the Welfare State*.

[11] Offe, *Contradictions of the Welfare State*, p. 247.

[12] Poulantzas, *Political Power and Social Classes*.

[13] W. Muller and C. Neususs, 'The "Welfare-State Illusion" and the Contradiction Between Labour and Capital', in J. Holloway and S. Picciotto,(eds), *State and Capital: A Marxist Debate*; see also R. Jessop, *The Capitalist State*; 'Capitalism and Democracy', in G. Littlejohn, (ed.), *Power and the State*; 'The Political Indeterminacy of Democracy', in A. Hunt, (ed), *Marxism and Democracy*.

[14] J. Hirsch, 'The State Apparatus and Social Reproduction', in Holloway and Picciotto,(eds), *State and Capital: A Marxist Debate*, p. 82.

[15] H. Gerstenberger, 'Class Conflict, Competition and State Functions', in Holloway and Picciotto,(eds), *State and Capital: A Marxist Debate*, p. 159.

[16] Ibid., pp. 158–9.

[17] A. Giddens, *A Contemporary Critique of Historical Materialism*, p. 249.

[18] Ibid., p. 249.

[19] J. Urry, *The Anatomy of Capitalist Societies*, p. 80.

[20] Ibid., p. 81.

[21] G. Esping-Andersen et al., 'Modes of Class Struggle and the Capitalist State', p. 191.

[22] Urry, *The Anatomy of Capitalist Societies*, p. 113.

[23] Giddens, *A Contemporary Critique of Historical Materialism*, p. 219.

[24] B. Frankel, *Beyond the State?*, p. 18; see also 'The State of the State'.

[25] Urry, *The Anatomy of Capitalist Societies*, p. 113.

[26] Esping-Andersen et al., 'Modes of Class Struggle and the Capitalist State', p. 198.

[27] Giddens, *A Contemporary Critique of Historical Materialism*, p. 220.

[28] Ibid., p. 250.

[29] P. Hall, 'Patterns of Economic Policy: an Organizational Approach', in D. Held et al., (eds), *States and Societies*, p. 366.

[30] Gorz, *Farewell to the Working Class*, p. 117; this was not always Gorz's position; see also *Strategy for Labour*; *Socialism and Revolution*; (ed.), *The Division of Labour*.

[31] Frankel, *Beyond the State?*, p. 181.

[32] Poulantzas, *State, Power, Socialism*, p. 251.

[33] Gorz, *Farewell to the Working Class*, p. 65.

[34] D. Held and J. Keane, 'Socialism and the Limits of State Action', in J. Curran, (ed.), *The Future of the Left*, p. 176.

[35] See footnote 3, above.

[36] Gorz, *Farewell to the Working Class*, p. 35.

[37] Ibid., p. 112.

[38] Ibid., pp. 113–4.

[39] Ibid., p. 116.

[40] Ibid., p. 79.

[41] Ibid., pp. 79–80.

[42] J. Cohen, *Class and Civil Society*, p. 184.

[43] Urry, *The Anatomy of Capitalist Societies*, p. 17.

[44] Ibid., pp. 17 ff.

[45] J. Keane, *Public Life and Late Capitalism*.

[46] Ibid., p. 2.

[47] Ibid., pp. 89; 95.

[48] Ibid., p. 141.

[49] Ibid., p. 144.

[50] Ibid., pp. 8; 256–7.

[51] Ibid., p. 256.

[52] Polan, *Lenin and the End of Politics*, p. 3.

[53] Ibid., p. 97.

[54] B. Hindess, *Parliamentary Democracy and Socialist Politics*, p. 52.

[55] J. Keane, 'Introduction', in Offe, *Contradictions of the Welfare State*.

[56] See, for example, J. Siltanen and M. Stanworth, (eds), *Women and the Public Sphere*.

Chapter 7

[1] E. B. Pashukanis, *Law and Marxism: A General Theory*, p. 68.

[2] Ibid., p. 81.

[3] Ibid., p. 96.

[4] Ibid., p. 81.

5 Ibid., p. 61.
6 Ibid., p. 158.
7 See H. Kelsen, *The Communist Theory of Law*.
8 H. Collins, *Marxism and Law*, p. 122.
9 Ibid., pp. 144; 146.
10 S. Picciotto, 'The theory of the state, class struggle and the rule of law', in R. Fine et al., (eds), *Capitalism and the Rule of Law*.
11 Ibid., p. 171.
12 Ibid., p. 171.
13 Ibid., p. 172.
14 Ibid., p. 177.
15 P. Hirst, 'Law, Socialism and Rights', in P. Carlen and M. Collinson, (eds), *Radical Issues in Criminology*.
16 Ibid., p. 70.
17 Ibid., pp. 77–8.
18 Ibid., pp. 92–3; 95.
19 Ibid., p. 97.
20 Ibid., pp. 95–6.
21 Ibid., p. 99; A. Macintyre, *After Virtue*.
22 Hirst, 'Law, Socialism and Rights', *Radical Issues in Criminology*, p. 104.
23 Ibid., p. 58.
24 A. Hunt, 'The Politics of Law and Justice', in Hunt (ed.), *Politics and Power*, 4, pp. 3-26.
25 Ibid., p. 16.
26 T. Campbell, *The Left and Rights: A Conceptual Analysis of Socialist Rights*.
27 Ibid., p. 4.
28 Ibid., p. 18.
29 Ibid., p. 81.
30 Ibid., p. 46.
31 Ibid., p. 95.
32 A. E. Buchanan, *Marx and Justice: The Radical Critique of Liberalism*, p. 64.
33 Ibid., p. 165.
34 Campbell, *The Left and Rights*, pp. 132-7.
35 A. Weale, *Political Theory and Social Policy*, p. 42.
36 E. P. Thompson, *Writing by Candlelight*, p. 153.
37 Ibid., p. 205.
38 Ibid., pp. 169; 246.
39 E. P. Thompson, *Whigs and Hunters*, pp. 264–7.
40 Ibid., p. 267.
41 R. Fine, *Democracy and the Rule of Law*, p. 175.
42 Hunt, 'The Politics of Law and Justice', p. 20.
43 Hirst, 'Law Socialism and Rights', p. 94.
44 S. Hall et al., *Policing the Crisis*, p. 193.
45 Ibid., p. 208.
46 Fine, *Democracy and the Rule of Law*, p. 157.
47 Ibid., p. 161.

[48] Ibid., p. 174.
[49] Ibid., p. 178.
[50] Ibid., p. 205.
[51] Ibid., p. 206.
[52] Ibid., p. 207.
[53] Ibid., p. 208.
[54] Ibid., p. 208.
[55] Ibid., p. 209.
[56] Ibid., p. 211.
[57] Buchanan, *Marx and Justice*, p. 162.
[58] Ibid., p. 163.
[59] Ibid., p. 163; see also G. A. Cohen, 'Freedom, Justice and Capitalism'; M. Cohen et al., *Marx, Justice and History*.
[60] Buchanan, *Marx and Justice*, pp. 64; 73.

Chapter 8

[1] Gorz, *Farewell to the Working Class*, pp. 73–4; on the former point, see K. Popper, *The Poverty of Historicism*.
[2] Cohen, *Class and Civil Society*, p. 103.
[3] B. Hindess, *Parliamentary Democracy and Socialist Politics*, p. 40.
[4] K. Middlemas, *Power and the Party*; see ch. 5, footnote 35.
[5] J. Habermas, 'The Public Sphere', p. 49–50; on the public sphere, see also R. Luxemburg, *The Russian Revolution*; H. Arendt, *The Human Condition*; J. Habermas, *Theory and Practice*; C. W. Mills, *Power, Politics and People*, F. Tonnies, *Community and Society*; *On Sociology*; J. J. Rodger, 'On the Degeneration of the Public Sphere'.
[6] Habermas, 'The Public Sphere', p. 54.
[7] J. Habermas, *Towards a Rational Society*, p. 75.
[8] Habermas, 'The Public Sphere', p. 55.
[9] Giddens, *A Contemporary Critique of Historical Materialism*, p. 213.
[10] See J. Habermas, *Knowledge and Human Interests*; *Legitimation Crisis*; *Communication and the Evolution of Society*; of the critics, see, for example, D. Held and J. Thompson, (eds), *Habermas: Critical Debates*; D. Held, *Introduction to Critical Theory*, pp. 375–6; A. Giddens, 'Habermas's Social and Political Theory', in *Profiles and Critiques*.
[11] A. Smith, *The Wealth of Nations*; J. Schumpeter, *Capitalism, Socialism and Democracy*; A. Downs, *An Economic Theory of Democracy*
[12] See, for example, Smith, *The Wealth of Nations*, (Penguin, 1970), A. Ferguson, *An Essay on the History of Civil Society*.
[13] See R. Dahl, *A Preface to Democratic Theory*; *Polyarchy*; D. B. Truman, *The Governmental Process*; S. Lipset, *Political Man*; G. Almond and S. Verba, *The Civic Culture*; B. Barry, *Sociologists, Economists and Democracy*; M. A. Crenson, *The Un-Politics of Air Pollution*; M. Mann, 'The Social Cohesion of Liberal Democracy', *The American Sociological Review*, 35, 1970; see also C. E. Lindblom, *Politics and Markets*.

[14] See Lindblom, *Politics and Markets*; G. McLennan, 'Capitalist State or Democratic Polity?', in G. McLennan et al. (eds), *The Idea of the Modern State*.

[15] McLennan, 'Capitalist State or Democratic Polity?'.

[16] Gorz, *Farewell to the Working Class*; C. Sirianni, 'Councils and Parliaments'; 'Production and Power in a Classless Society'.

Bibliography

1 Classical Marxism

Marx and Engels

Althusser, L., *For Marx*, (New Left Books, London, 1977)

Avineri, S., *The Social and Political Thought of Karl Marx*, (Cambridge University Press, Cambridge, 1968)

Hegel's Theory of the Modern State, (Cambridge University Press, Cambridge, 1972)

Buchanan, A. E., *Marx and Justice: The Radical Critique of Liberalism*, (Methuen, London, 1982)

Carver, T., *Marx and Engels: The Intellectual Relationship*, (Wheatsheaf, Brighton, 1983)

Cerroni, U., 'Democracy and Socialism', *Economy and Society*, 7, 3, 1978

Cohen, G. A., *Karl Marx's Theory of History: A Defence*, (Oxford University Press, Oxford, 1978)

Colletti, L., *Marxism and Hegel*, (Verso, London, 1973)

From Rousseau to Lenin, (New Left Books, London, 1972)

'Introduction', in K. Marx, *Early Writings*, (Penguin, Harmondsworth, 1975)

Della Volpe, G., *Rousseau and Marx and Other Writings*, (Lawrence and Wishart, London, 1978)

Draper, H., *Karl Marx's Theory of Revolution: 1: State and Bureaucracy; 2: The Politics of Social Classes*, (Monthly Review Press, London, 1977)

'Marx and the Dictatorship of the Proletariat', *New Politics*, 1, 4, 1962

Edwards, S., *The Paris Commune 1871*, (Quadrangle, New York, 1973)

Engels, F., *Anti-Dühring: Herr Eugen Dühring's Revolution in Science* (Lawrence and Wishart, London, 1969)

Selected Writings, (Penguin, Harmondsworth, 1967)

'Socialism: Utopian and Scientific', in Marx, K., and Engels, F., *Selected Works*.

'Ludwig Feuerbach and the End of Classical German Philosophy', in Marx, K., and Engels, F., *Selected Works*.

'The Origins of the Family, Private Property and the State', in Marx, K., and Engels, F., *Selected Works*.

'The Condition of England II: The English Constitution', in Marx, K., and Engels, F., *Collected Works*, 3

'Progress of Social Reform on the Continent', in Marx, K., and Engels, F., *Collected Works*, 3

'Introduction to Marx's *Class Struggles in France*, (1895)', in F. Engels, *Selected Writings*.

'Introduction to Marx's *Civil War in France*, (1891)', in K. Marx and F. Engels, *Selected Works*.

Gilbert, A., *Marx's Politics: Communists and Citizens*, (Martin Robertson, Oxford, 1981)

Harding, N., 'Socialism, Society and the Organic Labour State', in Harding, N., (ed.), *The State in Socialist Society*, (Macmillan/St Antonys, London, 1984)

Harrington, M., 'Marxism and Democracy', *Praxis International*, 1,1, 1981

Hegel, G. W. F., *The Philosophy of Right*, (Oxford University Press, Oxford, 1945)

Hindess, B., *Parliamentary Democracy and Socialist Politics*, (Routledge and Kegan Paul, London, 1983)

Hippolyte, S., 'Marx, l'Etat et la Liberté, Révolution ou émancipation', *Esprit*, 11, 1977

Studies on Marx and Hegel, (Heinemann, London, 1969)

Hook, S., *From Hegel to Marx*, (University of Michigan Press, Oxford, 1945)

Hunt, R. N., *The Political Ideas of Marx and Engels: 1: Marxism and Totalitarian Democracy 1818–1850*, (Macmillan, London, 1975)

Jessop, R., 'Marx and Engels on the State', in Hibbin, S., (ed.), *Politics, Ideology and the State*, (Lawrence and Wishart, London, 1981)

Johnstone, M., 'Marx, Blanqui and Majority Rule', in Miliband, R., and Saville, J., *The Socialist Register*, 1983, (Merlin, London, 1983)

Kamenka. E., *Marxism and Ethics*, (Macmillan, London, 1969)

Laurat, L., *Marxism and Democracy*, (Gollancz, London, 1940)

Levin, M., 'Deutschmarx: Marx, Engels and the German Question', *Political Studies*, 29, 4, 1981

Lichtheim, G., *The Origins of Socialism*, (Weidenfield and Nicholson, London, 1969)

Marxism, (Routledge and Kegan Paul, London, 1981)

Liebich, A., 'On the Origins of a Marxist Theory of Bureaucracy in *The Critique of Hegel's "Philosophy of Right"*', *Political Theory*, 10, 1, 1982,

Lukács, G., *The Young Hegel. Studies in the Relation Between Dialectics and Economics*, (Merlin, London, 1975)

McLellan, D., *The Young Hegelians and Marx*, (Macmillan, London, 1969)

Maguire, J., *Marx's Paris Writings*, (Dublin, 1972)

Marx's Theory of Politics, (Cambridge University Press, Cambridge, 1978)

Marcuse, H., *Reason and Revolution: Hegel and the Rise of Modern Social Theory*, (Beacon, Boston, 1960)

Marx, K., *Early Writings*, ed. Colletti, L., (Penguin, Harmondsworth, 1975)
'Critique of Hegel's Doctrine of the State, pp. 57–198
'On the Jewish Question', pp. 211–241

'Contribution to the Critique. Introduction', pp. 243–257
'Economic and Philosophical Manuscripts', pp. 279–400
'Critical Notes on the Article "The King Of Prussia and Social Reform. By a Prussian"', pp. 401–420
The Revolutions of 1848, (Penguin, Harmondsworth, 1973)
'The Communist Manifesto', pp. 62–98
'Address of the Central Committee to the Communist League, (March 1850)', pp. 319–330
'Address of the Central Committee to the Communist League, (June 1850)', pp. 331–338
Surveys From Exile, (Penguin, Harmondsworth, 1973)
'The Class Struggles in France 1848 to 1850' pp. 35–142
'The Eighteenth Brumaire of Louis Bonaparte', pp. 143–249
'The Chartists', pp. 262–271
The First International and After, (Penguin, Harmondsworth, 1974)
'Inaugural Address of the IWMA', pp. 73–81
'The Civil War in France', pp. 187–236
'First Draft of "The Civil War in France"', pp. 236–268
'Resolution of the London Conference on Working-Class Political Action', (1871), pp. 269–270
'Instructions for Delegates', pp. 85–94
'Letter to Schweitzer', pp. 146–148
'Speech on the Hague Congress', pp. 323–326
'Conspectus of Bakunin's *Statism and Anarchy*', pp. 333–338
'Critique of the Gotha Programme', pp. 339–359
Critique of Hegel's 'Philosophy of Right', (Cambridge University Press, Cambridge, 1970)
The Poverty of Philosophy, (Lawrence and Wishart, London, 1979)
'Preface to *A Contribution to the Critique of Political Economy*', (International, London, 1970)
Grundrisse, (Penguin, Harmondsworth, 1973)
Capital, (Penguin, Harmondsworth, 1973)
Marx, K., and Engels, F., *Collected Works*, (Lawrence and Wishart, London, 1975)
Selected Works, (1 vol., Lawrence and Wishart, London, 1968)
'The Holy Family', *Collected Works*, 4
The German Ideology, (Lawrence and Wishart, London, 1970)
'The Trial of the Rhenish District Committee of Democrats', *Collected Works*, 8
'The Prussian Counter-Revolution', *Collected Works*, 8
Selected Correspondence, (Lawrence and Wishart, London, 1934)
Mayo, H.B., *An Introduction to Marxist Theory*, (Oxford University Press, Oxford, 1960)
Melzer, A. M., 'Rousseau and the Problem of Bourgeois Society', *American Political Science Review*, 74, 1980,
Moore, S. W., *The Critique of Capitalist Democracy*, (Kelley, New York, 1969)

Moorhouse, H. F., 'The Political Incorporation of the British Working Class: An Introduction', *Sociology*, 7, 3, 1973

Pelczynski, Z. A., (ed.), *Hegel's Political Philosophy*, (Cambridge University Press, Cambridge, 1971)

Perez-Diaz, V. M., *State, Bureaucracy and Civil Society*, (Macmillan, London, 1978)

Phillips, P., *Marx and Engels on Law and Laws*, (Martin Robertson, Oxford, 1980)

Ritter, J., *Hegel and the French Revolution*, (M.I.T., London, 1982)

Rosenberg, A., *Democracy and Socialism*, (Beacon, Boston, 1965)

Rubel, M., 'Notes on Marx's Conception of Democracy', *New Politics*, 1, Winter 1962

Spencer, M. E., 'Marx on the State', *Theory and Society*, 7, 1/2, 1979

Taylor, C., *Hegel and Modern Society*, (Cambridge University Press, Cambridge, 1979)

Therborn, G., 'The Rule of Capital and the Rise of Democracy', *New Left Review*, 103, 1977

Tucker, R. C., *The Marxian Revolutionary Idea*, (Oxford University Press, Oxford, 1970)

Welty, G., 'Marx, Engels and "Anti-Dühring"', *Political Studies*, 31, 1983

The Second and Third Internationals

Anderson, E., *Hammer or Anvil. The Story of the German Working Class Movement*, (Gollancz, London, 1945)

Angel, P., *Eduard Bernstein et l'Evolution du Socialisme Allemande*, (Paris, 1961)

Arato, A., 'The Second International: A Re-examination', *Telos*, 18, 1973/4

Bahro, R., *The Alternative in Eastern Europe*, (Verso, London, 1978)

Bernstein, E., *Evolutionary Socialism*, (Independent Labour Party, London, 1909)

Bottomore, T., and Goode, P., (eds), *Austro-Marxism*, (Oxford University Press, Oxford, 1978)

Braunthal, J., *History of the Second International 1864-1914*, (Gollancz, London, 1966)

Bronner, S. E., 'Karl Kautsky and the Twilight of Orthodoxy', *Political Theory*, 10, 4, 1982

Bukharin, N., Fabri, L., Rocker, R., *The Poverty of Statism. Anarchism vs. Marxism*, (Cienfuegos, Orkney, 1981)

Claudin, F., 'Democracy and Dictatorship in Lenin and Kautsky', *New Left Review*, 106, 1977,

Cole, G. D. H., *The Second International 1889-1914*, (Macmillan, London, 1967)

Colletti, L., *From Rousseau to Lenin*, (New Left Books, London, 1972)

Corrigan, P., et al. 'Bolshevism and the USSR', *New Left Review*, 125, 1981

d'Encausse, H. Carrere, *Lenin Revolution and Power*, (Longman, London, 1982)

Engels, F., and Kautsky, K., 'Juridical Socialism', *Politics and Society*, 7, 2, 1977

Ensor, R. C. K., (ed.), *Modern Socialism*, (Harper, London, 1910)

Gay, P., *The Dilemma of Democratic Socialism*, (Octagon, New York, 1952)

Geras, N., *The Legacy of Rosa Luxemburg*, (New Left Books, London, 1976)
    'Classical Marxism and Proletarian Representation', *New Left Review*, 125, 1981

Harding, N., *Lenin's Political Thought: vol. 1: Theory and Practice in the Democratic Revolution; vol. 2: Theory and Practice in the Socialist Revolution*, (Macmillan, London, 1977-81)

Holmes, L., (ed.) *The Withering Away of the State?*, (Sage, London, 1981)

Hulse, J. W., *Revolutionists in London*, (Clarendon, Oxford, 1970)

Ionescu, G., 'Lenin, the Commune and the State', *Government and Opposition*, 5, 2, 1970

Jacoby, R., 'Towards a Critique of Automatic Marxism', *Telos*, 10, 1971

Kautsky, K., *The Class Struggle*, (C. H. Kerr, New York, 1910)
    The Road to Power, (S. A. Bloch, Chicago, 1909)
    The Dictatorship of the Proletariat, (University of Michigan Press, Ann Arbor, 1964)
    Terrorism and Communism, (George Allen and Unwin, London, 1920)
    Selected Political Writings, (Macmillan, London, 1983)

Kolakowski, L., *Main Currents of Marxism*, (3 vols, Oxford University Press, Oxford, 1978)

Korsch, K., *Marxism and Philosophy*, (New Left Books, London, 1970)

Lenin, V. I. *Collected Works*, (Lawrence and Wishart, London, 1960)
    'Working-Class and Bourgeois Democracy,' *Collected Works*, 8, pp. 72–82
    'Plan of a Lecture on the Commune', *Collected Works*, 8, pp. 206–208
    'The Proletariat and the Bourgeois Democrats', *Collected Works*, 8, pp. 228–230
    'The Proletariat and the Peasantry', *Collected Works*, 8, pp. 231–236
    'The Revolutionary-Democratic Dictatorship of the Proletariat and the Peasantry', *Collected Works*, 8, pp. 293–294
    'The Democratic Tasks of the Revolutionary Proletariat', *Collected Works*, 8, pp. 511–518
    'Playing at Parliamentarism', *Collected Works*, 9, pp. 265–280
    'The Proletariat and the Peasantry', *Collected Works*, 10, pp. 40–43
    'Preface to the Russian translation of K. Kautsky's pamphlet *Social Democracy Wiped Out*', *Collected Works*, 10, pp. 196–197
    'Lessons of the Commune', *Collected Works*, 13, pp. 475–478
    Marxism and Revisionism', *Collected Works*, 15, pp. 29–39
    'Imperialism, the Highest Stage of Capitalism', *Collected Works*, 22, pp. 185–304
    'Letters from Afar', *Collected Works*, 23, pp. 295–342
    'The Tasks of the Proletariat in the Present Revolution', (April Theses), *Collected Works*, 24, pp. 19–26
    'The Dual Power', *Collected Works*, 24, pp. 38–41
    'The Tasks of the Proletariat in Our Revolution', *Collected Works*, 24, pp. 55–91

'The State and Revolution', *Collected Works*, 25, pp. 385–497
'Letter to American Workers', *Collected Works*, 28, pp. 61–74
'The Proletarian Revolution and the Renegade Kautsky', *Collected Works*, 28, pp. 227–326
'"Democracy" and Dictatorship', *Collected Works*, 28, pp. 368–372
'Theses and Report on Bourgeois Democracy and the Dictatorship of the Proletariat. March 4th', *Collected Works*, 28, pp. 457–474
'First All-Russia Congress on Adult Education', *Collected Works*, 29, pp. 333–376
'Foreword to the Published Speech "The Deception of the People with Slogans of Freedom and Equality"', *Collected Works*, 29, pp. 377–381
'The "Dictatorship of the Proletariat"', *Collected Works*, 30, pp. 93–104
'Economics and Politics in the Era of the Dictatorship of the Proletariat', *Collected Works*, 30, pp. 107–117
'The Constituent Assembly Elections and the Dictatorship of the Proletariat', *Collected Works*, 30, pp. 253–275
'"Left-Wing" Communism – An Infantile Disorder', *Collected Works*, 31, pp. 17–118
'The Essence of the Dictatorship of the Proletariat and of Soviet Power', *Collected Works*, 31, pp. 185–188
'A Contribution to the History of the Question of the Dictatorship', *Collected Works*, 31, pp. 340–361
Marxism on the State, (Progress, Moscow, 1972)
Lukács, G., *Lenin: A Study in the Unity of His Thought*, (New Left Books, London, 1970)
History and Class Consciousness, (Merlin, London, 1971)
Luxemburg, R., *Selected Political Writings*, ed. Howard, D., (Monthly Review Press, New York, 1971)
Selected Political Writings, ed. Looker, R., (Cape, London, 1972)
The Accumulation of Capital, (Routledge and Kegan Paul, London, 1971)
Reform or Revolution, (Pathfinder, New York, 1970)
The Mass Strike, (Harper and Row, New York, 1971)
The Russian Revolution and Marxism or Leninism?, (University of Michigan Press, Ann Arbor, 1961)
Mattick, P., *Anti-Bolshevik Communism*, (Merlin, London, 1978)
Nettl, J. P., *Rosa Luxemburg*, (Oxford University Press, Oxford, 1966)
Plekhanov, G. V., *Fundamental Problems of Marxism*, (Lawrence and Wishart, London, 1969)
Polan, A. J., *Lenin and the End of Politics*, (Methuen, London, 1984)
Roth, G., *The Social Democrats in Imperial Germany*, (Bedminster, Totowa, 1963)
Salvadori, M., *Karl Kautsky and the Socialist Revolution: 1880–1938*, (New Left Books, London, 1979)
Schorske, C., *German Social Democracy 1905–1917*, (Harvard University Press, Cambridge, Mass., 1955)
Steenson, G. P., *Karl Kautsky, 1854–1938. Marxism in the Classical Years*, (University of Pittsburgh, Pittsburgh, 1978)

Trotsky, L., *1905*, (Penguin, Harmondsworth, 1973)
  Terrorism and Communism, (University of Michigan Press, Ann Arbor, 1969)
  The History of the Russian Revolution, (Monad, New York, 1980)
Tucker, R.C., *The Marxian Revolutionary Idea*, (George Allen and Unwin, London, 1970)

2 The 'Third Road'

Italian Communism

Allum, P. A., *Italy – Republic Without Government?*, (Norton, Guilford, 1974)
Amyot, G., *The Italian Communist Party. The Crisis of the Popular Front Strategy*, (Croom Helm, London, 1981)
Anderson, P., 'The Antinomies of Antonio Gramsci', *New Left Review*, 100, 1977
Balibar, E., *On the Dictatorship of the Proletariat*, (New Left Books, London, 1977)
Berlinguer, E., 'Sixty Years of Democratic Struggle', *The Italian Communists*, 1, 1981
  'Opening Address to the 16th Congress of the PCI (1983)', *Communist Affairs*, 2, 1983
Bellamy, R., *Modern Italian Social Thought*, (Polity Press, Cambridge, forthcoming)
Blackmer, L.M., Tarrow, S., *Communism in Italy and France*, (Princeton University Press, Princeton, 1975)
Bobbio, N., *What is Socialism?*, (Polity Press, Cambridge, forthcoming)
Boggs, C., 'Eurocommunism: The state and the crisis of legitimation', *Berkeley Journal of Sociology*, 23, 1978/9
  The Impasse of European Communism, (Westview, Boulder, Colorado, 1982)
Boggs, C., and Plotke, D., *The Politics of Eurocommunism. Socialism in Transition*, (Macmillan, London, 1980)
Brown, B. E., (ed.), *Eurocommunism and Eurosocialism*, (Irvington, New York, 1979)
Buci-Glucksmann, C., *Gramsci and the State*, (Lawrence and Wishart, London, 1980)
Cammett, J., *Antonio Gramsci and the Origins of Italian Communism*, (Stanford University Press, Stanford, 1967)
Carillo, S., *'Eurocommunism' and the State*, (Lawrence and Wishart, London, 1977)
Carrieri, M., and Radice, L. L., 'Italy Today: A Crisis of a New Type of Democracy', *Praxis International*, 1, 3, 1982
Childs, D., *The Changing Face of Western Communism*, (Croom Helm, London, 1980)
Claudin, F., *Eurocommunism and Socialism*, (New Left Books, London, 1978)

CPGB *The British Road to Socialism*, (CPGB, London, 1978)

Davis, J. A., (ed.), *Gramsci and Italy's Passive Revolution*, (Croom Helm, London, 1979)

Dunhamel, L., 'Lenin, Violence and Eurocommunism', *Canadian Journal of Political Science*, 13, 1, 1980

Femia, J. V., *Gramsci's Political Thought*, (Oxford University Press, Oxford, 1981)

Fiori, G., *Antonio Gramsci: Life of a Revolutionary*, (New Left Books, London, 1970)

Frank, A. G., 'Eurocommunism: Left and Right Variants', *New Left Review*, 108, 1978

Gati, C., 'The "Europeanization" of Communism', *Foreign Affairs*, 55, 33, 1977

Gordon, R., and Haseler, S., *'Eurocommunism'*, (St. Martin's, London, 1978)

Gramsci, A., *Selections from Political Writings 1910-1920*, (Beekman, London, 1977)
Selections from Political Writings 1921-1926, (International, London, 1977)
The Prison Notebooks, (Lawrence and Wishart, London, 1971)

Gruppi, L., (ed.), *Il Compresso Storico*, (Riuniti, Rome, 1977)

Gundle, S., 'The 16th Congress of the PCI', *Communist Affairs*, 2, 1983,
'In Search of the Arab Phoenix: The PCI and the Italian Elections of 26th June 1983', *Communist Affairs*, 1984, 3, 1

Kautsky, J., 'Karl Kautsky and Eurocommunism', *Studies in Comparative Communism*, 14, 1, 1981, pp. 3–44

Kindersley, R., (ed.), *In Search of Eurocommunism*, (Macmillan, London, 1981)

Kriegel, A., *Eurocommunism: A New Kind Of Communism?*, (Hoover Institute Press, Stanford, 1978)

Lange, P., and Tarrow, S., (eds), *Italy in Transition: Conflict and Consensus*, (Cass, London, 1980)

Le Gloannec, A.-M. 'Eurocommunism...', *International Studies*, 11,1, 1980
'RDA and Eurocommunism', *Revue Française de Science Politique*, 29,1, 1979

Machin, H., (ed.), *National Communism in Western Europe: A Third Way to Socialism?*, (Methuen, London, 1983)

Mandel, E., *From Stalinism to Eurocommunism*, (New Left Books, London, 1978)

Marchais, G., *Le Défi Démocratique*, (Editions Sociales, Paris, 1973)

Marko, K., 'Real Communism or Eurocommunism', *Studies in Socialist Thought*, 18, 1978

Middlemas, K., *Power and the Party: Changing Faces of Communism in Western Europe*, (Deutsch, London, 1980)

Mouffe, C., (ed.), *Gramsci and Marxist Theory*, (Routledge and Kegan Paul, London, 1979)

Mouffe, C., and Sassoon, A. S., 'Gramsci in France and Italy', *Economy and Society*, 6, 1977

Napolitano, G., *The Italian Road to Socialism*, (Journeyman, London, 1977)

PCI, 'PCI: 1983 Manifesto', *Communist Affairs*, 1984, 3, 1,

'For a Democratic Alternative', *The Italian Communists*, 1982, 4

'The Democratic Alternative', *Communist Affairs*, 1983, 2

Piccone, P., 'Labriola and the Roots of Eurocommunism', *Berkeley Journal of Sociology*, 22, 1977/8

Italian Marxism, (University of California Press, Berkeley, 1983)

'Gramsci's Marxism: Beyond Lenin and Togliatti', *Theory and Society*, 3, 1976

Pontusson, J., 'Gramsci and Eurocommunism: A Comparative Analysis of Conceptions of Class Rule and Socialist Transition', *Berkeley Journal of Sociology*, 25, 1980

Poulantzas, N., *Political Power and Social Classes*, (Verso, London, 1973)

Classes in Contemporary Capitalism, (New Left Books, London, 1975)

The Crisis of the Dictatorships, (New Left Books, London, 1976)

State, Power, Socialism, (Verso, London, 1978)

Pozzolini, A., *Antonio Gramsci: An Introduction to his Thought*, (Pluto, London, 1970)

Prevost, G., 'Eurocommunism and the Spanish Communists', *West European Politics*, 4, 1, 1981

Przeworski, A., 'Social Democracy as an Historical Phenomenon', *New Left Review*, 122, 1980

'Proletariat into a Class. . .', *Politics and Society*, 7, 4, 1977

Capitalism and Social Democracy, (Cambridge University Press, Cambridge, 1985)

Ranney, A., and Sartori, G., (eds), *Eurocommunism: The Italian Case*, (American Enterprise Institute, Washington, 1978)

Rodano, F., *Sulla Politica dei Communista*, (Boringhieri, Turin, 1975)

Ruscoe, J., *On the Threshold of Government: The Italian CP, 1976-81*, (St. Martin's, New York, 1982)

Sassoon, A. S., *Gramsci's Politics*, (St. Martin's, London, 1980)

Sassoon, D., *The Italian Communists Speak For Themselves*, (Spokesman, Nottingham, 1978)

The Strategy of the PCI, (Pinter, London, 1981)

Schwab, G., (ed.), *Eurocommunism: The Ideological and Political-Theoretical Foundations*, (Greenwood, Westport, 1981)

Serfaty, S., and Gray, L., *The Italian Communist Party: Yesterday, Today and Tomorrow*, (Greenwood, Westport, 1980)

Shaw, E., 'The Italian Historical Compromise', *Political Quarterly*, 49, 1978

Spriano, P., *Antonio Gramsci and the Party: The Prison Years*, (Lawrence and Wishart, London, 1979)

Studies in Comparative Communism: *Special Issue on the PCI*: 13, 2/3, 1980

Therborn, G., *What Does the Ruling Class Do When It Rules?*, (New Left Books, London, 1978)

Togliatti, P., *On Gramsci and Other Writings*, (Lawrence and Wishart, London, 1979)

'Parliament and the Struggle for Socialism', *Marxism Today*, 21, 1977

Tokes, R. L., *Eurocommunism and Detente*, (New York University Press, New York, 1978)

Torre, P.F. de, et al., *Eurocommunism: Myth or Reality?*, (Penguin, Harmondsworth, 1979)

Urban, G. R.,(ed.), *Euro-Communism*, (Temple Smith, London, 1978)

Vacca, G., *Saggio sv Togliatti e la tradizione communista*, (Bari, De Donato, 1973)

Weber, H., 'Eurocommunism, Socialism and Democracy', *New Left Review*, 110, 1978

Williams, G. A., *Proletarian Order: Antonio Gramsci, Factory Councils and the Origins of Italian Communism, 1911-1921*, (Pluto, London, 1975)

Woolacott, J., 'The Portuguese CP and the April 1983 General Elections in Portugal', *Communist Affairs*, 3, 1984

Swedish Social Democracy

Adler-Karlsson, G., *Functional Socialism*, (Prisma, Stockholm, 1967)

Ahrne, G., Himmelstrand, U. and Lundberg, L., '"Middle-Way" Sweden at a Crossroad', *Acta Sociologica*, 21,4, 1978

Bornstein, S., et al., (eds), *The State in Capitalist Europe*, (George Allen and Unwin, 1984)

Castles, F. G., *The Social Democratic Image of Society*, (Routledge and Kegan Paul, London, 1978)
'Scandinavian Social Democracy: Achievements and Problems', *West European Politics*, 1, 1, 1978

Castles F. G. and Mackinlay, R. D., 'Public Welfare, Scandinavia...', *British Journal of Political Science*, 9, 2, 1979

Childs, M., *Sweden: The Middle Way*, (Yale University Press, New Haven, 1961)

Crosland, A., *The Future of Socialism*, (Cape, London, 1964)

Emmanuel, A., 'The State in the Transitional Period', *New Left Review*, 113/4, 1979

Ersson, S., and Lane, J.-E., 'Polarisation and Political Economy Crisis: The 1982 Swedish Elections,' *West European Politics*, 6, 3, 1983

Esping-Andersen, G. 'Recasting Sweden's Middle Way', *Working Papers*, 7, 4, 1980
'Social Democracy', in Zeitlin, M., *Classes, Class Conflict and the State*, (Winthrop, Cambridge, Mass., 1980)
'Social Class, Social Democracy and the State', *Comparative Politics*, 11, 1, 1978
Politics Against Markets, (Princeton University Press, Princeton, forthcoming)

Esping-Andersen, G., Friedland, R., and Wright, E. O., 'Modes of Class Struggle and the Capitalist State', *Kapitalistate*, 4, 5, 1976

Fry, J. A., *Limits of the Welfare State: Critical Views on Post-War Sweden*, (Saxon House, Westmead, Hants., 1980)

Fry, J. A., (ed.), *Industrial Democracy and Labour Market Policy in Sweden*, (Pergamon, Oxford, 1979)

Fulcher, R., 'Class Conflict in Sweden', *Sociology*, 7, 1973

Gustaffson, B., Giddens, A., and Offe, C., 'Beyond Welfare Capitalism: Review Symposium', *Acta Sociologica*, 25, 3, 1982

Himmelstrand, U., et al., *Beyond Welfare Capitalism*, (Heinemann, London, 1981)

Kesselman, M., 'Prospects for Democratic Socialism in Advanced Capitalism: Class Struggle and Compromise in Sweden and France', *Politics and Society*, 11, 4, 1982

Korpi, W., 'Social Democracy in Welfare Capitalism', *Acta Sociologica*, Supplement, 1978
The Working Class in Welfare Capitalism, (Routledge and Kegan Paul, London, 1979)
'Social Policy Strategies and Distributional Conflicts in Capitalist Democracies', *West European Politics*, 3, 3, 1980
The Democratic Class Struggle, (Routledge and Kegan Paul, London, 1983)

Lindberg, L., et al., (eds), *Stress and Contradiction in Modern Capitalism*, (D.C. Heath, Lexington, 1975)

Martin, A., 'Is Democratic Control of Capitalist Economies Possible?', in Lindberg, L., et al., *Stress and Contradition in Modern Capitalism*
'Sweden: Industrial Democracy and Social Democratic Strategy', in Garson, G. D., (ed.), *Worker Self-Management in Industry: The West European Experience*, (Praeger, New York, 1977)
'From Joint Consultation to Joint Decision-Making, in J. A. Fry, *Industrial Democracy*

Meidner, R., *Employee Investment Funds*, (George Allen and Unwin, London, 1978)

Otter, C. von, 'Sweden: Labour Reformism shapes the system', in Barkin, S., (ed.), *Worker Militancy and Its Consequences, 1965-1975*, (Praeger, New York, 1983)
'Swedish Welfare Capitalism: The Role of the State', in Scase, R., (ed.), *The State in Western Europe*, (Croom Helm, London, 1980)

Pontusson, J., 'Behind and Beyond Social Democracy in Sweden', *New Left Review*, 143, 1984

Scase. R., *Social Democracy in Capitalist Society: Working Class Politics in Britain and Sweden*, (Croom Helm, London, 1977)

Scase, R., (ed.), *Readings in the Swedish Class Structure*, (Pergamon, London, 1977)
The State in Western Europe, (Croom Helm, London, 1980)

Stephens, J., *The Transition from Capitalism to Socialism*, (Macmillan, London, 1979)

Tilton, T. A., 'A Swedish Road to Socialism: Ernst Wigforss and the Ideological Foundations of Swedish Social Democracy', *American Political Science Review*, 73, 1979

Tingsten, H., *The Swedish Social Democrats: Their Ideological Development*, (Bedminster, Totowa, 1973)

Tomasson, R. F., *Sweden: Prototype of Modern Society*, (Random House, New York, 1970)
'The Extraordinary Success of the Swedish Social Democrats', *Journal of Politics*, 31, 3, 1969

3 Contemporary Political Theory

Almond, G., and Verba, S., *The Civic Culture*, (Princeton University Press, Princeton, 1963)

Anderson, P., *Considerations on Western Marxism*, (New Left Books, London, 1976)

Arendt, H., *The Human Condition*, (Chicago University Press, Chicago, 1958)

Barry, B., *Sociologists, Economists and Democracy*, (Collier-Macmillan, London, 1970)

Blackburn, R., (ed.), *Revolution and Class Struggle* (Fontana, London, 1977)

Birnbaum, P., Lively, J., and Parry, G., (eds), *Democracy, Consensus and Social Contract*, (Sage, London, 1978)

Bornstein, S., et al., *The State in Capitalist Europe*, (George Allen Unwin, London, 1984)

Braverman, H., *Labour and Monopoly Capital*, (Monthly Review, New York, 1974)

Campbell, T. C., *The Left and Rights: A Conceptual Analysis of the Idea of Socialist Rights*, (Routledge and Kegan Paul, London, 1983)

Cohen, G. A., 'Freedom, Justice and Capitalism', *New Left Review*, 126, 1981

Cohen, J., *Class and Civil Society: The Limits of Marxian Theory*, (Martin Robertson, Oxford, 1983)

Cohen, M., Nagel, T. and Scanlon, T., (eds), *Marx, Justice and History*, (Princeton University Press, Princeton, 1980)

Colletti, L., 'Power and Democracy in Socialist Society', *New Left Review*, 56, 1969

Collins, H., *Marxism and Law*, (Oxford University Press, Oxford, 1982)

Crenson, M. A., *The Un-Politics of Air Pollution*, (Johns Hopkins Press, Baltimore, 1971)

Curran, J., (ed.), *The Future of the Left*, (Polity Press/New Socialist, Cambridge, 1984)

Cutler, A., et al., *Marx's 'Capital' and Capitalism Today*, (2 vols, Routledge and Kegan Paul, London, 1977)

Dahl, R., *A Preface to Democratic Theory*, (University of Chicago Press, Chicago, 1956)

Polyarchy, (Yale University Press, New Haven, 1971)

Downs, A., *An Economic Theory of Democracy*, (Harper and Row, New York, 1957)

Dunn, J., *Western Political Theory in the Face of the Future*, (Cambridge University Press, Cambridge, 1979)

The Politics of Socialism: An Essay in Political Theory, (Cambridge University Press, Cambridge, 1984)

Ferguson, A., *An Essay on the History of Civil Society*, (Edinburgh University Press, Edinburgh, 1966)

Fine, R., *Democracy and the Rule of Law: Liberal Ideals and Marxist Critque*, (Pluto, London, 1984)

Fine, R., et al., (eds), *Capitalism and the Rule of Law: From Deviancy Theory to Marxism*, (Hutchinson, London, 1979)

Fine, R., et al., *Class Politics: An Answer to Its Critics*, (Central Books, London, 1984)

Frankel, B., *Beyond the State? Dominant Theories and Socialist Strategies*, (Macmillan, London, 1983)

'The State of the State', *Theory and Society*, 7, 1/2, 1979

Gamble, A., *An Introduction to Modern Social and Political Thought*, (Macmillan, London, 1981)

Giddens, A., *The Class Structure of the Advanced Capitalist Societies*, (Hutchinson, London, 1973)

Central Problems in Social Theory, (Macmillan, London, 1979)

A Contemporary Critique of Historical Materialism, (Macmillan, London, 1981)

Profiles and Critiques in Social Theory, (Macmillan, London, 1982)

The Nation-State and Violence, (Polity Press, Cambridge, 1985)

Gorz, A., *Strategy for Labour*, (Beacon, Boston, 1967)

Socialism and Revolution, (Allen Lane, London, 1975)

The Division of Labour , (Harvester, Hassocks, 1976)

Farewell to the Working Class, (Pluto, London, 1982)

Gough, I., *The Political Economy of the Welfare State*, (Macmillan, London, 1979)

Gouldner, A. W., *The Two Marxisms*, (Macmillan, London, 1980)

Habermas, J., 'The Public Sphere', *New German Critique*, 1, 3, 1974

Theory and Practice, (Heinemann, London, 1974)

Toward a Rational Society, (Heinemann, London, 1971)

Knowledge and Human Interests, (Heinemann, London, 1972)

Legitimation Crisis, (Heinemann, London, 1976)

Communication and the Evolution of Society, (Heinemann, London, 1979)

Hall, S., et al., *Policing the Crisis: Mugging, the State and Law and Order*, (Macmillan, London, 1978)

Held, D., *Introduction to Critical Theory*, (Hutchinson, London, 1980)

Held, D, and Thompson, J., *Habermas: Critical Debates*, (Macmillan, London, 1982)

Held, D., et al., (eds,) *States and Societies*, (Open University/Martin Robertson, Oxford, 1983)

Hindess, B., *Parliamentary Democracy and Socialist Politics*, (Routledge and Kegan Paul, London, 1983)

Hirst, P., 'Law, Socialism and Rights', in Carlen P., and Collinson, M., (eds), *Radical Issues in Criminology*, (Martin Robertson, Oxford, 1980)

Hoffman, J., *Coercion and Consent in Marxist Political Theory*, (Martin Robertson, Oxford, 1984)

Holloway, J., and Picciotto, S., (eds), *State and Capital: A Marxist Debate*, (Arnold, London, 1978)

Hunt, A., (ed.), *Marxism and Democracy*, (Lawrence and Wishart, London, 1980)

'The Politics of Law and Justice', in Hunt, A., et al., (eds), *Politics and Power 4*, (Routledge and Kegan Paul, London, 1981)

Jessop, R., *The Capitalist State: Marxist Theories and Methods*, (Martin Robertson, Oxford, 1982)

'Recent Theories of the Capitalist State', *Cambridge Journal of Economics*, 1, 1977

'Capitalism and Democracy', in Littlejohn, G., et al., (eds), *Power and the State*

'The Political Indeterminacy of Democracy', in Hunt, A., (ed.), *Marxism and Democracy*

'Nicos Poulantzas on Political Strategy', *Politics*, 2, 1982

Jessop, R., et al., 'Authoritarian Populism, Two Nations and Thatcherism', *New Left Review*, 147, 1984, pp. 32–60

Keane, J., *Public Life and Late Capitalism: Toward a Socialist Theory of Democracy*, (Cambridge University Press, Cambridge, 1984)

Kelsen, H., *The Communist Theory of Law*, (Stevens, London, 1975)

Laclau, E., *Politics and Ideology in Marxist Theory*, (New Left Books, London, 1977)

Lindblom, C.E., *Politics and Markets*, (Basic, New York, 1977)

Lipset, S., *Political Man*, (Heinemann, London, 1969)

Littlejohn, G., et al., (eds), *Power and the State*, (Croom Helm, London, 1978)

Macintyre, A., *After Virtue*, (Duckworth, London, 1981)

McLennan, G., Held, D., and Hall, S., (eds), *The Idea of the Modern State*, (Open University, Milton Keynes, 1984)

Macpherson, C.B., *The Political Theory of Possessive Individualism*, (Oxford University Press, Oxford, 1962)

'Post-liberal Democracy?', *Canadian Journal of Economic and Political Science*, 30, 1964

The Real World of Democracy, (Oxford University Press, Oxford, 1966)

Democratic Theory: Essays in Retrieval, (Oxford University Press, Oxford, 1973)

The Life and Times of Liberal Democracy, (Oxford University Press, Oxford, 1978)

Mandel, E., *Revolutionary Marxism Today*, (New Left Books, London, 1979)

Mattick, P., *Anti-Bolshevik Communism*, (Merlin, London, 1978)

Medvedev, R., *Leninism and Western Socialism*, (Verso, London, 1981)

Miliband, R., *Parliamentary Socialism*, (Merlin, London, 1961)

Marxism and Politics, (Oxford University Press, Oxford, 1977)

The State in Capitalist Society, (Weidenfield and Nicholson, London, 1969)

Capitalist Democracy in Britain, (Oxford University Press, London, 1982)

Class Power and State Power: Political Essays, (Verso/New Left Books, London, 1983)

Mills, C. W., *Power, Politics and People: The Collected Essays of C. Wright Mills*, (Oxford University Press, Oxford, 1963)

Moore, S., *Marx on the Choice Between Socialism and Communism*, (Harvard University Press, London, 1980)

O'Connor, J., *The Fiscal Crisis of the State*, (St. Martin's, New York, 1973)

Offe, C., *Contradictions of the Welfare State*, (Hutchinson, London, 1984)

Parkin, F., *The Social Analysis of Class Structure*, (Tavistock, London, 1974)

Class Inequality and Political Order, (Paladin, London, 1972)

Marxism and Class Theory: A Bourgeois Critique, (Tavistock, London, 1979)

Pashukanis, E. B., *Law and Marxism: A General Theory. Towards a Critique of the Fundamental Juridical Concepts*, (Ink Links, London, 1978)

Plamenatz, J., *Democracy and Illusion*, (Longman, Harlow, 1973)
German Marxism and Russian Communism, (Greenwood, London, 1954)

Popper, K., *The Open Society and Its Enemies*, (2 vols, Routledge and Kegan Paul, London, 1962)
The Poverty of Historicism, (Routledge and Kegan Paul, London, 1961)

Rodger, J. J., 'On the Degeneration of the Public Sphere', *Political Studies*, 33, 2, 1985

Schumpeter, J., *Capitalism, Socialism and Democracy*, (Oxford University Press, Oxford, 1976)

Siltanen, J., and Stanworth, M., (eds), *Women and the Public Sphere*, (Hutchinson, London, 1984)

Sirianni,C., 'Production and Power in a Classless Society', *Socialist Review*, 59, 1981/2
'Councils and Parliaments: The Problems of Dual Power and Democracy in Comparative Perspective', *Politics and Society*, 12, 2, 1983

Smith, A., *The Wealth of Nations*, (Penguin, Harmondsworth, 1970)

Stephens, J. D., *The Transition from Capitalism to Socialism*, (Macmillan, London, 1979)

Sweezy, P. M., and Bettelheim, C., *On the Transition to Socialism*, (Monthly Review Press, New York, 1971)

Talmon, J. L., *The Origins of Totalitarian Democracy*, (Sphere, London, 1970)
Political Messianism: The Romantic Phase, (Secker and Warburg, London, 1960)

Thompson, E. P., *The Making of the English Working Class*, (Penguin, Harmondsworth, 1970)
The Poverty of Theory and Other Essays, (Merlin, London, 1978)
Writing By Candlelight, (Merlin, London, 1980)
Whigs and Hunters, (Allen Lane, London, 1977)

Tonnies, F., *Community and Society*, (Harper and Row, New York, 1957)
On Sociology: Pure, Applied and Empirical, (Chicago University Press, Chicago, 1971)

Truman, D. B., *The Governmental Process*, (Knopf, New York, 1951)

Tucker, D. F. B., *Marxism and Individualism*, (Blackwell, Oxford, 1980)

Tucker, R. C., *The Marxian Revolutionary Idea*, (George Allen and Unwin, London, 1970)

Urry, J., *The Anatomy of Capitalist Societies*, (Macmillan, London, 1981)

Weale, A., *Political Theory and Social Policy*, (Macmillan, London, 1983)

Wilensky, H., *The Welfare State and Equality*, (University of California Press, Berkeley, 1975)

Williams, R., 'Democracy and Parliament', *Marxism Today*, 26, 6, 1982

Index